Texts in Philosophy

Volume 32

Experience and the Ultimate Structure of Reality Husserl's Pursuit of Truth

Volume 22
The Good, the Right & the Fair – an introduction to ethics
Mickey Gjerris, Morten Ebbe Juul Nielsen, and Peter Sandøe

Volume 23
The Normative Structure of Responsibility. Law, Language, Ethics
Federico Faroldi

Volume 24
Karl Popper. A Centenary Assessment. Volume I. Life and Times, and Values in a World of Facts
Ian Jarvie, Karl Milford and David Miller, eds

Volume 25
Karl Popper. A Centenary Assessment. Volume II. Metaphysics and Epistemology
Ian Jarvie, Karl Milford and David Miller, eds

Volume 26
Karl Popper. A Centenary Assessment. Volume III Science
Ian Jarvie, Karl Milford and David Miller, eds

Volume 27
Unorthodox Analytic Philosophy
Guillermo E. Rosado Haddock

Volume 28
Quantum Heresies.
Kent A. Peacock, with a foreword by James Robert Brown

Volume 29
Carrollian Notes
George Englebretsen

Volume 30
Problems from Hume
David Bostock

Volume 31
The Labyrinth of Infinity or the Enigma of Existence
Stathis Livadas

Volume 32
Experience and the Ultimate Structure of Reality, Huserl's Pursuit of Truth
Claire Ortiz Hill

Texts in Philosophy Series Editors
Vincent F. Hendriks vincent@hum.ku.dk
John Symons jsymons@utep.edu
Dov Gabbay dov.gabbay@kcl.ac.uk

Experience and the Ultimate Structure of Reality

Husserl's Pursuit of Truth

Claire Ortiz Hill

© Individual authors and College Publications 2024
All rights reserved.

ISBN 978-1-84890-451-4

College Publications
Scientific Director: Dov Gabbay
Managing Director: Jane Spurr

http://www.collegepublications.co.uk

Original cover design by Laraine Welch
Cover art by Jacqueline Wegmann
Photograph of Claire Ortiz Hill with previous co-authors, Jairo da Silva (left) and Guillermo Rosado Haddock (right) taken by Tinna Stoyanova de Rosado Haddock

---

All rights reserved. No part of this publication may be reproduced, stored in a retrieval system or transmitted in any form, or by any means, electronic, mechanical, photocopying, recording or otherwise without prior permission, in writing, from the publisher.

Experience and the Ultimate Structure of Reality, On Husserl's Pursuit of Truth

Table of Contents

This book is dedicated to the memory of

Jaakko Hintikka

who was always looking for ways to be of service.

Photograph taken by Claire Ortiz Hill in Paris in 2003

PREFACE

Experience and the Ultimate Structure of Reality, Husserl's Pursuit of Truth follows the evolution of Edmund Husserl's thought through those crucial years at the end of the nineteenth century and the beginning of the twentieth century when reason compelled the young doctor of mathematics to forsake empirical psychology and to strive to find the theories respecting the central traits of reality necessary to buttress the ultimate knowledge of reality he was seeking. Those theories about, to borrow Willard Quine's expression, "limning the true and ultimate structure of reality",[1] were to be the spine he needed to back up his nascent phenomenology, which would put flesh on the purely logical skeleton he was uncovering and give it a brain and a heart.

The book's chapters chronicle Husserl's anguished search for answers to the spiny questions at the intersection of what he called the "strange" worlds of actual consciousness and the purely logical that unnerved him as he worked on logic and the foundations of arithmetic at the University of Halle during the last fourteen years of the nineteenth century. They explore discoveries that he made about those worlds during those many years of mental travels in them as he struggled to come to clarity regarding the underlying objective structure of reality. I particularly use his lecture courses on logic, theory of knowledge and science which the Husserl Archives has been publishing since the 1980s to recuperate the map of the underlying logical form grounded in the deep nature of things that he strove to provide.

It is essential to keep in mind that during those years Husserl was not philosophizing about logic and mathematics in a vacuum and he was not just extemporizing about things that he liked to believe about them. He was as well-versed in them, if not more so, than the makers and champions of the theories about logic and philosophy of mathematics embraced by the Analytic school of philosophy which has dominated those fields, and philosophy in general, in English-speaking countries, since those days.

He was a mathematician by training, who for decades kept company with the most outstanding and pioneering mathematicians of his time. He had been Karl Weierstrass' student and assistant in Berlin. During his

---

[1] Willard Quine, *Word and Object*, Cambridge MA: MIT Press, 1960, p. 221.

years in Halle he was befriended by the father of set theory, Georg Cantor, who was hard at work earnestly mixing philosophy, mathematics, logic epistemology, metaphysics, theology and occultism in thought-provoking ways while exploring and defending the strange world of the transfinite sets he was engendering and encountering the antinomies of set theory, the later reactions to which Husserl's future friend and colleague at the University of Göttingen, the great mathematician David Hilbert, once described as "dramatic" and "violent" and as having had "a downright catastrophic effect in the world of mathematics".[2]

Husserl left dramatic accounts of the distress and intellectual isolation he experienced during the long, intense intellectual crisis he suffered in his quest for answers to his thorny questions. In "Personal Notes" penned in 1906, he recalled having been powerfully gripped by the deepest problems during the late 1880s and the early 1890s as he wracked his brain trying to answer questions raised by the logic of mathematical thought and of the mathematical calculus. He described himself as having been "tormented by those incredibly strange realms: the world of the purely logical and the world of actual consciousness". He believed that "they had to interrelate and form an intrinsic unity", but he did not know how to unite them.[3] He described himself as having striven to arrive at ultimate and deepest knowledge of reality, as being "close to the most obscure parts of the theory of knowledge", as facing "great unsolved puzzles" about the very possibility of knowledge in general. However, he only saw all around him inchoate, ambiguously described problems, prickly questions, profoundly unclear theories, thick clouds of confusion.[4]

The bewilderment that invaded him during those years marked the crucial turning point in his philosophizing. His brain-wracking questions impressed upon him an urgent need to develop the more sophisticated logical and epistemological tools needed to arrive at a deeper, clearer understanding of how the human mind interacted with the world of pure logic. He finally felt compelled to set aside his philosophical mathematical

---

[2] David Hilbert, "On the Infinite", in *From Frege to Gödel: A Source Book in Mathematical Logic, 1879-1931*, Jean van Heijenoort (ed.), Cambridge MA: Harvard University Press, 1967 (1925), p. 375.

[3] Edmund Husserl, "Personal Notes", in his *Early Writings in the Philosophy of Logic and Mathematics*, Dordrecht: Kluwer, 1994, pp. 490-93.

[4] Edmund Husserl, *Introduction to the Logical Investigations, A Draft of a Preface to the Logical Investigations*, The Hague: Martinus Nijhoff, 1975 (1913), pp. 16-17.

investigations until he came to clarity about basic questions about the relationship between the subjectivity of knowing and the objectivity of what is known. Profoundly shaken, cast intellectually adrift, weary of the confusion and afraid of sinking in a sea of unending criticism, he decided that, for the sake of philosophical self-preservation, he had to set out on his own in search of answers.[5]

His search for answers pushed him over the borderline and into the world of pure logic. He would write that only someone who like himself had been profoundly distressed by the issues in the most intense way, who had felt compelled by the failures of psychologism to recognize the realm of the purely logical, but also compelled to recognize the essential relationships between the psychological and the ideal, could see the need for psychological critiques to force recognition of the ideal as something given prior to all theories. Only such a person could see that the being-in-itself of the ideal sphere in its relation to consciousness brings with it a dimension of puzzles that had to be solved through the phenomenological methods he was developing.[6] The early years of the twentieth century found him teaching that all objectivity of thinking was grounded in purely logical forms, that the ultimate meaning and source of all objectivity making it possible for thinking to reach beyond contingent, subjective, human acts and lay hold of objective being in itself was to be found in ideality and in the ideal laws defining it.[7]

In his 1900 abstract for his *Prolegomena to Pure Logic*, he defined pure logic as "the scientific system of ideal laws and theories which are purely grounded in the sense of the ideal categories of meaning; that is, in the fundamental concepts which are common to all sciences because they determine in the most universal way what makes sciences objectively sciences at all: unity of theory. In this sense, pure logic is the science of the ideal 'conditions of the possibility' of science generally, or of the ideal constituents of the idea of theory".[8] He saw it as including all of the pure "analytical" theories and suggested that instead of pure logic one might

---

[5] See, for example, Edmund Husserl, *Logical Investigations*, London: Routledge and Kegan Paul, 1970, pp. 42-43; his *Early Writings*, pp. 15-17, 50-51; his *Introduction to the Logical Investigations*, p. 17.

[6] Husserl, *Introduction to the Logical Investigations*, pp. 21-22.

[7] Edmund Husserl, *Allgemeine Erkenntnistheorie, Vorlesung 1902/03*, Dordrecht: Kluwer, 2001, pp. 41, 47, 53, 58, 200, 206.

[8] Husserl, *Introduction to the Logical Investigations*, p. 4.

speak of analytics or the science of what is analytically knowable in general, the science that establishes and systematically grounds analytic laws.[9]

He was furthermore persuaded that completely new radical dimensions of philosophical problems were illuminated in the idealist systems and that the ultimate and highest goals of philosophy only opened up when the philosophical method that such systems require was clarified and developed.[10] However, he endeavored to make it perfectly clear that that did not mean that he was advocating any sort of mysticism or magical view of nature. The ideal entities he was talking about, he insisted, were not mythical or mystical entities suspended between being and non-being, not the metaphysical abstrusities eschewed by empirical psychologists, not the creatures of darkness that would later spook so many analytic philosophers. They had not been artificially invented by him or anyone else, but were given beforehand by the meaning of the universal talk of propositions and truths indispensable in all the sciences. He considered that indubitable fact to be the starting point of all logic. He even asserted that the ideal objects he was talking about were what was the very most ordinary, like ordinary stones on the road, that all people know them in a certain naive way since they talk of numbers and do so on in ideal ways. It was only philosophers, he said, who did not want to know them.[11]

In his "Personal Notes" of 1907, he went on to confide that finally, after "many years of confused struggling", his hopes had soared as he saw himself nearing his goal of "gaining genuine insight in logic, in the critique of knowledge, and in the critique of reason in general: of establishing a nature order among the problems, of discovering the natural sequence in investigations, of raising the problems themselves to the highest level of precision, of refining the methods to the point of total consistency and complete assuredness – and then, within this clarity of goals and methods of doing what it in each case: dictated, step by step". He vowed not to

---

9 Edmund Husserl, *Alte und neue Logik, Vorlesung 1908/09*, Dordrecht: Kluwer, 2003, p. 244.
10 Edmund Husserl, "Recollections of Franz Brentano", in *Husserl: Shorter Works*, Notre Dame IN: University of Notre Dame Press, 1981 (1919), p. 345.
11 Edmund Husserl, *Logic and General Theory of Science 1917/18*, Cham, Switzerland: Springer, 2019, §§5a, 8, 19a.

waste "a life of impassioned struggle, of the most extreme labors". It was his intention "never to give up", and he said he never would.[12]

"Without getting clear on the general outlines of the sense, essence, methods and main points of a critique of reason", he had written in 1906,

> without having thought out, outlined, formulated and justified a general sketch of such a critique, I cannot live truly and sincerely. I have had enough of the torments of unclarity, of tottering back and forth in doubt. I have to come to an inner stability. I know that this concerns high, even the highest matters.... I simply cannot go on without clarity.... I will – I must – approach these sublime goals, through self-sacrificing labor and purely disinterested absorption in the work.... Only one thing will fulfil me: I must come to clarity. Otherwise I cannot live. I cannot endure life without believing that I shall attain it.... Pure inner conviction, purely inward life, inward gestation of the problems, being devoted purely to them and only to them: that is the hope of my future. If I do not succeed in this, then I can only live a life which is, rather, a death.[13]

Then in 1908, he confided: "I intend to triumph or die. To perish in spirit, so succumb in the battle for inner clarity, for philosophical integrity – and yet to live on physically: that I hope, will not be my lot, not be possible for me"[14], an expression of determination evoking his contemporary Alfred Tennyson's "Ulysses", who reflected:

> I... have suffer'd greatly, both with those that loved me, and alone... all experience is an arch wherethro' gleams that untravell'd world whose margin fades for ever and forever when I move... yearning in desire to follow knowledge like a sinking star beyond the utmost bound of human thought... 'T is not too late to seek a newer world... for my purpose holds to sail beyond the sunset, and... all the western stars, until I die... strong in will, to strive, to seek, to find, and not to yield.

Husserl finally wrote the answers that he found during his years of painful searching into the foundations of his science of objectivity, namely, his philosophy of pure analytic logic and mathematics, and into those of his nascent science of subjectivity, which would become his much-studied

---

[12] *Ibid.*, p. 498.

[13] *Ibid.*, pp. 494, 497.

[14] *Ibid.*, p. 500.

phenomenology.[15] By outlining what he found in each world and how the two worlds interconnect, Husserl provided guidelines for avoiding confusion in many areas of philosophy. If he was right in believing that his new understanding of the structure of the world of pure logic was of the greatest significance for a genuine understanding of the true sense of logic and all of philosophy and that his radical clarification of the relationship between formal logic and formal mathematics could lead to a definitive clarification of the sense of pure formal mathematics as a pure analytics of non-contradiction,[16] then philosophers need to be particularly lucid about the really important questions that his insights raise for philosophy of logic and mathematics now. If Husserl had been heeded they could have avoided many problems and those fields might have followed a different, less error-ridden course.

***

I would like to add a few more comments. For the sake of accuracy, consistency of terminology, style, and spelling I have often had to modify published translations of German texts, something that I have not always acknowledged in the texts themselves. I would also like to say that the three reviews figuring in the appendix at the end of the book may at first appear to address issues only of relevance to analytic philosophers. However, the issues raised in them bear upon those raised in the essays making up the body of the work in thought-provoking ways and so are directly relevant to the discussions of Husserl's theories found there.

I would also like to say that this book is exclusively comprised of contributions that I was invited to present to diverse publications and audiences in Belgium, Brazil, England, Germany, Italy, Poland, Portugal, Puerto Rico, Romania and the United States. The subjects of the papers being interrelated, there is sometimes more repetition, at times, even word for word repetition, than I consider desirable, something which I find a little distressing. I have eliminated repetitious passages where I could, but have had to retain some of them where I believe they were necessary for the development of my arguments.

---

[15] See, for example, Husserl, *Introduction to the Logical Investigations,* p. 33; his *Early Writings*, pp. 13-17, 48-49, 345-46; his "Double Lecture: On the Transition through the Impossible ('Imaginary') and the Completeness of an Axiom System," Essay III in his *Philosophy of Arithmetic, Psychological and Logical Investigations with Supplementary Texts from 1887-1901*, Dordrecht: Kluwer, 2003, pp. 430-47.

[16] Husserl, *Formal and Transcendental Logic*, p. 11.

Permissions

All the papers anthologized here were previously published elsewhere. The Taylor & Francis Group has given me permission to reprint "From Empirical Psychology to Phenomenology", first published in *The Brentano Puzzle*, R. Poli (ed.) (Aldershot: Ashgate) 1998, pp. 151-68 and "The Strange Worlds of Actual Consciousness and the Purely Logical", first published in the *New Yearbook for Phenomenology and Phenomenological Philosophy*, B. Hopkins (ed.) (Abingdon: Routledge) vol. 13, 2013, pp. 62-83. Springer Verlag has given me permission to reprint "Husserl's Purely Logical Chastity Belt", first published in *Constructive Semantics, Meaning in Between Phenomenology and Constructivism*, C. Weiss (ed.) (Cham, Switzerland: Springer Nature) 2019, pp. 135-46; "Husserl and Cantor", first published in *Essays on Husserl's Logic and Philosophy of Mathematics*, S. Centrone (ed.) (Dordrecht: Springer) 2017, pp. 169-96; "Husserl and Phenomenology, Experience and Essence", first published in *Phenomenology and Existentialism* Book I, A-T. Tymieniecka (ed.) (Dordrecht: Springer) 2009, pp. 9-22 and "Review of W. Demopoulos' *Frege's Philosophy of Mathematics*", first published in *Synthese* 133, 2002, pp. 441-52. Rachel Twombly of Rowman & Littlefield has given me permission to reprint "Limning the Ultimate Structure of Reality", first published in *Mereologies, Ontologies, and Facets: The Categorial Structure of Reality*, P. Hackett (ed.) (Lanham MD: Lexington Books) 2018, pp. 37-64. Marco Ruffino has given me permission to reprint "Husserl, Frege and 'the Paradox'", first published in *Manuscrito, Revista Internacional de Filosofia* 23, 2, October 2000, pp. 101-32. George Bondor has assured me that I may reprint "Husserl on Sets and the Causes of the Set-theoretical Paradoxes", first published in *After Husserl: Phenomenological Foundations of Mathematics*, I. Apostolescu (ed.), a special issue of *Meta: Research in Hermeneutics, Phenomenology, and Practical Philosophy*, Vol. XI, No. 2, December 2019, pp. 450-72. Ashleen Sauerborn of de Gruyter has given me permission to reprint "Husserl's Way Out of Frege's Jungle", first published in *Objects and Pseudo-Objects Ontological Deserts and Jungles from Brentano to Carnap*, B. Leclercq, S. Richard and D. Seron (eds.) (Berlin: de Gruyter) 2015, pp. 183-96. Etienne Helmer has given me permission to reprint "Circling Gottlob Frege, Review of M. Schirn's *Frege Importance and Legacy*", first published in *Diálogos* 73, 1999, pp. 203-13. Annabel Flude of the journals department of the Taylor & Francis Group has given me permission to reprint "Review of *The New Theory of Reference*, P. Humphreys and J. Fetzer (eds.)", first published in *History and Philosophy of Logic* 20, 1999, pp. 125-27. Their web site is: https://www.tandfonline.com/

Acknowledgments

I must continue to thank those who so generously made it possible to me to pursue my philosophical work as I saw fit on my own terms. In 1967, my neighbor Dr. Frank Blume suggested to me that I might want to study philosophy with his friend Roger Schmidt, who turned me into a philosopher when I was 16 years old and remained a faithful friend until his death in 2018. In 1970, Bernd Magnus, my teacher at the University of California, Riverside, sponsored my Senior Honors Thesis on Descartes and Husserl, which turned me into a Husserlian when I was 19 years old. Seven years later, he oriented me towards the work of Dagfinn Føllesdal, Jaakko Hintikka, David Woodruff Smith and Ronald Mc Intyre on Husserl, Frege and Possible World Semantics. Then, one thing led to another. Maurice Clavelin of the University of Paris-Sorbonne agreed to sponsor my Master's thesis on their work and then later gave me completely free rein to write the doctoral thesis I wanted to write, which was published as my first book, *Word and Object in Husserl, Frege and Russell, the Roots of Twentieth Century Philosophy.* For years and years after that Paul Gochet, Ivor Grattan-Guinness, Jaakko Hintikka, Ruth Barcan Marcus, Barry Smith and Dallas Willard generously and unselfishly helped me professionally whenever I needed it. I must also continue to thank my friends and successive spiritual directors Fr. Tom Russmann OFM.cap., Fr. Jean Diot S.S., Fr. Jacques Sommet S.J. and Fr. François Delpit for their faithful support.

Claire Ortiz Hill
Paris
February 2024

Photo by Gene Hill

1

FROM FRANZ BRENTANO'S EMPIRICAL PSYCHOLOGY TO PHENOMENOLOGY[1]

Gustave Flaubert is known to have believed that writers should be like God in the universe, present in all parts of their creation but in none of them visible. In what follows I want to suggest that Flaubert's conviction may provide some insight into the puzzle of Franz Brentano's invisibility in his student Edmund Husserl's work. For the influence teachers exercise on their disciples is often one of invisible form, rather than of visible content, and this may be particularly so in the case of students who, like Husserl, become original thinkers in their own right.

Indeed, when we try to assess the influence that Brentano obviously had on Husserl, the impression of intellectual kinship blurs and Brentano's imprint fades away. Brentano definitely gave Husserl the conviction that encouraged him to choose philosophy as his life's work and headed him in the direction he wanted to go. But once out of Brentano's sight, Husserl embarked upon an independent path, transforming Brentano's basic intuitions to such an extent that he almost might be said to have turned Brentano on his head.

Brentano's invisibility here can be seen in the following facts:

1) There is no doubt that Brentano imparted to Husserl the conviction that philosophy was a serious discipline which could and must be dealt with in the spirit of the strictest science. But for Brentano the ideal of a strict philosophic science was most nearly realized in the exact natural sciences. After a painful experience of the shortcomings of Brentano's empirical psychology, though, Husserl eradicated this most distinctive feature of Brentano's teaching from phenomenology.

2) Husserl's search for answers he did not believe empirical psychology could provide led him to embrace metaphysical and epistemological views that Brentano considered odious and despicable. Husserl came to consider idealistic systems as being of the highest value and compatible with the goals of a strict scientific philosophy. He believed

---

[1] This was originally a paper presented at a conference about the puzzle of Brentano's invisibility entitled "The Brentano Puzzle: At the Origins of the Contemporary Idea of Exact Philosophy", held November 14-16, 1996 in Bolzano, Italy.

that the idea of a pure phenomenology as eidetic and resting on the transcendental reduction was entirely alien to Brentano's descriptive psychology.

3) Though the pre-eminent role Husserl accorded to the theory of intentionality guaranteed Brentano's presence in all parts of phenomenology, Husserl believed he had utterly transformed Brentano's insight. He considered Brentano to be so bound to the prejudices of the naturalistic tradition that the unique sense of intentional analysis and the proper method of intentional psychology remained foreign to him.

4) While Brentano's clear, rigorous, insightful, objective and precise philosophical analyses and ability to transform unclear beginnings into clear thoughts and insights had a profound impact on the man in whom Karl Weierstrass had awakened an interest in seeking radical foundations for knowledge, Husserl believed that Brentano's methods left him in the lurch at the crucial turning point in his philosophical career.

In what follows, I let Husserl speak for himself. I use parts of his autobiographical and philosophical writings[2] to piece together a picture of his relationship to the teacher he revered.

Initial enthusiasm

"The good fortune of attending Brentano's lectures was mine for only two years... At that time I had just finished my university studies and was still a beginner in philosophy, which was the minor subject for my doctorate in mathematics".[3]

"My great teacher Weierstrass was the one who... by his lectures on function theory awakened my interest in seeking radical foundations for mathematics. I came to understand the pains he was taking to transform analysis from the mixture of reason, and irrational instincts and knowhow it was at the time into a pure rational theory. His aim was to expose its original roots, its elementary concepts and axioms on the basis of which the whole system of analysis might be deduced in a completely rigorous, perspicuous way".[4]

---

[2] Since this paper is almost entirely composed of translations from German texts, I have at times been obliged to modify those translations for the sake of consistency of terminology, style, and spelling.

[3] Edmund Husserl, "Recollections of Franz Brentano", *Husserl: Shorter Works*, Notre Dame IN: University of Notre Dame Press, 1981 (1919), p. 342.

[4] Karl Schuhmann, *Husserl Chronik*, The Hague: Martinus Nijhoff, 1977, p. 7.

"At a time when my philosophical interests were increasing and I was uncertain whether to make my career in mathematics or to dedicate myself totally to philosophy, Brentano's lectures settled the matter".[5] "Brentano's lectures gave me for the first time the conviction that encouraged me to choose philosophy as my life's work, the conviction that philosophy too was a serious discipline which also could be and must be dealt with in the spirit of the strictest science".[6] "Brentano was entirely devoted to the austere ideal of a strict philosophic science, an ideal he saw in the exact natural sciences".[7]

"At first I attended these lectures just out of curiosity, simply to hear the man who was then being talked about so much in Vienna".[8] "The very first impression Brentano made upon me struck me quite a bit".[9] "Brentano stood before his young students like a seer of eternal truths and a herald of a celestial world".[10]

"Sometimes it was the subject matter which overcame me, other times the quite singular clearness and dialectical sharpness of his expositions, the cataleptic power as it were of his way of developing problems and of his theories".[11] "He was completely certain of his method and he strove constantly to satisfy the highest claims of an almost mathematical rigor. Brentano believed that his sharply polished concepts, his strongly constructed and systematically ordered theories, and his all round aporetic refutation of alternative interpretations, captured final truths…."[12]

"Although his intuitive analyses were deeply penetrating and often ingenious, Brentano relatively quickly moved from intuition to theory, to the delimitation of sharp concepts, to theoretical formulation of working problems".[13] "Brentano was a master of Socratic maieutic. How well he knew how to use questions and objections to guide the unsure groping beginner, to encourage sincere efforts, and to transform the unclear beginnings of vaguely felt truths into clear thoughts and insights".[14]

5 Husserl, "Recollections of Franz Brentano", p. 342.

6 *Ibid.*, p. 343.

7 *Ibid.*, p. 344-45.

8 *Ibid.*, p. 342.

9 *Ibid.*

10 *Ibid.*, p. 343.

11 *Ibid.*

12 *Ibid.*, p. 344.

13 *Ibid.*

14 *Ibid.*, p. 343.

"What made me marvel and filled me with confidence was the completely impartial way Brentano attacked all problems, his way of dealing with problems in terms of *aporiai*, his finely dialectical measuring of various possible arguments, his clarifying of equivocations, and bringing back of all philosophical concepts to their original intuitive sources".[15] "Brentano's preeminent and admirable strength was in logical theory. Yet the extraordinary and still lasting effect of Brentano's philosophy in the long run rests on his having drawn as an original thinker from original intuitive sources".[16]

"In his university lectures *Franz Brentano* always placed the greatest of emphasis upon the distinction between 'authentic' and 'inauthentic' or 'symbolic' presentations".[17] "Any content which is not given to us as what it is, but rather is given only indirectly by means of some sort of sign, is one that is symbolically presented".[18]

"To him I owe the deeper understanding of the vast significance of inauthentic presentations for our whole psychical life, which before him, as far as I can tell, no one had fully grasped".[19] "They begin to take hold on the earliest levels of psychic development, and accompany that development – ever expanding, and fulfilling ever more inclusive and more complicated functions – up to the highest levels of development. Indeed, we may claim still more: They do not merely *accompany* psychic development, but rather they essentially *condition* it, making it possible to begin with. Without the possibility of external, enduring marks of reference as support for our memory, without the possibility of symbolic presentations serving in place of actual presentations that are more abstract or too difficult to keep distinct and to operate with (or, indeed, serving in place of presentations that *as* actual are altogether denied to us), there would simply be no higher mental life – much less, then, science. Symbols are the great natural instrument by which the limits of our psychical life, originally so narrow, are broken through, and by which the essential imperfections of our intellect are, at least to a certain degree, rendered harmless. Through

---

15 *Ibid.*

16 *Ibid.*, p. 345.

17 Edmund Husserl, *Philosophy of Arithmetic, Psychological and Logical Investigations with Supplementary Texts from 1887-1901*, Dordrecht: Kluwer, 2003 (1891), p. 205 n. 1.

18 Edmund Husserl, "On the Logic of Signs (Semiotic)" (1890), in his *Early Writings in the Philosophy of Logic and Mathematics*, Dordrecht: Kluwer, 1994, p. 30.

19 Husserl, *Philosophy of Arithmetic*, p. 205 n. 1.

characteristic detours, sparing of higher thought, they enable the human mind to accomplish things which directly, in the workings of actual knowing, it could never bring about. Symbols serve the economy of mental achievement as tools and machines do the economy of mechanical achievement... Take the symbolic tools away from the greatest genius and he becomes less capable than the most limited of minds".[20]

Analyzing the concepts of mathematics

"For a long time I worked on philosophical investigations into the principles of general mathematics".[21] "From Antiquity – in fact, for millennia – there have been repeated attempts at the analysis of the concepts upon which mathematics is based, of the elementary truths from which it is built up, and of the methods owing to which it has always stood as the model of rigorously scientific deduction".[22] "A series of new and very far reaching instruments of investigation was found, and an almost boundless profusion of important pieces of knowledge was won. It was an exhilaratingly creative period... It is easy to understand... how reflections concerning the logical nature of all the puzzling, auxiliary concepts... had to be postponed in favor of the quest for results, for discoveries, and for the utilization of all those admirable tools. Only later – when... errors which arose in consequence of the unclarity about the nature of the auxiliary means used, and about the limits of reliability of the operations involved, became more and more numerous... arose the need... to logically clarify, survey and secure what had been attained, to analyze the primitive and mediating concepts closely, to gain logical insight into the interdependency of the various mathematical disciplines... and, finally, to develop the whole of mathematics out of the smallest possible number of self-evident principles in a rigorously deductive manner".[23]

"*Weierstrass* usually opened his epoch-making lectures on the theory of analytical functions with the sentences: 'Pure arithmetic (or pure analysis) is a science based solely and only on the concept of number

[20] Husserl, "On the Logic of Signs (Semiotic)" (1890), pp. 28-29.

[21] Schuhmann, *Husserl Chronik*, p. 13.

[22] Edmund Husserl, *On the Concept of Number: Psychological Analyses* (1887), in his *Philosophy of Arithmetic, Psychological and Logical Investigations with Supplementary Texts from 1887-1901*, p. 305.

[23] *Ibid.*, pp. 306-07.

[*Zahl*]".[24] "Therefore", I believed in my youth, "it is with the analysis of the concept of number that any philosophy of mathematics must begin.... The means which it employs to this end", I wrote, "belong to psychology, and they must do so if such an investigation is to attain solid results".[25] "In truth, not only is psychology indispensable for the analysis of the concept of number, but rather this even *belongs within* psychology".[26] I thought that "analyses of elementary concepts... may nowadays be counted among the more essential tasks of psychology. For how otherwise could it attain insight into the internal structure of the fantastically interwoven tissue of thoughts which constitutes the substance of our thought-life? The understanding of the first and most simple modes of composition of presentations is the key to the understanding of those higher levels of complication with which our consciousness constantly operates as with seamless and fixed formations".[27]

Doubts arise

"There were connections, however, in which such a psychological foundation never came to satisfy me".[28] "Much as I saw in my analyses helpful and new beginnings, they still left me deeply dissatisfied".[29] "Where one was concerned with questions as to the origin of mathematical presentations, or with the elaboration of those practical methods which are indeed psychologically determined, psychological analyses seemed to me to promote clearness and instruction. But once one has passed from the psychological connections of thinking, to the logical unity of the thought-content (the unity of theory), no true continuity and unity could be established".[30]

"The presentation of 'set' was supposed to arise out of the collective combination (out of unifying consciousness of being intended together, in being conceived as one) and certainly, there was some truth in that. The

24 Husserl, *Philosophy of Arithmetic*, p. 13, n. 3.
25 Husserl, *On the Concept of Number*, p. 311.
26 *Ibid.*
27 *Ibid.*
28 Edmund Husserl, *Logical Investigations*, London: Routledge and Kegan Paul, 1970, p. 42.
29 Edmund Husserl, *Introduction to the Logical Investigations, A Draft of a Preface to the Logical Investigations*, The Hague: Martinus Nijhoff, 1975 (1913), p. 34.
30 Husserl, *Logical Investigations*, p. 42.

collective is no substantial unity grounded in the content of the collected items... It could not be physical: hence the concept of collection arises... through psychological reflection in Brentano's sense, through 'reflection' upon the concept of collecting... But then is the concept of number not something basically different from the concept of collecting which is all that can result from the reflection on acts? Such doubts unsettled – even tormented – me already in the very beginning and then extended to all categorial concepts... and finally... to all concepts of objectivities of any sort whatsoever. The customary appeal in the Brentano school to symbolic presentation... could not help. That was only a phrase in the place of a solution".[31]

"I became more and more disquieted by doubts of principle as to how to reconcile the objectivity of mathematics, and of all science in general, with a psychological foundation for logic... My whole method that sought to illuminate the given science through psychological analyses, became shaken, and I felt myself more and more pushed towards general critical reflections on the essence of logic, and on the relationship, in particular, between the subjectivity of knowing and the objectivity of the content known.[32]

"And while laboring over projects concerning the logic of mathematical thought, and of the mathematical calculus in particular, I was tormented by those incredibly strange realms: the world of the purely logical and the world of actual consciousness – or as I would say now, that of the phenomenological and also the psychological. I had no idea how to unite them; and yet they had to interrelate and form an intrinsic unity".[33] "I was gripped by deep, and by the deepest problems".[34]

"The immense importance that 'purely symbolical thinking' has for consciousness could, after all sorts of difficulties, theoretically be comprehended by external logic, as it were, in the case of mathematics. But how symbolic thinking is 'possible', how the objective, mathematical and logical relations constitute themselves in subjectivity, how the insight into this is to be understood, and how the mathematical in itself, is given

---

31 Husserl, *Introduction to the Logical Investigations,* pp. 34-35.

32 Husserl, *Logical Investigations*, p. 42.

33 Edmund Husserl, "Personal Notes" (1906-1908), in his *Early Writings in the Philosophy of Logic and Mathematics*, pp. 490-91.

34 *Ibid.*, pp. 492-93.

in the medium of the psychical, could be valid, this all remained mystery".[35]

"Here lie great, unsolved puzzles. We stand close to the most obscure parts of the theory of knowledge... Scientific knowledge... is totally based upon the possibility of our being able to abandon ourselves completely to thought that is merely symbolic or is otherwise most removed from intuition, or of our being able purposively to prefer such thinking, with certain precautions, over thought more fully adequated to intuition. But how, then, is rational insight possible in science? And how with such a style of thought does one even come to mere empirically correct results?"[36] "We proceed *without* any justification; we are guided, not by a motive of knowledge, but rather by a psychological mechanism. But this does not settle the second or objective aspect of the question, the one about *truth*. Indeed, a logically unjustified procedure can quite well lead to true results".[37]

"One will search logical works in vain for light on what really makes such mechanical operations, with mere written characters, capable of vastly expanding our actual knowledge concerning the number concepts – making possible for us accomplishments which were unconceivable to the greatest thinkers of antiquity".[38] "Vainly we turn, for the resolution of such doubts, to the old logic or the new. They leave us totally in the lurch. Logic, the 'theory of science', must concede... that all science is a mystery to it... Now I certainly will not deny that one can considerably advance logical understanding of the soundness of symbolic (and above all, of course, mathematical thought) without a more penetrating insight into the essence of those elementary processes of intuition and the Representation which everywhere make that thought possible. But without such insight one surely cannot obtain a full and truly satisfactory understanding of symbolic thought or of any logical process".[39]

---

[35] Husserl, *Introduction to the Logical Investigations*, p. 35.

[36] Edmund Husserl, "Psychological Studies in the Elements of Logic" (1894), in his *Early Writings in the Philosophy of Logic and Mathematics*, p. 167.

[37] Edmund Husserl, "On the Logic of Signs (Semiotic)" (1890), p. 37.

[38] *Ibid.*, p. 50.

[39] Husserl, "Psychological Studies in the Elements of Logic", pp. 168-69.

Entering the realm of the ideal

"I was eventually compelled to lay aside my philosophical mathematical investigations, until I had succeeded in reaching a certain clearness on the basic questions of epistemology and in the critical understanding of logic as a science".[40] "In the decade of solitary, arduous labor... I still saw all around me only inchoate, ambiguously defined problems, and profoundly unclear theories. Weary of the confusions and fearing lest I sink into the ocean of endless criticism, I felt myself compelled... for the sake of philosophical self-preservation, to risk attempting to start some place on my own... from which I could perhaps eventually work my way up step by step".[41]

"The course of my development... led to my drawing apart as regards basic logical convictions from men and writings to whom I owe most of my intellectual training, and to my drawing rather closer to a group of thinkers whose writings I was not able to estimate rightly, and whom I consulted all too little in the course of my labors".[42] "Completely under Brentano's influence in my beginnings, I developed rather late the conviction which is shared today by so many scholars intent on a strict scientific philosophy, namely that the Idealistic systems... must be seen rather as immature and yet of the highest value... Entirely new and totally radical dimensions of philosophical problems are illuminated in the Idealist systems. Moreover the ultimate and highest goals of philosophy are opened up only when the philosophical method which these particular systems require is clarified and developed".[43]

"The transformation was prepared by the study of Leibniz and by the considerations occupying me ever anew of the sense both of the distinction between *vérités de raison* and *vérités de fait* and also at the same time of Hume's expositions concerning knowledge about 'relations of ideas' and 'matters of fact'. I became keenly aware of the contrast between this latter distinction and Kant's distinction between analytic and synthetic judgments, and this became important for the later positions I took".[44]

"The empirical sciences – natural sciences – are sciences of 'matters of fact'... Pure Mathematics, the whole sphere of the genuine Apriori in

---

40 Husserl, *Logical Investigations*, p. 43.

41 Husserl, *Introduction to the Logical Investigations,* pp. 16-17.

42 Husserl, *Logical Investigations*, p. 43.

43 Husserl, "Recollections of Franz Brentano", p. 345.

44 Husserl, *Introduction to the Logical Investigations,* p. 36.

general, is free of all matter of fact suppositions... We stand not within the realm of nature, but within that of Ideas, not within the realm of empirical... generalities, but within that of the ideal, apodictic, general system of laws, not within the realm of causality, but within that of rationality... Pure logical, mathematical laws are laws of essence...".[45] "Thus no psychologistic empiricism... can change the fact that pure mathematics is a strictly self-contained system of doctrines which is to be cultivated using methods that are essentially different from those of natural science".[46]

"For the fully conscious and radical turn and for the accompanying 'Platonism', I must credit the study of Lotze's logic".[47] "My concepts of the 'Ideal' significations, and 'Ideal' contents of presentations and judgments... originally derive... – as the term 'Ideal' all by itself indicates – from *Lotze*. In particular, Lotze's reflections about the interpretation of *Plato*'s theory of ideas had a profound effect on me".[48] "Little as Lotze himself had gone beyond... psychologism, still his brilliant interpretation of Plato's doctrine of Ideas gave me my first big insight and was a determining factor in all further studies. Lotze already spoke of truths in themselves, and so the idea suggested itself to transfer all of the mathematical and a major part of the traditionally logical in to the realm of the ideal".[49]

"Only by thinking out these thoughts from *Lotze* – and in my opinion he failed to get completely clear on them – did I find the key to the curious conceptions of Bolzano, which in all their phenomeno-logical naiveté were at first unintelligible, and to the treasures of his *Wissenschaftslehre*".[50]

"Bolzano as a mathematician was brought to my attention (I was a student of Weierstrass at the time) through an article by Stolz... and above all through Brentano's critical discussion (in his lectures) of the 'paradoxes

---

45 Edmund Husserl, "Husserl an Brentano, 27. III. 1905", in his *Briefwechsel, Die Brentanoschule I*, Dordrecht: Kluwer, 1994, p. 37.
46 Husserl, *Introduction to the Logical Investigations,* p. 29.
47 *Ibid.*, p. 36.
48 Edmund Husserl, "Review of Melchior Palagyi's *Der Streit der Psychologisten und Formalisten in der modernen Logik*" (1903), in his *Early Writings in the Philosophy of Logic and Mathematics*, Dordrecht: Kluwer, 1994, p. 201.
49 Husserl, *Introduction to the Logical Investigations,* p. 36.
50 Husserl, "Review of Melchior Palagyi's *Der Streit der Psychologisten und Formalisten in der modernen Logik*", p. 201.

of infinity' and through G. Cantor... However, his original thoughts about ideas, propositions and truths 'in themselves', I misinterpreted as metaphysical abstrusities".[51] "Then it suddenly occurred to me... that the first two volumes of Bolzano's *Wissenschaftslehre* (entitled "A Theory of Ideas in Themselves" and "A Theory of Propositions in Themselves") were to be looked upon as a first attempt at a unified presentation of the area of pure ideal doctrines – in other words, that here a complete plan of a 'pure' logic was already available. Understandably, this insight offered me an immense benefit: step by step using Bolzano's account, I could verify the "Platonic" interpretation...".[52]

"If... his 'propositions in themselves' previously appeared to me as mythical entities, suspended between being and non-being, it then became clear to me... that here we basically have a quite obvious conception... I saw that under 'proposition in itself' is to be understood what is designated in ordinary discourse – which always hypostasizes the Ideal – as the "sense" of a statement. It is that which is explained as one and the same where, for example, different persons are said to have asserted the same thing. Or, again, it is what, in science, is simply called a theorem, e.g., the theorem about the sum of the angles in a triangle, which no one would think of taking to be someone's lived experience of judging. And it further became clear to me that this identical sense could be nothing other than the universal, the species, which belongs to a certain Moment present in all actual assertions with the same sense, and which makes possible the identification just mentioned, even where the descriptive content of the individual lived experiences of asserting varies considerably in other respects... Now with this view of things... Bolzano's theory, that propositions are objects which nonetheless have no 'existence', comes to have the following quite intelligible signification: – They have the 'Ideal' being or validity of objects which are universals – and, thus, that being which is established, for example, in the 'existence proofs' of mathematics".[53]

"I must say besides that I am far from any mystico-metaphysical exploitation of 'Ideas', ideal possibilities and such. Likewise, Bolzano did not hypostasize his 'presentations' and propositions 'in themselves'. These conceptions of Bolzano's have had a powerful effect on me just as Lotze's

---

[51] Husserl, *Introduction to the Logical Investigations,* p. 37.

[52] *Ibid.*

[53] Husserl, "Review of Melchior Palagyi's *Der Streit der Psychologisten und Formalisten in der modernen Logik*", pp. 201-02.

new interpretation of Plato's theory of Ideas... What I set forth are fragments of a theory of knowledge and of a phenomenology of knowledge. Both are foreign to Bolzano. He was an eminent mathematical and logical mind, but with him precise conceptual analyses and formal-logical theories go hand in hand with a plainly naive theory of knowledge. There is no trace in his work (as in Lotze's) of any thought of a pure phenomenological elucidation of knowledge".[54]

Brentano and the science of intentionality

"The whole approach whereby the overcoming of psychologism is phenomenologically accomplished shows that what... was given as analyses of immanent consciousness must be considered as a pure a priori analysis of essence. In this way were opened up for the first time, and in far-reaching analyses actually carried out, the immense fields of the givens of consciousness as fields for 'ontological' investigations".[55]

"This is the place to recall the extraordinary debt we owe to Brentano for the fact that he began his attempt to reform psychology with an investigation of the peculiar characteristics of the psychic (in contrast to the physical) and showed intentionality to be one of these characteristics".[56] "Brentano conducts his enquiry in the form of a two-edged separation of the two main classes of 'phenomena'... the psychical and the physical... Of his two principal differentiations, one directly reveals the essence of psychical phenomena or acts... In perception something is perceived, in imagination, something imagined, in a statement, something stated, in love, something loved, in hate hated. Brentano looks to what is graspably common to such instances, and says that 'every mental phenomenon is characterized by what the mediaeval schoolmen called the intentional (or mental) inexistence of an object, and by what we... call the relation to a content, the direction to an object... or an immanent objectivity. Each mental phenomenon contains something as object in itself, though not all in the same manner".[57]

"Brentano's separation of the 'psychical' from 'physical phenomena'... is particularly important, since it blazed a fresh trail for the development

---

54 Husserl, "Husserl an Brentano, 27. III. 1905", p. 39.

55 Husserl, *Introduction to the Logical Investigations,* p. 42.

56 Edmund Husserl, *The Crisis of European Sciences and Transcendental Phenomenology*, Evanston IL: Northwestern University, 1970 (1954), §68.

57 Husserl, *Logical Investigations*, p. 554.

of phenomenology – although Brentano himself remained a stranger to phenomenological ground, and although with his sharp distinction he failed to reach that for which he sought, namely, the separation of the empirical domains of psychology and the physical natural sciences... Brentano... took no account of the separation on grounds of principle of the 'physical phenomena' as material phases (sensory data) from 'physical phenomena' as the objective phases that appear in the noetic apprehension of the former (the color of a thing, the shape of a thing, and the like); but as against this he marked off on the other side the concept of 'psychical phenomenon'... through the unique feature of Intentionality".[58]

"Among the demarcations of classes in descriptive psychology, there is none more remarkable nor more important philosophically than the one offered by Brentano under his title of 'psychical phenomena'....[59] "A sharply defined class of experiences is here brought before us, comprising all that enjoys mental, conscious experience... Turning aside from psychology, and entering the field of the philosophical disciplines proper, we perceive the fundamental importance of our class of experiences, since only its members are relevant in the highest ranks of the normative sciences. They alone, seized in their phenomenological purity, furnish concrete bases for abstracting the fundamental notions that function systematically in logic, ethics and aesthetics, and that enter into the ideal laws of these sciences".[60]

"It was *Franz Brentano* who first opened up the trail here – but only through his formal indicating of the general descriptive uniqueness of 'mental phenomena'. He had never overcome the naturalistic prejudice in his psychology, and precisely because of this the unique sense of intentional analysis and the proper method of an intentional psychology remained inaccessible to him. The idea of a pure phenomenology however was completely beyond his reach".[61]

"It is not enough to say that all consciousness is consciousness-of and go on to distinguish by type the various modes of consciousness, in the manner of... Brentano's classification (with which I cannot

---

58 Edmund Husserl, *Ideas, General Introduction to Pure Phenomenology*, New York: Collier Books, 1962 (1913), p. 229.

59 Husserl, *Logical Investigations*, p. 552.

60 *Ibid.*, p. 554.

61 Husserl, *Introduction to the Logical Investigations*, p. 61.

agree)... On the contrary, what must be undertaken is an inquiry into the various categories of 'objects' – but purely as objects of possible consciousness – and a questioning back to the essential forms of possible 'manifolds', ones that are to be joined together synthetically and through whose synthesis, itself something to be described, there arises the consciousness of the identity of the present object of the respective category. One and the same 'object in general', as meant object, traverses these manifolds".[62]

"Thus Brentano set up a psychology of intentionality as a task only formally, but had no way of attacking it. The same is true of his whole school, which also, like Brentano himself, consistently refused to accept what was decisively new in my *Logical Investigations* (even though his demand for psychology of intentional phenomena was put into effect here). What is new in my *Logical Investigations* is found not at all in the merely ontological investigations..., but rather in the subjectively directed investigations... in which for the first time the *cogitata qua cogitata*, as essential moments of each conscious experience as it is given in genuine inner experience, come into their own and immediately come to dominate the whole method of intentional analysis".[63]

"However great is the veneration and gratitude with which I remember my teacher and his genius, and as much as I consider his transformation of the scholastic concept of intentionality into a descriptive foundational concept of psychology to be a great discovery, without which phenomenology would never have been possible, nevertheless an essential distinction has to be drawn between pure psychology in my sense, a psychology contained implicitly in transcendental phenomenology, and Brentano's psychology".[64] "Descriptive psychology offers a genuine and natural point of departure for the working out of the idea of phenomenology. This was in fact the way which led me to phenomenology. On the other hand, it is to be fully established in a deeper investigation that phenomenology, the way *we* understand it – as eidetic, but, at the same time, as resting on

[62] Edmund Husserl, *Ideas Pertaining to a Pure Phenomenology and to a Phenomenological Philosophy, Second Book, Studies in the Phenomenology of Constitution*, Dordrecht: Kluwer, 1989, pp. 424-25.

[63] Husserl, *The Crisis of European Sciences and Transcendental Phenomenology*, §68.

[64] Husserl, *Ideas Pertaining to a Pure Phenomenology and to a Phenomenological Philosophy, Second Book*, p. 422.

the *transcendental reduction* – is in no way descriptive psychology and has, in strict truth, not even one part in common with it".[65]

"The basic error of Psychologism consists, according to my view, in its obliteration of this fundamental distinction between pure and empirical generality, and in its misinterpretation of the *pure* laws of logic as empirical laws of psychology".[66] "What is essentially new, broken open in transcendentally oriented phenomenology and at the same time a breakthrough for descriptive psychology, transforming completely the face of this psychology, its entire method and its concrete aims, is the insight that a concrete description of the sphere of consciousness as a self-enclosed sphere of intentionality... has a totally different sense than descriptions of nature, thus than the exemplary descriptions in the descriptive natural sciences".[67]

Final meeting

"I did not see him again until 1908 in Florence".[68] "He let me report cohesively on the sense of the phenomenological way of investigation and my past struggle against psychologism. But we did not understand each other... I was hindered by the inner conviction that... Brentano was no longer adaptable enough to be able to understand the necessity which had forced me to transform his basic intuitions".[69]

"Brentano was sure of his philosophy... His inner certainty of being on the right path and of founding a purely scientific philosophy never wavered... I would like to stress this pure doubt free conviction as being plainly the basic fact of Brentano's life".[70] "Brentano was sensitive about any deviation from his fixed convictions".[71] "I knew... how much it bothered him when someone took another path even though it emanated from his own".[72] "No one surpassed him in educating students to think

65 *Ibid.*, p. 326.

66 Husserl, "Review of Melchior Palagyi's *Der Streit der Psychologisten und Formalisten in der modernen Logik*", p. 204.

67 Husserl, *Ideas Pertaining to a Pure Phenomenology and to a Phenomenological Philosophy, Second Book*, p. 424.

68 Husserl, "Recollections of Franz Brentano", p. 347.

69 *Ibid.*

70 *Ibid.*, p. 345.

71 *Ibid.*

72 *Ibid.*, p. 346.

independently, yet no one took it harder when such thinking was directed against his own entrenched convictions".[73]

"There was a kind of radiance about him, as if he belonged no longer to this world, as if he lived half here and half already in that higher world... This last image I have of him from that time in Florence has impressed itself most profoundly in my spirit. This is the way Brentano lives now always in my memory, an image from a higher world".[74]

"Initially I was his enthusiastic student... But I could not remain a member of his school".[75] "That was not easy for me. Nothing runs deeper in my nature than to revere... But... there unfortunately dwells within me an intractably critical sense unmindful of my natural inclinations... By nature bound, intellectually free, so I go... my way... I am... still a poor beginner ... As always, I work, and often with despairing doggedness, as if to rid myself of some of the endless shame of my dullness, unclarity, and ignorance".[76]

---

73 *Ibid.*, p. 345.

74 *Ibid.*, p. 348.

75 *Ibid.*, p. 346.

76 Edmund Husserl, *Briefwechsel, Die Brentanoschule I*, pp. 20-21.

2

HUSSERL AND PHENOMENOLOGY, EXPERIENCE AND ESSENCE[1]

For Husserl, which came first, experience or essence? That question is as slippery as the famous one about the chicken and the egg. And, since there is probably no completely satisfactory answer to it, it is surely something that is going to be debated as long as there are philosophers to debate it.

However, whether or not there is a definitive answer, the question is well worth asking. For Husserl's search to fathom the complex interplay between experience and essence was at the heart of the dynamic that brought phenomenology into being, and the slipperiness of the question harbors one of the secrets of phenomenology's impact.

The underlying paradox is that Husserl's science of subjectivity was his science of objectivity. He taught that the ultimate meaning and source of all objectivity making it possible for thinking to reach beyond contingent, subjective, human acts and lay hold of objective being-in-itself was to be found in ideality and the ideal laws defining it.[2] In *Experience and Judgment*, he presented the world constituted by transcendental subjectivity as a pre-given world that is not a pure world of experience, but a world determined and determinable in itself with exactitude, a world in which any individual entity is given beforehand in an perfectly obvious way as in principle determinable in accordance with the methods of exact science.[3]

Yet, while insisting on the primacy of the objective order, Husserl stressed that, for example, logic turns *both* towards ideal objects, towards a world of concepts where truth is an analysis of essences or concepts, where knowing subjects and the material world play no role, *and* towards the deeply hidden subjective forms in which reason does its work. He considered that almost everything concerning the fundamental meaning of logic was laden with misunderstandings owing to the fact that objectivity arises out of subjective activity. He considered that even the ideal objectivity

---

1 This was originally a paper presented at the Fourth International Congress of Phenomenology held in Cracow, Poland from August 17-21, 2008.

2 Edmund Husserl, *Allgemeine Erkenntnistheorie, Vorlesung 1902/03*, Dordrecht: Kluwer, 2001, p. 200.

3 Edmund Husserl, *Experience and Judgment*, London: Routledge and Kegan Paul, 1973 (1939), §11.

of logical structures and *a priori* nature of logical theories especially pertaining to this objectivity, and the meaning of that a priori, suffered from this lack of clarity since what is ideal appears as located in the subjective sphere and arises from it.[4]

Fortunately, texts and research published during the last few decades are shedding light on many of phenomenology's puzzles. Here, I want to take a new look at what I have called Husserl's paradox by integrating some of this less familiar material into the familiar picture of the genesis of phenomenology. In particular, I want to look at Husserl's conversion from experience to essences during the last decade of the nineteenth century, a time that resembles our times in some respects.

From experience to essences

To see in what way Husserl's paradox about subjectivity and objectivity is at the heart of the dynamic that brought phenomenology into being, we need to review the evolution his ideas underwent at the time the foundations of phenomenology were laid.

At first, as recounted in the last chapter, experience came first. As a student of Franz Brentano, Husserl was not receptive to the claims of metaphysical idealism. Brentano was entirely devoted to the austere ideal of a strict philosophical science as realized in the exact natural sciences. He considered metaphysical idealism odious and despicable.[5]

It was only after experiencing the shortcomings of Brentano's empirical psychology that Husserl begin veering in the direction of essences. The further he delved into his philosophical investigations into the principles of mathematics, the more he grew troubled by doubts as to how to reconcile the objectivity of mathematics and all science in general, with empirical foundations for logic, and the more he saw the need to engage in general critical reflections on the essence of logic and the relationship between the subjectivity of knowing and the objectivity of the content known.[6]

---

4 Edmund Husserl, *Formal and Transcendental Logic*, The Hague: Martinus Nijhoff, 1969 (1929), §§7, 8.

5 Edmund Husserl, "Recollections of Franz Brentano", in *Husserl: Shorter Works*, P. McCormick and F. Elliston (eds.), Notre Dame IN: University of Notre Dame Press, 1981, pp. 342-49.

6 Edmund Husserl, *Logical Investigations*, London: Routledge and Kegan Paul, 1970, p. 42; his *Introduction to the Logical Investigations, A Draft of a Preface to the Logical Investigations*, The Hague: Martinus Nijhoff, 1975, pp. 34-35.

He left dramatic descriptions of ten years of hard, lonely work and struggling during which he felt tormented by the incredibly strange worlds of the purely logical and actual consciousness that he saw opening up on all sides. He aspired after clarity, but only encountered confusion.[7] He was assailed by questions. Facing only riddles, tensions, puzzles and mysteries, and seeing all around him only unclear, undeveloped, ambiguous ideas, weary of all the confusion, he felt he had to risk setting out on his own.[8] This crisis could be thought of as the birth pangs of phenomenology.

During those years, Husserl kept company with Georg Cantor,[9] the eccentric creator of set theory, who was hard at work discovering and exploring the strange worlds of the pure mathematics and actual consciousness. However psychologistic his mysterious references to inner intuition or to experiences helping produce concepts in his mind might seem, Cantor was strictly opposed to any philosophy that located the sources of knowledge and certainty in the senses or in the supposedly pure forms of intuition of the world of presentation. A good measure of the freedom he felt he possessed as a mathematician came from distinguishing between an empirical treatment of numbers and Plato's pure, ideal *arithmoi eidetikoi,* which by their very nature were detached from things perceptible by the senses. Originally untainted by the metaphysical idealism that Brentano disdained, Husserl drew near the Platonic idealism that Cantor espoused and renounced the psychologism, empiricism, and naturalism that he renounced.[10]

Husserl's fully conscious and radical turn away from empirical psychology and his espousal of Platonism, we have seen, came about

---

[7] Edmund Husserl, "Personal Notes" (1906-1908), in his *Early Writings in the Philosophy of Logic and Mathematics*, Dordrecht: Kluwer, 1994, pp. 490-91.

[8] Husserl, "Psychological Studies in the Elements of Logic" (1894), pp. 167-69, his "Personal Notes", pp. 492-93, 497-98, his *Introduction to the Logical Investigations*, p. 17, his *Logical Investigations*, pp. 42-43.

[9] Malvine Husserl, "Skizze eines Lebensbildes von E. Husserl", *Husserl Studies* 5, 1988, pp. 105-25.

[10] Claire Ortiz Hill, "Did Georg Cantor Influence Edmund Husserl?", *Synthese* 113 (October 1997), pp. 145-70 and "Abstraction and Idealization in Georg Cantor and Edmund Husserl", in *Idealization IV. Historical Studies on Abstraction and Idealization*, F. Coniglione, R. Poli, R. Rollinger (eds.), Amsterdam: Rodopi, 2004, pp. 217-43, both papers are anthologized in Claire Ortiz Hill and G. E. Rosado Haddock, *Husserl or Frege, Meaning, Objectivity, and Mathematics*, La Salle IL: Open Court, 2000.

through his study of Hermann Lotze's logic. Husserl said that his own concepts of ideal significations and ideal contents of presentations and judgments originally derived from Lotze, whose interpretation of Plato's Theory of Ideas gave Husserl the key to understanding Bernhard Bolzano's ideas about propositions and truths in themselves, which under Brentano's influence, Husserl had thought of as metaphysical abstrusities, mythical entities suspended somewhere between being and non-being.[11]

The last years of the nineteenth century and the early years of the twentieth century found Husserl teaching that the ideal entities so unpleasant for empiricistic logic, and so consistently disregarded by it, had not been artificially devised either by himself, or by Bolzano, but were given beforehand by the meaning of the universal talk of propositions and truths indispensable in all the sciences. This indubitable fact, Husserl now stressed, had to be the starting point of all logic. This constant talk of propositions, of true and false means something identical and atemporal. No more is meant by the ideality than that it is a matter of a kind of possible objects of knowledge, whose particular characteristics can, and in scientific investigation must, be determined, while they are just not objects in the sense of real objects.[12]

As regards its essential, theoretical makeup, Husserl taught, science is a system of ideal meanings that unite into a meaning unit. The theory of gravity, the system of analytic mechanics, the mechanical theory of heat, the theory of metric or projective geometry are all units, not of mental experiences of one person or another, or of states of mind, but units entirely made up of ideal material, of meanings. And, in this lies truth and falsehood, what science makes into an objective, supra-individual unit of validity logically grasping and dealing with a sphere of objectivity.[13]

All truly scientific thinking, all proving and theorizing, operates in forms that correspond to purely logical laws. Pure logic embraces all the concepts and propositions without which science would not be possible,

---

[11] Husserl, *Introduction to the Logical Investigations*, pp. 36-38, 46-49; his "Review of Melchior Palagyi's *Der Streit der Psychologisten und Formalisten in der modernen Logik*" (1903), in his *Early Writings in the Philosophy of Logic and Mathematics*, pp. 200-03, 209; Hermann Lotze, *Logic*, New York: Garland, 1980, Chapter II.

[12] Edmund Husserl, *Alte und neue Logik, Vorlesung 1908/09*, Dordrecht: Kluwer, 2003, pp. 45, 47, 241.

[13] Edmund Husserl, *Introduction to Logic and Theory of Knowledge, Lectures 1906/07*, Dordrecht: Springer, 2008, §12.

would not have any sense or validity.[14] While all of natural science is an a posteriori discipline grounded in experience with its actual occurrences, the world of the purely logical is a world of ideal objects, a world of "concepts". Pure logic is an a priori discipline entirely grounded in conceptual essentialities. There all truth is nothing other than the analysis of essences or concepts. With them, we are just not in psychology, in any sphere of empiricism and probability.[15]

A science of ideal being

A rediscovery of metaphysics took place at the end of the nineteenth century, which had seen a positivistic revolt against idealism and Kantian inspired psychologism and a yearning for the real and the palpable that turned the thoughts of many in the direction of the natural world of perceptible facts and events. There had also been a revolt against the various forms of positivism, empiricism, naturalism and materialism that others felt the modern age was foisting upon them. Subsequently, still others wanted to unite what seemed to be two contradictory worlds. They wanted a scientific metaphysics, a scientific idealism.

Lotze played a preeminent role in rehabilitating the respectability of metaphysical inquiry. Trained in medicine, he was initially caught up in the naturalistic movement that sought to extend natural science and its methods over the entire realm of intelligible existence. It taught that what science could not know, could not be. It did not admit any unknowable, supra-sensuous reality and easily evolved into materialistic philosophy that denied it. He rebelled. He judged the basic ideas of the natural sciences inadequate, disconnected, and often inconsistent. His antagonism was directed toward their pretensions to deal with all the phenomena of human experience. He believed that they had nothing to say about what was most worth knowing. He wanted to show their inadequacy and that there was room and need for philosophy side by side with science.

However, his genuine respect for the methods and results of the natural sciences, as long as they confined themselves to their own proper domain, deepened his aversion to idealism, which he saw as having turned its back upon the realm of facts and as having lost itself in the realm of empty thoughts. So to create his new philosophical outlook, Lotze had to

---

[14] Husserl, *Allgemeine Erkenntnistheorie*, p. 47.

[15] Husserl, *Introduction to Logic and Theory of Knowledge*, §13c.

clear the way by combating the errors of both philosophers inspired by the natural sciences and the idealists.[16]

In his 1902 Paris doctoral thesis on Lotze's metaphysics, Henri Schoen explained how Lotze inspired courage in worried and tormented consciences and communicated faith in the triumph of a spiritualistic conception of the world to young people whose confidence had been shaken by the ineffectiveness of idealism and the successes of materialism. To those impressed by positivism, Schoen explains, Lotze gave an exact method starting from observation and not a priori reasoning. He taught a generation disgusted with abstractions to start from given facts.

Schoen saw his generation as being disgusted with materialism, with vague and confused aspirations and disposed to accept a metaphysics not in contradiction with its scientific views. He explains how he was guided and had tried to guide students through the philosophical and psychological crisis of German metaphysics, how he considered a return to the old dogmatism impossible, but saw the inadequacy of pure reason, how eclipsed by idealism, Kant's realism wrought vengeance on the modern metaphysics that aimed to develop the seeds of realism contained in his theory, and not the idealism there as well. For Schoen, an equal balance had to be maintained between ideality and reality, between the supra-sensible world and the real world. He was completely confident about the future of metaphysics. It was a matter of creating a new philosophical outlook that could satisfy both the modern need for reality and concrete facts and the idealistic and mystical needs of the times.[17]

In his eccentric way, Georg Cantor too was part of the post-Kantian movement to reconcile the findings of modern science with metaphysical views. He made no secret of his intention to supply his new transfinite numbers with adequate philosophical and metaphysical foundations. His views were deeply pro-idealistic. He was an avowed enemy of the new empiricism, of all psychologism, empiricism, positivism, naturalism, sensualism, skepticism, and Kantianism. In 1894, he confided that "in the realm of the spirit" mathematics had no longer been "the essential love of

---

16 Henry Jones, *A Critical Account of the Philosophy of Lotze, the Doctrine of Thought*, Glasgow: James Maclehouse and Sons, 1895, pp. 8, 28, 29.

17 Henri Schoen, *La Métaphysique de Hermann Lotze, ou la philosophie des actions et des réactions réciproques*, Paris: Librairie Fischbacher, 1902, pp. 8-9, 18, 22-23.

his soul" for more than twenty years. Metaphysics and theology, he "openly confessed", had taken possession of his soul.[18]

Pope Leo XIII was also intent upon reconciling modern science and metaphysics. His influential encyclical *Aeterni Patris* of 1879 captured the attention of Cantor, who engaged in exchanges with a number of Catholic philosophers involved in the revival of scholastic philosophy in the spirit of the encyclical. Cantor scholar Joseph Dauben has described the interest generated by *Aeterni Patris* as a tonic for Cantor's declining spirits.[19]

In talking about what Husserl's contemporaries were searching for, it is important to realize that, while the end of the nineteenth century witnessed attempts to rehabilitate the respectability of metaphysical inquiry and to situate it centrally on the philosophical agenda alongside rigorous, rational, scientific thinking, alongside this metaphysical revival there was an occult revival. Like our times, the end of the nineteenth century witnessed a rise in cults, spiritism, Satanism, occultism, magic, witchcraft, and so on. As many were hard at work destroying the superstition of religion, some were indulging in irrational, superstitious, and unsavory pursuits, something that surely fanned antagonism towards any uncritical, unscientific metaphysics, or even a fear of it.

Carl Jung once described the times as having prepared the way for crime. As he saw it, people were living in a lifeless nature bereft of gods. Enlightenment might have destroyed the spirits of nature, but it did not destroy the psychic factors corresponding to them, such as suggestibility, an uncritical attitude, fearfulness, propensity to superstition and prejudice. Even though nature is depsychized, demons do not really disappear, Jung insisted. He saw the psychic conditions breeding them to be as actively at work as ever. "Just when people were congratulating themselves on having abolished all spooks, it turned out that instead of haunting the attic or old ruins, the spooks were flitting about in the heads of apparently normal Europeans. Tyrannical obsessive, intoxicating ideas and delusions were abroad everywhere, and people began to believe the most absurd things...".[20]

---

18 George Cantor, *Georg Cantor Briefe*, H. Meschkowski and W. Nilson (eds.), Springer, New York, 1991, p. 350; Hill, "Did Georg Cantor Influence Edmund Husserl?" and "Abstraction and Idealization in Georg Cantor and Edmund Husserl".

19 Joseph Dauben, *Georg Cantor, His Mathematics and Philosophy of the Infinite*, Princeton: Princeton University Press, 1979, pp. 140-48.

20 Carl Jung, *Jung on Evil*, Murray Stein (ed.), London: Routledge, 1995, p. 194.

Historian Nicholas Goodrick-Clarke has explained that, though there were many forms of modern occultism, its function was relatively uniform. Behind the mantic systems of astrology, and palmistry, the doctrines of theosophy, the quasi-sciences of animal magnetism and hypnotism, the study of the esoteric literature of Cabalists, Rosicrucians, and alchemists, there was a strong desire to reconcile the findings of modern natural science with a religious view. Occult science strove to counter materialist science, with its emphasis upon tangible and measurable phenomena and its neglect of invisible qualities respecting the spirit and the emotions.[21] Cantor's unpublished correspondence shows that he was very knowledgeable about Rosicrucianism in particular.[22]

Intentionality, a sign of contradiction

Into this intellectual climate, Husserl introduced a science of intentionality that was suitably ambiguous because intentionality points in two directions, towards the world of subjectivity and towards the world of objects. I said that Husserl's paradox about subjectivity and objectivity harbors one of the secrets of phenomenology's impact, because I think that his science of intentionality had, and still has, the impact that signs of contradiction have.

According to Brentano's definition of intentionality, every mental phenomenon is characterized by the intentional or mental inexistence of an object, by relation to a content, direction to an object or an immanent objectivity.[23] As seen in the last chapter, Husserl considered that by indicating the uniqueness of mental phenomena, Brentano had blazed the way for the development of phenomenology and made it possible, but that the idea of a pure phenomenology was beyond his reach because he held fast to his ideal of a strict philosophical science based on the exact natural sciences.[24]

---

21 Nicholas Goodrick-Clarke, *The Occult Roots of Nazism, Secret Aryan Cults and their Influence on Nazi Ideology*, New York: I. B. Tauris 1985, p. 29.

22 Cantor's letter books as found in the Niedersächsische Staats-und Universitäts-bibliothek Göttingen, Abteilung Handschriften und Seltene Drücke reveal this.

23 Franz Brentano, *Psychology from an Empirical Standpoint*, London: Routledge and Kegan Paul, 1973 (1874), p. 88.

24 Edmund Husserl, *Ideas, General Introduction to Pure Phenomenology*, New York: Collier Books, 1962 (1913), p. 229; his *Ideas Pertaining to a Pure Phenomenology and to a Phenomenological Philosophy, Second Book, Studies in the Phenomenology of Constitution*, Dordrecht: Kluwer, 1989, p. 422; his *Logical Investigations*, p. 554; his *Introduction to the Logical Investigations*, p. 61.

The entire approach whereby the overcoming of psychologism was phenomenologically accomplished, Husserl stressed in 1913, showed that analyses of immanent consciousness had to be seen as pure a priori analyses of essence, that it was in this way that the immense fields of the givens of consciousness as fields for "ontological" investigations" were opened up for the first time.[25] What was new in the *Logical Investigations*, he maintained in *The Crisis of European Sciences and Transcendental Phenomenology*, was "found not at all in the merely ontological investigations..., but rather in the subjectively directed investigations... in which for the first time the *cogitata qua cogitata*, as essential moments of each conscious experience as it is given in genuine inner experience, come into their own and immediately come to dominate the whole method of intentional analysis".[26]

So Husserl's science of intentionality produced masterpieces as diverse as Edith Stein's *Finite and Eternal Being* and *Science of the Cross,* Emmanuel Levinas' *Otherwise than Being or Beyond Essence*, Maurice Merleau-Ponty's *Phenomenology of Perception*, Martin Heidegger's *Being and Time,* and even strongly anti-metaphysical works like and Jean-Paul Sartre's *Being and Nothingness* and *Existentialism is a Humanism.*

Levinas saw phenomenology as reversing the scientific attitude that turned away from the subject for the greater glory of the object and decreed the expulsion of every so-called subjective element from the object.[27] In comparison, Sartre considered that for centuries there had not been a philosophical movement that so "plunged human beings back into the world".[28] He proposed that the profound meaning of the discovery expressed by, "All consciousness is consciousness of something" could be grasped by imagining "a connected series of bursts that tear us out of ourselves, throw us beyond them into the dry dust of the world, onto the plain earth, amidst things…".[29]

---

25 Husserl, *Introduction to the Logical Investigations*, p. 42.

26 Edmund Husserl, *The Crisis of European Sciences and Transcendental Phenomenology.* Evanston: Northwestern University, 1970, §68.

27 Richard Sugarman, "Emmanuel Levinas: the Ethics of 'Face to Face', the Religious Turn", in *Phenomenology World Wide*, Anna-Teresa Tymieniecka (ed.), Dordrecht: Kluwer, 2002, p. 412.

28 Yvanka Raynova, "Jean-Paul Sartre, A Profound Revision of Husserlian Phenomenology", in *Phenomenology World Wide*, Tymieniecka (ed.), p. 324.

29 Jean-Paul Sartre, "Intentionality: A Fundamental Idea of Husserl's Phenomenology", *Journal of the British Society of Phenomenology* 1, 2, May 1970, pp. 4-5.

The great mathematician David Hilbert wrote of how Husserl was a product of Brentano's school, which was oriented toward the creation of an exact theory of acts of judgment and logic with the goal of constructing a theory of science of the kind Bolzano had in mind, but how, in contrast to other representatives of the school, Husserl had adopted an a priori method and rejected psychologism. From this theoretical stance, Hilbert continued, Husserl befriended the speculative trend in philosophy by strengthening it enormously. For since he had expounded a far-reaching grounding of logic and related sciences, after he came out in favor of the methods of speculative dogmatics, he deflected the criticism of sterility normally attached to its application in the exact sciences. But, the problem was solved only apparently. For his method was in fact psychological, and it was only owing to misunderstandings about its true nature that he was able to post successes on the "a priori dogmatism" side of the ledger.[30]

The democratic socialist philosopher Leonard Nelson complained to Hilbert that even if Husserl himself remained protected from mystical degeneration by inhibitions and restraints imposed by secure connections to mathematics that he could not strip away, after his schools had burned its bridges to mathematics, it was frightening to see how unrestrainedly his students fell victim to every excess of Neo-platonic mysticism.[31]

Metaphysics, theory of knowledge and the natural sciences

Husserl communicated the new vision of metaphysics, theory of knowledge and the natural sciences that he developed during the 1890s to the new generation of students in search of a scientific metaphysics that could stand up to the challenges of the natural sciences. He told them of how he saw the metaphysical needs of his time going unmet and gave this as an explanation as to why spiritism and the occult were thriving and superstition of every kind was spreading.[32]

---

30 Unpublished Extracts from Hilbert's *Denkschrift* for Leonard Nelson, undated, archived in the Niedersächsische Staats-und Universitätsbibliothek Göttingen, Abteilung Handschriften und Seltene Drücke.

31 Leonard Nelson, letter of December 29, 1916 to David Hilbert archived in the Niedersächsische Staats-und Universitätsbibliothek Göttingen, Abteilung Handschriften und Seltene Drücke.

32 See for example, Husserl's "Aus der Einleitung der Vorlesung 'Erkenntnistheorie und Hauptpunkte der Metaphysik 1898/99'", in his *Allgemeine Erkenntnistheorie*, pp. 225-55.

He blamed the overriding role and authoritative influence that the natural sciences had acquired in the lives of educated people for the prevailing contempt for metaphysics and its transformation into "a kind of a hobgoblin" (*eine Art Popanz*), or its being considered a relic of scientifically backward times on a par with alchemy and astrology. As he saw it, the natural sciences had taken abundant revenge for the injustice they endured from the pseudo-scientific natural philosophy of the Romantics, but in speaking of metaphysics, natural scientists still had in mind a kind of philosophizing that was up to the old tricks of the Hegelian school.[33]

As Husserl told the story, after the collapse of idealistic philosophy in the mid-nineteenth century, a great awkward lull set in when the philosophical race of Titans of Romanticism, with their extravagant promises and flaunting of the requirements of rigorous science, trained to storm the Mount Olympus of philosophy with their dialectical tricks, were flung down into the dark Tartarus of dissension and unclarity, and uneasy disenchantment, even disillusionment, followed the earlier exuberance. Then sounded ever louder the call back to Kant, who had set limits on the presumptuousness of uncritical metaphysics and established the critique of knowledge as the true foundation for philosophy. With the revival of Kantianism, for which an a priori science of concepts was impossible, the word 'metaphysics' took on ominous overtones and people preferred not to use it.[34]

The extent to which the hard questions about the objectivity of knowledge raised by Kant's work could determine one's entire conception of being in the world was a matter of concern to Husserl,[35] for whom such problems could only be solved through a pure phenomenological elucidation of knowledge for which it was completely obvious that theory of knowledge was prior to all natural knowledge and science and on an entirely different plane.

As long as we are in the state of epistemological innocence and have not bitten the fateful apple of the tree of philosophical knowledge, then every science suits us fine, Husserl taught. But, the moment the sphinx of critique of knowledge asks its questions, all sciences, no matter how

---

33 *Ibid.*, pp. 230-33.

34 Husserl, *Allgemeine Erkenntnistheorie*, pp. 9, 229, 232-33; his *Logik, Vorlesung 1902/03*, Dordrecht: Kluwer, 2001, pp. 12-13.

35 See for example, Husserl's, "Aus der Einleitung der Vorlesung 'Erkenntnistheorie und Hauptpunkte der Metaphysik 1898/99'", p. 232.

beautiful, are nothing to us. All the puzzling questions combined signify that we do not understand sciences in general. No naturally obtained scientific result is free of the worm of doubt or unclarity. Therefore, we cannot use any as a premise from which to derive the answer to these questions.[36]

He called for a science of metaphysics to study problems lying beyond empirical investigation, to engage in the exploration of what is *realiter* in the ultimate and absolute sense, and so provide ultimate and deepest knowledge of reality. He believed that such a science of metaphysics was possible, justifiable, and that human beings could attain knowledge of reality.[37]

Husserl taught that the sciences were in need of metaphysical foundations. But, he strove to make it perfectly clear that by that he "meant anything but a dialectical spinning of the concrete results of these sciences out of some abstract conceptual mysticism".[38] He proposed to have metaphysics understood in a broad sense as radical ontology, as the radical science of Being in the absolute sense, instead of the science of Being in the empirical sense, which we think we know, but upon closer inspection at times turns out to be deceptive and an illusion.[39]

It is certain, he argued, that the knowledge of the world provided by the natural sciences is not definitive knowledge of reality. They are merely sciences of being in the relative, provisional sense sufficient for practical orientation in the phenomenal world. Through them, we attain the practical mastery of nature, a far-reaching orienting of empirical reality, the possibility of formulating laws by which we exactly foresee, foretell and redirect the course of empirical processes, but we are not in possession of definitive knowledge, of ultimate, conclusive knowledge of the essence of nature. Lack of critical insight into the meaning of fundamental concepts and principles makes it impossible to be clear about what has been ultimately achieved and so about the sense in which the results may be considered expressions of ultimate Being.[40]

---

36 Husserl, *Introduction to Logic and Theory of Knowledge*, §32c.

37 Husserl, "Aus der Einleitung der Vorlesung 'Erkenntnistheorie und Hauptpunkte der Metaphysik'", pp. 232, 233, 252; his *Introduction to Logic and Theory of Knowledge*, §§20, 21.

38 Edmund Husserl, *Logik, Vorlesung 1896*, Dordrecht: Kluwer, 2001, p. 5; his *Logik, Vorlesung 1902/03*, pp. 12-13.

39 Husserl, *Introduction to Logic and Theory of Knowledge*, §20.

40 Husserl, *Introduction to Logic and Theory of Knowledge*, §20; his *Logik, Vorlesung 1902/03*, pp. 12-13.

Husserl believed that it was certain that a most universal concept of what is real in general, of the particularities grounded in the essence of what is real, could and must be delineated. He reasoned that concepts like that of an individual real thing, Being for itself, or thing in the broadest sense, real property in the broadest sense, real relation, time, cause and effect, are surely necessary thoughts concerning possible reality and require a study of the analysis of essence and of essential laws. There must therefore be, he concluded, a science of real Being as such in the most universal universality, and this a priori metaphysics would be the necessary foundation for empirically based metaphysics, which not only claims to know what lies in the idea of reality in general, but claims to know what is now actually actual.[41]

Husserl saw a science of metaphysics as being so necessary for science that even natural scientists could not do without it. The empirical sciences, he taught, are not creations of a purely theoretical mind. They are not based on absolutely scrupulously laid foundations in accordance with a rigorous logical method. They are subject to principles that govern thinking and research in the natural sciences, that make them possible, and that consequently cannot be searched for by investigations into the natural sciences. Even the most highly developed, most exact natural sciences uncritically use concepts and presuppositions originating in a prescientific understanding of the world. In fact, as soon as they begin reflecting on the principles of their science, natural scientists fall into metaphysics, though they most certainly do not want to call it by that forbidden name.[42]

The realm of truth, Husserl insisted, is no disorderly hodgepodge. Truths are connected in systematic ways, governed by consistent laws and theories, and so the inquiry into truth and its exposition must be systematic. The systematic representation of knowledge must to a certain degree reflect the systematic representation grounded in the things themselves. All invention and discovery involves formal patterns without which there is no testing of given propositions and proofs, no methodical construction of new proofs, no methodical building of theories and whole systems. No blind omnipotent power has heaped together some pile of propositions P, Q, R, strung them together with a proposition S, and then organized the human mind so that the knowledge of the truth of P

---

[41] Husserl, *Introduction to Logic and Theory of Knowledge*, §21.

[42] *Ibid.*, §20; Husserl, *Allgemeine Erkennthistheorie*, p. 233.

unfailingly must entail knowledge of S. Not blind chance, but the reason and order of governing laws reigns in argumentation.[43]

Wherever it is a question of reality, in life and in all empirical sciences, he explained, we apply concepts like thing, real property, real relation, state, process, coming into being and passing away, cause and effect, space and time, that seem to belong necessarily to the idea of a reality. Whether or not all these concepts are actually intrinsic to the idea of reality, there surely are such concepts, the basic categories in which what is real as such is to be understood in terms of its essence. Thus, investigations must be possible that simply reflect everything without which reality in general cannot be conceived. This is where the idea of a metaphysical a priori ontology comes in.[44]

For Husserl, the most radical reason why the natural sciences do not provide definitive knowledge of physical and mental reality and therefore require a metaphysics as the science of absolute being is that the possibility and meaning of the objective validity of knowledge is a mystery to us. So, the ultimate meaning of any reality, which for knowledge is just what it posits as real and has determined in a given way, is also problematical for us. In spite of all of natural science, we therefore do not know what reality is and in what sense we may claim to take the results of the natural sciences as being definitive for reality. Therefore, only by theory of knowledge and critique of knowledge practiced upon the natural sciences does metaphysics become possible.[45]

He warned against caving into the old temptation of grounding theory of knowledge upon metaphysics and wanting to solve the radical problems of the elucidation of knowledge by metaphysical underpinnings. Drawing in premises from metaphysics means radically missing the meaning of the genuine problems of theory of knowledge. Metaphysics presupposes theory of knowledge. Therefore, it cannot undergird theory of knowledge.[46] And that brings us back to the paradox about the science of subjectivity being the science of objectivity.

---

43 Husserl, *Logik, Vorlesung 1896*, pp. 9, 13, 16-17.

44 Husserl, *Introduction to Logic and Theory of Knowledge*, §21.

45 *Ibid.*, §32c.

46 *Ibid.*

3

HUSSERL AND CANTOR[1]

In 1886, Edmund Husserl arrived at the University of Halle to prepare his *Habilitationsschrift* called *On the Concept of Number*. He studied the calculus of probabilities with Georg Cantor, the creator of set theory, who then served on his *Habilitationskommittee* and approved the mathematical portion of the work.[2]

Cantor took a liking to his younger colleague, and the two became close friends during the last fourteen years of the nineteenth century, when Cantor was at the height of his creative powers and Husserl in the throes of an intellectual struggle during which his ideas changed considerably and definitively. During those years, he published the *Philosophy of Arithmetic*, numerous articles and reviews[3] and the groundbreaking *Logical Investigations*, where he began laying the foundations of his phenomenology that went on to shape the course of philosophy in Continental Europe.

While Husserl labored as a *Privat Dozent* – meaning that he gave courses, but did not have a regular position – Cantor multiplied efforts to find him a professorship. Surviving books of Cantor's correspondence show him "most warmly" recommending Husserl in "good conscience" for a position of full professor. He praised Husserl's "exceptional academic qualifications beyond all question" and cited the great respect generated by his writings, the *Philosophy of Arithmetic*, in particular. Cantor described Husserl as "a person highly-valued and generally loved by us because of his peaceable and sterling character", as being thoroughly honest. He assured that "his personality and character justify the belief that he would discharge his duties with desirable tact". He said that he knew for certain from courses that Husserl had given on the proofs for the existence of God and against Darwinism that he was a theist. In response to reservations about the fact that Husserl was a Jewish convert to Protestantism, Cantor

---

[1] This essay was originally written for *Essays on Husserl's Logic and Philosophy of Mathematics*, Stefania Centrone (ed.), Dordrecht: Springer, 2017.

[2] Hans Martin Gerlach and Hans Rainer Sepp (eds.), *Husserl in Halle,* Bern: Peter Lang, 1994.

[3] These articles and reviews are now published in English in Husserl's *Early Writings in the Philosophy of Logic and Mathematics*, Dordrecht: Kluwer, 1994 and his *Philosophy of Arithmetic, Psychological and Logical Investigations with Supplementary Texts from 1887-1901*, Dordrecht: Kluwer, 2003.

appealed to the "holiest traditions of the Church" and to the fact that "the most holy person of our Savior, his twelve apostles were all Jews".[4]

In 1901, when he was in his forties, Husserl was appointed associate professor at the University of Göttingen. Cantor died in 1918 after bouts of mental illness. Of the relationship between the two men, Husserl's wife recalled that "Cantor, the greatest mathematician since Gauss, the creator of set theory" loved her husband tenderly ("*liebte H. zärtlich*"). "They were alike in many ways", she added, "but with otherwise great dissimilarity. The Cantors' house was like home…"[5] In what follows, I discuss respects in which Husserl and Cantor might be said to have been alike while pointing to dissimilarities between them.

On the borderline between mathematics and philosophy

In the 1880s, Husserl and Cantor (along with Frege) figured among the small number of their contemporaries intent upon marrying mathematics and philosophy. A mathematician by training,[6] Husserl had just been transformed into a philosopher by Franz Brentano. In *On the Concept of Number*, he wrote of definitively removing the real and imaginary difficulties on the borderline between mathematics and philosophy. He regretted that mathematicians had failed to examine the logic of the concepts and methods they were introducing and using and he saw the need for logical clarification, precise analyses.[7]

According to its 1882 foreword, Cantor's *Mannigfaltigkeitslehre* was a work, "written with two groups of readers in mind – philosophers who have followed the developments in mathematics up to the present time, and mathematicians who are familiar with the most important older and

---

[4] See Cantor's letters of reference for Husserl translated in Claire Ortiz Hill and Jairo José da Silva, *The Road Not Taken, On Husserl's Philosophy of Logic and Mathematics*, London: College Publications, pp. 367-69, 374-75, 377.

[5] Malvine Husserl, "Skizze eines Lebensbildes von E. Husserl", *Husserl Studies* 5: 1988, §E, pp. 105-25.

[6] Claire Ortiz Hill, "On Husserl's Mathematical Apprenticeship and Philosophy of Mathematics", *Phenomenology World Wide*, Anna-Teresa Tymieniecka (ed.) Dordrecht: Kluwer, 2002, pp. 76-92, also anthologized in Hill & da Silva.

[7] Edmund Husserl, "On the Concept of Number" (1887), in his *Philosophy of Arithmetic, Psychological and Logical Investigations with Supplementary Texts from 1887-1901*, p. 310.

newer publications in philosophy".[8] Joseph Dauben has noted that in the *Mannigfaltigkeitslehre*, "Cantor made philosophy an equal and intentional partner to mathematics.... In the German version issued as a separate monograph by Teubner in 1883, a simple introduction was added in which he stressed that the mathematical and the philosophical sections were inextricably connected".[9]

During the late 1880s, the embattled creator of set theory was in fact hard at work trying to put the new numbers he was inventing on solid foundations and philosophically justifying the claims he was making about them.[10] Those attempts found expression in his correspondence and most particularly in the "Mitteilungen zur Lehre vom Transfiniten",[11] which he said he published in the *Zeitschrift für Philosophie und philosophische Kritik* because he had grown disgusted with mathematical journals.[12]

Over the years, Cantor's thoughts had been turning increasingly to philosophy and he was ready to abandon mathematics for philosophy. He had come to see himself as a sort of philosopher *manqué*. He tried to teach philosophy[13] and was seasoning his writings with philosophical reflections and references to Democritus, Plato, Aristotle, Augustine, Boethius, Aquinas, Descartes, Nicolas von Cusa, Spinoza, Leibniz, Kant, Auguste Comte, Francis Bacon, Locke and so on. In 1883, Gösta Mittag-Leffler saw fit to warn him that his work would be much better received in the mathematical world "without the philosophical and historical explanations"[14] and in 1885 that he risked shocking most mathematicians and damaging his reputation with his philosophical way of expressing himself.[15] Despite those warnings, Cantor continued to clothe his theories in philosophical garb.

---

8 Michael Hallett, *Cantorian Set Theory and Limitation of Size*, Oxford: The Clarendon Press, 1984, p. 7.

9 Joseph Dauben, *Georg Cantor: His Mathematics and Philosophy of the Infinite*, Princeton: Princeton University Press, 1979, p. 120.

10 *Ibid.*, Chapter 6.

11 Georg Cantor, "Mitteilungen zur Lehre vom Transfiniten" (1887/88), as found in his *Gesammelte Abhandlungen*, Ernst Zermelo (ed.), Berlin: Springer, p. 416.

12 Dauben, *Georg Cantor, His Mathematics and Philosophy of the Infinite*, pp. 139, 336 n. 29.

13 Georg Cantor, *Briefe*, Herbert Meschkowski and Winfried Nilson (eds.), Berlin: Springer, 1991, pp. 210, 218; Dauben, *Georg Cantor: His Mathematics and Philosophy of the Infinite*, pp. 282, 337 n. 31.

14 Cantor, *Briefe*, p. 118.

15 *Ibid.*, p. 244.

Cantor's Platonic idealism

In the *Mannigfaltigkeitslehre*, Cantor emphasized that the idealist foundations of his theories were essentially in agreement with the basic principles of Platonism according to which only conceptual knowledge in Plato's sense afforded true knowledge.[16] By "manifold" or "set", he said, he was defining something related to the Platonic *eidos* or *idea*.[17] He once wrote to Giuseppe Peano that he conceived of numbers as 'forms' or 'species', general concepts, of sets and that in essentials that was the conception of the ancient geometry of Plato, Aristotle, Euclid etc.[18] His talk of awakening and bringing to consciousness the knowledge, concepts and numbers slumbering in us[19] was an unmistakable allusion to Plato's theory of recollection and Socratic theories of concept formation.

In the "Mitteilungen", Cantor described the realm of the transfinite as "a rich, ever growing field of ideal research" and his transfinite numbers as a special form of Plato's *arithmoi noetoi* or *eidetikoi*.[20] There, he was particularly intent upon proving that his theorems about transfinite numbers were firmly secured "through the logical power of proofs" which, proceeding from his definitions were "neither arbitrary nor artificial, but originate naturally out of abstraction, have, with the help of syllogisms, attained their goal".[21]

He considered that his technique for abstracting numbers from reality provided the only possible foundations for his Platonic conception of numbers.[22] In the "Mitteilungen", he repeatedly gave the same recipe for extracting cardinal numbers from reality through abstraction:[23] By abstracting from both the characteristics of the elements of the set and the order in which they are given, one obtains the cardinal numbers;

---

16 Georg Cantor, *Grundlagen einer allgemeinen Mannigfaltigkeitslehre. Ein mathematisch-philosophischer Versuch in der Lehre des Unendlichen* (1883), as published in his *Gesammelte Abhandlungen*, pp. 181, 206 n. 6.

17 *Ibid.*, p. 204 n. 1.

18 Cantor, *Briefe*, p. 365.

19 Cantor, *Grundlagen einer allgemeinen Mannigfaltigkeitslehre*, p. 207 nn. 6, 7, 8; his "Mitteilungen zur Lehre vom Transfiniten", p. 418 n. 1.

20 Cantor, "Mitteilungen zur Lehre vom Transfiniten", pp. 406, 420.

21 *Ibid.*, p. 418.

22 Cantor, *Briefe*, pp. 363, 365; his "Mitteilungen zur Lehre vom Transfiniten", pp. 380, 411.

23 Cantor, "Mitteilungen zur Lehre vom Transfiniten", pp. 379, 387, 411, 418 n. 1.

abstracting only from the characteristics of the elements and leaving their order intact, one obtains the ideal numbers or *eidetikoi.*[24]

Cantor saw his theory of abstraction as the distinctive feature of his number theory and believed it was an entirely different method for providing the foundations of the finite numbers than was found in the theories of his contemporaries. He envisioned it as a technique for focusing on pure, abstract arithmetical properties and concepts that would divorce them from any sensory apprehension of the particular characteristics of the objects figuring in the sets and so free mathematics from psychologism, empiricism, Kantianism and insidious appeals to intuitions of space and time. He believed that with it he was laying bare the roots from which the organism of transfinite numbers develop with logical necessity. A good measure of the freedom he felt was his as a mathematician derived from his distinguishing between an empirical treatment of numbers and Plato's pure, ideal *arithmoi eidetikoi,* which by their very nature are detached from things perceptible by the senses.[25]

In his 1885 review of Frege's *Foundations of Arithmetic*, Cantor praised Frege for requiring that all psychological factors and intuitions of space and time be banned from arithmetical concepts and principles because that was the only way their strict logical purity and validity might be secured.[26] In so doing, Cantor was in step with Karl Weierstrass' aims, which Husserl also shared. Sections of *On the Concept of Number* and the *Philosophy of Arithmetic* were devoted to discussions aimed at obtaining pure arithmetical concepts by detaching the concept of number from any spatio-temporal intuitions and so also from any taint of Kantianism in keeping with goals Weierstrass had set.[27] The early years of the twentieth century would find Husserl

---

24 Cantor, "Mitteilungen zur Lehre vom Transfiniten", pp. 379-80; his *Grundlagen einer allgemeinen Mannigfaltigkeitslehre*, pp. 180-81; also his *Briefe*, pp. 329, 330.

25 Cantor, *Grundlagen einer allgemeinen Mannigfaltigkeitslehre*, pp. 191-92; his "Mitteilungen zur Lehre vom Transfiniten", pp. 380-81 n. 1, p. 411; his *Briefe*, pp. 363, 365; Claire Ortiz Hill, "Abstraction and Idealization in Georg Cantor and Edmund Husserl", *Abstraction and Idealization. Historical and Systematic Studies*, F. Coniglione et al. (eds.), Amsterdam: Rodopi, 1999, also published in Claire Ortiz Hill & G. E. Rosado Haddock, *Husserl or Frege? Meaning, Objectivity, and Mathematics*, La Salle: Open Court, 2000.

26 Georg Cantor, "Rezension von Freges *Grundlagen der Arithmetik*", *Deutsche Literatur-zeitung* VI (20), pp. 728-29, 1885, as published in his *Gesammelte Abhandlungen*, p. 440.

27 Husserl, "On the Concept of Number", Section 2; his *Philosophy of Arithmetic*, Chapter 2.

teaching that numbers could not concern what happens in or to the real temporal matters of fact that we call mental experiences of experiencing individuals. He stated unequivocally that Kant had brought pure arithmetic into an entirely inadmissible relationship to time.[28]

Husserl's early theory of abstraction

Husserl owned offprints of the "Mitteilungen" and marked and underlined precisely (and almost exclusively) those passages in which Cantor explained the abstraction process.[29] Calling Cantor a mathematician of genius in *Philosophy of Arithmetic*, Husserl further commended him for having written with a great deal of precision in the "Mitteilungen" that for "the formation of the general concept 'five' one needs only a set (for example, all the fingers of my right hand) which corresponds to this cardinal number; the act of abstraction with respect to both the properties and the order in which I encounter these wholly distinct things, produces or rather awakens the concept 'five' in my mind".[30]

In *On the Concept of Number*, Husserl himself characterized the distinctive abstractive process yielding the concept of number of a concrete set of objects as follows:

> It is easy to characterize the abstraction which must be exercised upon a concretely given multiplicity in order to attain to the number concepts under which it falls. One considers each of the particular objects merely insofar as it is a "something" or a "one," simultaneously retaining the collective combination; and in this manner there is obtained the corresponding general form of multiplicity, one and one and... and one, with which a number name is associated. In this process there is total abstraction *from* the specific characteristics of the particular objects. But this neither means nor implies that the concrete objects have to disappear from our consciousness. To "abstract" from something merely means to pay no special attention to it. Thus, also in our case at hand, no special interest is directed upon the peculiarities of content in the separate individuals....[31]

---

[28] Edmund Husserl, *Introduction to Logic and Theory of Knowledge, Lectures* 1906/1907, Dordrecht: Springer, 2008, §§11, 13b, 23.
[29] These offprints can be examined at the Husserl Archives in Leuven, Belgium.
[30] Cantor, "Mitteilungen zur Lehre vom Transfiniten", p. 418 n. 1; Husserl, *Philosophy of Arithmetic*, p. 121 n.
[31] Husserl, "On the Concept of Number", pp. 310, 354-55.

In *Philosophy of Arithmetic*, he studied this same process in greater detail, especially underscoring the uniqueness of the abstraction process that yields the number concept. He made a point of disassociating his theory from the better known abstraction theories of Locke and Aristotle, something it is important to call attention to because philosophers have been all too wont to assimilate the process Husserl advocated to theories more familiar to them.[32]

Since Cantor was propounding this theory of abstraction at the very time Husserl was writing *On the Concept of Number* and the *Philosophy of Arithmetic* where a similar theory was advocated, it is worth noting here that in the latter work, Husserl approvingly noted that the definition of number in the "Mitteilungen" was profoundly different from that of the *Mannigfaltigkeitslehre*.[33] He specifically pointed to two passages of the "Mitteilungen". In the first, Cantor had written:

> By the *power* or *cardinal number* of a set *M* (which is made up of distinct, conceptually separate elements *m*, *m'*,... and is to this extent determined and limited), I understand the general concept or species concept (universal) obtained by abstracting from the properties of the elements of the set, as well as from all the relations which the elements may have, whether themselves or to other things, but especially from the order reigning among the elements and only reflect upon what is common to all sets *equivalent* to *M*.[34]

Psychologism

However, as similar as Husserl's and Cantor's theories of abstracttion might seem to have been in the late 1880s, there was a major difference between them that reflected deep contradictions in both men's philosophies of arithmetic and soon brought Husserl to transform his entire approach to philosophy. For, however psychologistic Cantor's mysterious references to inner intuition[35] or to experiences helping to produce concepts in his mind[36] may seem, he opposed empiricism, naturalism, sensualism, skepticism,

---

[32] Husserl, *Philosophy of Arithmetic*, p. 86; Hill, "Abstraction and Idealization in Georg Cantor and Edmund Husserl".

[33] Husserl, *Philosophy of Arithmetic*, 121 n.

[34] Cantor, "Mitteilungen zur Lehre vom Transfiniten", p. 387; Cantor *Briefe*, p. 178.

[35] For example, Cantor, *Grundlagen einer allgemeinen Mannigfaltigkeitslehre*, pp. 168, 170, 201.

[36] Cantor, "Mitteilungen zur Lehre vom Transfiniten", p. 418 n. 1.

psychologism and Kantianism which, he argued, mistakenly locate the sources of knowledge and certainty in the senses or in the "supposedly pure forms of intuition of the world of presentation". He maintained that certain knowledge could "only be obtained through concepts and ideas which, at most stimulated by external experience, are on the whole formed through inner induction and deduction as something which in a way already lay within us and was only awakened and brought to consciousness".[37]

Husserl, on the other hand, began writing *On the Concept of Number* as a committed empirical psychologist *à la* Brentano, whose philosophical ideal was most nearly realized in the exact natural sciences.[38] There and in the *Philosophy of Arithmetic*, he tried to anchor arithmetical concepts in direct experience by analyzing the actual psychological processes to which he believed the concept of number owed its genesis. He considered the analysis of elementary concepts to be one of the more essential tasks of psychology.

However, Husserl's confidence in empirical psychology eroded quickly and the enthusiastic espousal of it in *On the Concept of Number* does not appear in the *Philosophy of Arithmetic*, – a sign that change was on the horizon. He later said that his doubts extended to all categorial concepts and to concepts of objectivities of any sort whatsoever, ultimately to include modern analysis and the theory of manifolds, and simultaneously mathematical logic and the entire field of logic in general. [39]

Husserl's idealistic turn

Franz Brentano taught his students to despise metaphysical idealism. So, Husserl came to Halle quite disinclined to traffic in the kind of idealism that pervades Cantor's writings,[40] and any such considerations are conspicuously absent from *On the Concept of Number* and *Philosophy of Arithmetic*.

Notwithstanding, he left Halle persuaded that there was "an essential, quite unbridgeable difference between the sciences of the ideal and the sciences of the real", the correct assessment of which presupposed "the complete abandonment of the empiricistic theory of abstraction, whose

---

37 Cantor, *Grundlagen einer allgemeinen Mannigfaltigkeitslehre*, p. 207 n. 6.

38 Edmund Husserl, "Recollections of Franz Brentano" (1919), in *Husserl: Shorter Works*, Notre Dame IN: University of Notre Dame Press, 1981, pp. 344-45.

39 Edmund Husserl, *Introduction to the Logical Investigations, A Draft of a Preface to the Logical Investigations* (1913), The Hague: M. Nijhoff, 1975, pp. 16-17, 34-35.

40 Husserl, "Recollections of Franz Brentano", pp. 344-45.

present dominance renders all logical matters unintelligible".[41] He began to accord idealist systems the highest value and to see them as shedding light on totally new, radical dimensions of philosophical problems.[42] Of his *Logical Investigations*, he stated that every possible effort had been made "to dispose the reader to the recognition of this ideal sphere of being and knowledge... to side with 'the ideal in this truly Platonistic sense', 'to declare oneself for idealism' with the author".[43] He had become a committed Platonic idealist. Phenomenology was to be an "eidetic" discipline.

However, although Husserl saw that empirical psychology could not solve the epistemological problems he was facing, he never considered utterly forsaking the world of actual consciousness. He said that it was troubling puzzles about the interrelationship and intrinsic unity of what he called the "incredibly strange" worlds of the purely logical and of actual consciousness that he saw opening up all around him while he was trying to understand the logic of mathematical thought and calculation and achieve clarity regarding the true meaning of the concepts of set theory and the theory of cardinal numbers in the *Philosophy of Arithmetic*[44] that launched him on his phenomenological voyage of discovery. He strove until the end of his life to solve those puzzles. He considered that only those who, like himself, deeply distressed by the issues in the most intense way,

> compelled by the critical dissolution of the blinding prejudices of psychologism to recognize the purely logical ideal... but... at the same time... compelled by the revealing emphasis upon the essential relationships between the ideal and the psychological... not to abandon by any means the psychological entirely but rather to keep it within view as somehow belonging with the ideal... can also have the insight that such psychological critiques are indispensable for forcing recognition of the ideal as something given prior to all theories.... can realize that the being-in-itself of the ideal sphere in its relation to consciousness brings with it a dimension of puzzles which remain untouched by all such argumentation against psychologism and hence must be solved through special investigations... through phenomenological ones.[45]

---

41 Edmund Husserl, *Logical Investigations* (1900-1901), New York: Humanities Press, 1970, p. 185.

42 Husserl, "Recollections of Franz Brentano", p. 345.

43 Husserl, *Introduction to the Logical Investigations*, p. 20.

44 Edmund Husserl, "Personal Notes" (1906-1908), in his *Early Writings in the Philosophy of Logic and Mathematics*, pp. 491-92.

45 Husserl, *Introduction to the Logical Investigations*, pp. 21-22.

Now, in Cantor's writings, the world of consciousness and the world of pure mathematics mingle together[46] in confusing and frustrating ways that cry out for clarification, so that the naive epistemological theorizing in which Cantor was so earnestly engaging while Husserl was grappling with analogous questions could easily have impressed upon his younger colleague an urgent need to develop the more sophisticated logical and epistemological tools needed to attain a deeper, clearer understanding of how the human mind interacted with the world of numbers.

For instance, Husserl might have fairly wondered in just what way the cardinal number belonging to a set is an abstract image in our intellect[47] or exactly how the act of abstraction awakened the number concepts in Cantor's mind.[48] In the same passage of the *Mannigfaltigkeitslehre* in which Cantor explicitly rejected the belief that "the source of knowledge and certainty is located in the senses or in the so-called form of pure intuition of the world of presentation", he wrote that "certain knowledge... can only be obtained through concepts and ideas, which are at best only stimulated by outer experience, but which are principally formed through inner induction, like something which, so to speak, already lay within us and is only awakened and brought to consciousness".[49] Frege was perfectly justified in qualifying Cantor's appeals to direct inner intuition[50] as "rather mysterious".[51]

So given the particular nature of Cantor's experiments, it is not surprising to find Husserl asking in those years how rational insight was possible in science,[52] how the mathematical in itself as given in the medium of the psychical could be valid, how logicians penetrated an objective realm entirely different from themselves, how objective, mathematical and logical relations constituted themselves in subjectivity, how symbolic thinking was possible,[53] how abandoning oneself completely to thought that is merely symbolic and removed from intuition could lead to

---

46 Hallett, *Cantorian Set Theory and Limitation of Size*, pp. 16-18, 34-35, 121, 128-33, 146-58.

47 Cantor, "Mitteilungen zur Lehre vom Transfiniten", p. 416.

48 *Ibid.*, p. 418 n. 1.

49 Cantor, *Grundlagen einer allgemeinen Mannigfaltigkeitslehre*, p. 207 n. 6; Hallett, *Cantorian Set Theory and Limitation of Size*, p. 15.

50 Cantor *Grundlagen einer allgemeinen Mannigfaltigkeitslehre*, pp. 168, 170, 201.

51 Gottlob Frege, *The Foundations of Arithmetic* (1884), Oxford: Blackwell, 1986, §86.

52 Edmund Husserl, "Psychological Studies in the Elements of Logic" (1894), in his *Early Writings in the Philosophy of Logic and Mathematics*, p. 167.

53 Husserl, *Introduction to the Logical Investigations*, pp. 35, 222.

empirically true results, or how mechanical operations with mere written characters could vastly expand our actual knowledge concerning number concepts.[54] These are all questions that Cantor's theories raise.

Cantor, Metaphysics, Mysticism and Occultism

The last chapter Husserl found communicating the new vision of metaphysics, epistemology and the natural sciences that he developed during the 1890s to a new generation of students in search of a scientific metaphysics that could stand up to the challenges of the natural sciences.[55]

As for Cantor, what remains of his correspondence reveals a great deal about his metaphysical views during those years in Halle. For example, in 1894, Cantor wrote to the French mathematician Charles Hermite that "in the realm of the spirit" mathematics had no longer been "the essential love of his soul" for more than twenty years. Metaphysics and theology, he "openly confessed", had so taken possession of his soul as to leave him relatively little time for his "first flame".[56]

Given Husserl's views on metaphysics as discussed earlier, he could have conceivably agreed with the Cantor who wrote to Fr. Thomas Esser in 1896, that the "grounding of the principles of mathematics and natural science is a matter for metaphysics. Metaphysics has therefore to look upon these two sciences not only as its servants and helpers but also as its children which it should not let out of its sight, but must watch over and control…",[57] or with Cantor's conviction that the "general *Mengenlehre*… belongs thoroughly to metaphysics. You can easily convince yourself of this by examining the basic concepts of *Mengenlehre*, the categories of cardinal number and ordinal type, and noticing not only the degree of their generality, but also how thinking [*Denken*] with them is fully pure, so that there is not the slightest room for fantasy".[58]

---

54 Husserl, "Psychological Studies in the Elements of Logic", p. 167 and his "On the Logic of Signs (Semiotic)" (1890), p. 50 in his *Early Writings in the Philosophy of Logic and Mathematics*.

55 Edmund Husserl, "Aus der Einleitung der Vorlesung Erkenntnistheorie und Hauptpunkte der Metaphysik 1898/99", in his *Allgemeine Erkennthistheorie, Vorlesung 1902/03*, Dordrecht: Kluwer, 2001, pp. 232, 233, 252; Husserl, *Introduction to Logic and Theory of Knowledge*, §§20, 21.

56 Cantor, *Briefe*, p. 350.

57 Quoted Hallett, *Cantorian Set Theory and Limitation of Size*, p. 10.

58 *Ibid.*

And Dauben's interpretation of what Cantor meant by metaphysics fits in with Husserl's later phenomenology:

> Whenever Cantor spoke of metaphysics he meant the philosophical study of the relations between the constructs of mind and the objects of the external world. Thus the study of the abstract theory of the transfinite numbers was the business of mathematics, but the study of the realization or embodiment of the transfinite numbers in terms of the objects of the phenomenological world was the concern of metaphysics. And so metaphysics assumed its place in Cantor's continuing program to establish the legitimacy of his new theory....[59]

More mystical, however, was Cantor's conviction that "the whole numbers both separately and in their actual infinite totality exist in that highest kind of reality as eternal ideas in the Divine Intellect"[60], or that contradictions in his own theories were but apparent and that one must distinguish between the numbers which we are able to grasp in our limited ways and "numbers as they are *in and for themselves, and in and for the Absolute intelligence*".[61] To Fr. Ignatius Jeiler, he wrote in 1888,

> Each individual *finite* cardinal number is in God's intellect both a representative idea and a unified form for the knowledge of innumerably many things, that is, those which possess the cardinal number in question. All *finite* cardinal numbers are thus distinct and simultaneously present in God's mind. They form in their *totality a manifold, unified thing for itself* [*Ding für sich*] *delimited* from the remaining content of God's intellect, and this thing is itself again an object [*Gegenstand*] of God's knowledge.[62]

And in another letter of the same year, Cantor wrote that he knew that his set theory stood "as firm as a rock", because he had studied it from all sides for many years, had examined all objections ever made against the infinite numbers and above had "followed its roots to the infallible cause of all created things".[63]

But, Cantor went rather further than that. In Dauben's opinion,

---

[59] Dauben, *Georg Cantor: His Mathematics and Philosophy of the Infinite*, p. 125.
[60] As quoted Hallett, *Cantorian Set Theory and Limitation of Size*, p. 149.
[61] Cantor, *Briefe*, pp. 326, 267, 282.
[62] As quoted Hallett, *Cantorian Set Theory and Limitation of Size*, p. 36.
[63] As quoted in Dauben, *Georg Cantor: His Mathematics and Philosophy of the Infinite*, p. 298.

> There can be no mistake about Cantor's identification of his mathematics with some greater absolute unity in God. This also paralleled his identification of transfinite set theory with divine inspiration.... Cantor... told Mittag-Leffler that his transfinite numbers had been communicated to him from a more powerful energy.... Cantor believed that God endowed the transfinite numbers with a reality making them very special. Despite all the opposition and misgivings of mathematicians in Germany and elsewhere, he would never be persuaded that his results could be imperfect.[64]

Such considerations may explain why Husserl wrote in the *Logical Investigations* of banishing "all metaphysical fog and all mysticism" from mathematical investigations into numbers and manifolds like those of Cantor.[65] Cantor's philosophy was mystical to say the least.[66]

It is important in this respect to remember that, as noted in the previous chapter, while the end of the nineteenth century witnessed attempts to rehabilitate the respectability of metaphysical inquiry and place it centrally on the philosophical agenda along with rigorous, rational, scientific thinking, alongside this there was an occult revival, a rise in cults, spiritism, Satanism, the occult, magic, witchcraft, irrationalism and superstitious practices. In fact, the same letter books that show Cantor multiplying efforts to obtain Husserl a satisfactory job reveal that, alongside interests in traditional theology and metaphysics, Cantor was extremely interested in occultism and occultist groups, Rosicrucianism especially.[67]

Frege's reviews of Husserl and Cantor

In 1894, Frege published a damaging, abusive review of Husserl's *Philosophy of Arithmetic.* In "Frege's Attack on Husserl and Cantor",[68] I endeavored to show the extent to which Frege directly incorporated into that review several criticisms he had already made of Cantor's work.

To begin with, Frege repeatedly criticized Husserl's use of a theory of number abstraction. He was perfectly correct to write that Husserl would have one "abstract from the peculiar constitution of the individual

---

64 *Ibid.*, pp. 290-91.

65 Husserl, *Logical Investigations*, p. 242

66 Dauben, *Georg Cantor: His Mathematics and Philosophy of the Infinite*, chapter 6; pp. 236-39; Hallett, *Cantorian Set Theory and Limitation of Size*, pp. 9-11, 35-36.

67 Cantor *Briefbücher I (1884-1888), II (1890-1895), III (1895-1896).*

68 Claire Ortiz Hill, "Frege Attacks Husserl and Cantor", *The Monist* 77(3), 1994, pp. 347-57.

contents that make up the multiplicity and retain each one only in so far as it is a something or a one". He was also correct in writing that Husserl's "process of abstracting the number goes hand in hand with a process of emptying all content".[69] But, unwilling just to condemn Husserl for holding views he had really advocated, Frege unfairly went on to charge that Husserl's procedure would "cleanse things of their peculiarities... in the wash-tub of the mind" where things "assume a quite peculiar pliancy…." There, Frege said, "we can easily change objects by directing our attention towards them or away from them.... We attend less to a property, and it disappears. By thus making one characteristic mark after another disappear, we obtain more and more abstract concepts".[70] And he went on to provide this caricature of Husserl's procedure.

> Suppose, e.g., that there are a black and white cat sitting side by side before us. We do not attend to their colour, and they become colourless – but they still sit side by side. We do not attend to their posture, and they cease to sit … but each of them is still in its place. We no longer attend to the place and they cease to occupy one – but they continue presumably to be separate. We have thus perhaps obtained from each of them a general concept of cat. By continued application of this procedure, each object is transformed into a more and more bloodless phantom.[71]

Frege maintained that it must surely be assumed that the process of abstraction effects some change in the objects and that they become different from the original objects which are either transformed or actually created by the abstraction process.[72] Nonetheless, in spite of the force of the charges he directed against Husserl in his review, Frege was honest enough to admit that Husserl himself did not hold that the mind creates new objects or changes old ones, and actually acknowledged that Husserl "disputes this in the most vehement terms (p. 139)".[73]

---

[69] Gottlob Frege, "Review of Dr. E. Husserl's *Philosophy of Arithmetic*" (1894), as published in his *Collected Papers on Mathematics, Logic und Philosophy*, Oxford: Blackwell, 1984, p. 196.

[70] *Ibid.*, p. 197.

[71] *Ibid.*, pp. 197-98.

[72] *Ibid.*, p. 204.

[73] *Ibid.*, p. 205; Claire Ortiz Hill, "The Varied Sorrows of Logical Abstraction", *Axiomathes* 1-3, 1997, pp.: 53-82, also in Hill & Rosado Haddock.

When Frege went on to charge that Husserl had taken "the road of magic rather than of science",[74] we have a good clue as to whom else he wished to attack, for in reviewing the "Mitteilungen", he had accused Cantor of the very same thing. He called the verb 'abstract' a psychological expression to be avoided in mathematics";[75] in a posthumously published draft of this review, he likened mathematicians who like Cantor talk of abstraction to "negroes from the heart of Africa". For them, words like 'abstraction' are supposed to have 'the kind of magical effects' that enable them to abstract from any properties of things that bother them.[76] In the spirit of the cat example of his review of Husserl, Frege complained that mathematicians like Cantor find a whole host of things in mice which are unworthy to form a part of the number. He wrote:

> Nothing simpler, one abstracts from the whole lot. Indeed when you get down to it everything in the mice is out of place: the beadiness of their eyes no less than the length of their tails and the sharpness of their teeth. So one abstracts from the nature of the mice ... one abstracts presumably from all their properties, even from those in virtue of which we call them animals, three-dimensional beings....[77]

Frege also alludes to someone whom he suspects is one of Cantor's pupils, who when asked what general concept he arrives at when given a pencil exerts himself "to the utmost in abstracting from the nature of the pencil and the order in which its elements are given", to answer 'the cardinal number one'.[78]

In his review, Frege further characterized Husserl's endeavor as "an attempt to justify a naïve conception of number". He called naïve "any view on which a statement of number is not a statement about a concept or about the extension of a concept". If Husserl had used 'extension of a concept' "in the same sense as I", Frege declared, "we should hardly differ in opinion about the sense of a number statement".[79] He also complained that for

---

[74] Frege, "Review of Dr. E. Husserl's *Philosophy of Arithmetic*", p. 205.

[75] Gottlob Frege, "Review of Georg Cantor, *Zur Lehre vom Transfiniten: Gesammelte Abhandlungen aus de Zeitschrift für Philosophie und philosophische Kritik*"(1892), in his *Collected Papers*, pp. 180, 181.

[76] Gottlob Frege, *Posthumous Writings*, Oxford: Blackwell, 1979, p. 69.

[77] *Ibid.*, p. 70.

[78] *Ibid.*, p. 71.

[79] Frege, "Review of Dr. E. Husserl's *Philosophy of Arithmetic*", pp. 201-02.

Husserl, multiplicities, sets, are more indeterminate and more general than numbers.[80] In addition, he wrote: "A concept under which only one object falls has a determinate extension, as does a concept under which no object falls, or a concept under which infinitely many objects fall".[81]

As it happens, Cantor had written in his review of Frege's *Foundations of Arithmetic* that it was unfortunate that Frege had used extensions of concepts as the foundation of the number concept, that that was "a reversal of the proper order", because the extension of a concept was generally something quantitatively completely undetermined, and that for such quantitative determination, the concept of number would have to have been given from somewhere else.[82] So Frege's criticism of Husserl's views on the relationship between numbers and extensions of concepts echoed criticisms Cantor had made of Frege.

Cantor's presence is again felt when Frege wrote that according to Husserl "numbers are supposed to be presentations *Vorstellungen*, the results of mental processes or activities" and charged Husserl with actually removing elements. Frege had also charged Cantor with "creating" numbers,[83] and with engaging in the "psychological and hence empirical" activity of psychically removing elements.[84] In addition, when criticizing Husserl for writing that when the number of items to be counted is beyond our capacity for presentation we are then to "idealize" our capacity for presentation,[85] Frege was surely also thinking of Cantor's statement in the *Mannigfaltigkeitslehre* that whenever "one comes to no greater number, one imagines a new one".[86]

Husserl's doubts about sets

In *On the Concept of Number* and *Philosophy of Arithmetic*, Husserl strove to make set theory the basis of mathematics. In *Formal and Transcendental Logic*, he explicitly described the *Philosophy of Arithmetic* as an initial attempt

---

80 *Ibid.*, p. 195.

81 *Ibid.*, p. 202.

82 Cantor, "Rezension von Freges *Grundlagen der Arithmetik*".

83 Frege, *The Foundations of Arithmetic*, §96 note.

84 Frege, "Review of Georg Cantor, *Zur Lehre vom Transfiniten*", pp. 180-81; Dauben, *Georg Cantor: His Mathematics and Philosophy of the Infinite*, pp. 220-28.

85 Frege, "Review of Dr. E. Husserl's *Philosophy of Arithmetic*", p. 207, re. Husserl's *Philosophy of Arithmetic*, p. 231.

86 Cantor, *Grundlagen einer allgemeinen Mannigfaltigkeitslehre*, p. 195; Dauben, *Georg Cantor: His Mathematics and Philosophy of the Infinite*, p. 206.

"to obtain clarity regarding the original genuine meaning of the fundamental concepts of the theory of sets and cardinal numbers".[87]

Stating that he would use the terms 'multiplicity' and 'set' interchangeably to neutralize any differences in meaning between the terms, and citing Euclid's classical definition of the concept of number as "a multiplicity of units", Husserl began his analyses by affirming that "the analysis of the concept of number presupposes the concept of multiplicity".[88] Just as cardinal numbers relate to sets, so ordinals relate to series that are themselves ordered sets, he maintained in the introduction to *Philosophy of Arithmetic*.[89] The most primitive concepts involved, he explained in the work, are the general concepts of set and number which are grounded in the concrete sets of specific objects of any kind whatsoever and to which particular numbers are assigned. There cannot be any doubt, Husserl went on to affirm there, as in *On the Concept of Number*, that the concrete phenomena that form the basis for the abstraction of the concepts in question are aggregates *(Inbegriffe)*, multiplicities of determinate objects. Everyone, he stressed, knew what was meant by this, for despite difficulties experienced in analyzing it, the concept of multiplicity itself was perfectly precise and the range of its extension exactly delimited. It might therefore be considered as a given, he maintained, even though we might still be in the dark about the essence and origination of the concept itself.[90]

However, Husserl quickly came to judge his first attempts to clarify the true meaning of the fundamental concepts of the theory of sets and cardinal numbers to have been a failure. He not only began to have doubts about psychological analyses of sets, but he expressed doubts about set theory itself. He confessed to having been disturbed, and even tormented, by doubts about sets right from the very beginning.[91] He specifically put Cantorian sets, "the *Mannigfaltigkeitslehre* in the broadest sense", into the category of pure logic that was a source of torment to him.[92] While working

---

87 Edmund Husserl, *Formal and Transcendental Logic* (1929), The Hague: Martinus Nijhoff, 1969, §27a; also §24 and note.

88 Husserl, *Philosophy of Arithmetic*, pp. 15-16; his "On the Concept of Number", pp. 313-14.

89 Husserl, *Philosophy of Arithmetic*, p. 12.

90 Husserl, *Philosophy of Arithmetic*, pp. 15-16; his "On the Concept of Number", pp. 314-15.

91 Husserl, *Introduction to the Logical Investigations*, p. 35.

92 Edmund Husserl, "Report on German Writings in Logic from the years 1895-1899, Third Article", in his *Early Writings in the Philosophy of Logic and Mathematics,*

on the logic of mathematical thought and mathematical calculation, he explained in introductions to the *Logical Investigations*, he had encountered disturbing problems while studying the logic of formal arithmetic and the theory of *Mannigfaltigkeiten*.[93]

In the early 1890s he was already expressing grave doubts about extensional logic, by which he meant the calculus of classes.[94] His chief target then was Ernst Schröder.[95] But his antipathy is evident in several articles of the period.[96] In those texts he sought to show "that the *total* formal basis upon which the class calculus rests is valid for the relationships between conceptual objects", and that one could solve logical problems without "the detour through classes".[97]

In Chapter XI of *Philosophy of Arithmetic*, Husserl warned against ascribing anything more to the concept of *infinite* sets than is actually logically permissible, and above all not the absurd idea of constructing the actual set. Treating "All S" as a closed set creates what he called a kind of "imaginary" concept whose anti-logical nature was harmless in everyday contexts precisely because its inherent contradictoriness was never obvious in life. However, he warned, the situation changes when such an imaginary construct is actually carried over into reasoning and influences judgments.[98] This warning came at a time when Cantor was busy exploring, mapping and inventing what he himself called the strange world of transfinite sets.

Indeed, it is not surprising to find that Husserl had doubts about sets when one considers that he was on hand as Cantor began discovering the antinomies of set theory[99] and so had a foretaste of the crisis in foundations that broke out once his proof by diagonal argument that there is no greatest cardinal number opened Bertrand Russell's eyes to the

---

p. 250; Husserl, *Introduction to the Logical Investigations,* p. 28.

93 Husserl, *Logical Investigations,* pp. 41-43.

94 Edmund Husserl, ex. p. 121 of his "A. Voigt's 'Elemental Logic,' in Relation to my Statements on the Logic of the Logical Calculus" (1893), in his *Early Writings in the Philosophy of Logic and Mathematics.*

95 Edmund Husserl, "Review of Ernst Schröder's *Vorlesungen über die Algebra der Logik*" (1891) and "From Husserl's Sketches for his Review of Schröder" in his *Early Writings in the Philosophy of Logic and Mathematics*, pp. 52-91, 421-41.

96 For example, see the articles anthologized on pp. 92-114, 115-20, 121-30, 135-38, 443-51 of Husserl's *Early Writings in the Philosophy of Logic and Mathematics.*

97 *Ibid.*, pp. 109, 123.

98 Husserl, *Philosophy of Arithmetic*, pp. 230-34.

99 Dauben, *Georg Cantor: His Mathematics and Philosophy of the Infinite*, pp. 240-70.

famous contradiction of the set of all sets that are not members of themselves.[100]

In a November 7, 1903 postcard, Hilbert informed Frege that Ernst Zermelo had discovered "Russell's" paradox three or four years earlier after he himself had communicated his examples to him.[101] A record of Zermelo's discovery is to be found in a note of April 16, 1902 that he conveyed to Husserl regarding the comments about the contradictions involving sets of sets that Husserl had made in his review of Schröder.[102]

Volker Peckhaus and Reinhard Kahle have tried to elucidate Hilbert's remark. They consider that it can be assumed that Hilbert formulated his paradox during exchanges with Cantor documented in their 1897-1900 correspondence.[103] That correspondence shows Cantor coping with the antinomies of set theory during Husserl's years in Halle. As Dauben has commented, it is "not a little ironic" that the first mathematician to discover the antinomies of set theory was Cantor himself, who had anticipated the problem and by 1895 was already "trying to remedy the paradoxes with a minimum of damage to his system of transfinite numbers".[104] Using his diagonalization proof of 1891, Cantor "could argue that the set of all sets had to give rise to a set of larger cardinality; the set of all its subsets. But since this set had to be a member of the set of all sets,

---

100 Bertrand Russell, *Principles of Mathematics*, New York: Norton, 1903, §§100, 344, 500 and his *My Philosophical Development*, London: Allen and Unwin, 1975, pp. 58-61; Ivor Grattan-Guinness, "How Russell Discovered His Paradox", *Historia Mathematica* 5, 1978, pp. 127-37, his "Georg Cantor's Influence on Bertrand Russell", *History and Philosophy of Logic* 1, 1980, pp. 61-93 and his *The Search for Mathematical Roots, Logics, Set Theories and the Foundations of Mathematics from Cantor through Gödel*, Princeton: Princeton University Press, 2000.

101 Gottlob Frege, *Philosophical and Mathematical Correspondence*, Oxford: Blackwell, 1980, p. 51.

102 Edmund Husserl, "Memorandum of a Verbal Communication from Zermelo to Husserl", in his *Early Writings in the Philosophy of Logic and Mathematics*, p. 442; Bernhard Rang and Wolfgang Thomas, "Zermelo's Discovery of Russell's Paradox", *Historia Mathematica* 8, 1981, pp. 16-22.

103 Volker Peckhaus and Reinhard Kahle 2000/2001, "Hilbert's Paradox", *Report No. 38, 2000/2001*, Institut Mittag-Leffler, The Royal Swedish Academy of Sciences, https://www.mittag-leffler.se/preprints/files/IML-0001-38.pdf, pp. 3-4; Cantor, *Briefe*, pp. 387-485.

104 Dauben, *Georg Cantor: His Mathematics and Philosophy of the Infinite*, p. 241.

the paradoxical conclusion was inevitable that a set of lower cardinality actually contained a set of higher cardinality".[105]

It is to be noted that Husserl did not ultimately conclude that set theory itself was false. In later writings, he viewed it as a legitimate mathematical discipline of the second level of the purely logical sphere. It was a matter of a rigorously scientific, a priori theory proceeding from purely logical concepts and axioms grounded in purely logical categories.[106] He concluded that it was faulty reasoning about a faulty concept of set had led to the set-theoretical paradoxes. He advocated making a fresh start and deriving set theory from a non-contradictory concept of set and element, or more universally of whole and part without resorting to an axiom of extensionality.[107] He was lucid enough to see that mathematics would not crumble if it did not have "a single object to represent an extension", as Russell believed it would.[108] All the rigmarole that Russell went through to evade the contradictions derivable from Frege's system with its axiom of extensionality[109] serves to illustrate what Husserl meant in *Formal and Transcendental Logic* when he said that extensions generate contradictions requiring every kind of artful device to make them safe for use in mathematical reasoning.[110]

Arithmetization

Much of the initial intellectual kinship between Husserl and Cantor can be explained by the influence that Karl Weierstrass exercised on both of them. Cantor had studied in Berlin from 1863 to 1869, where he had come under the influence of Weierstrass. In Halle, Husserl found him immersed himself in a project aimed at demonstrating that the positive whole numbers formed the basis of all other mathematical conceptual formations inspired by Weierstrass' famous theory to that effect. Any further progress of

---

105 *Ibid.*, pp. 165-68, 242.

106 Husserl, *Introduction to Logic and Theory of Knowledge*, §18d.

107 Edmund Husserl, *Ms A 1 35*, untitled, undated manuscript on set theory available at the Husserl Archives in Cologne, Leuven, and Paris, now partially published in German by Carlos Ierna and Dieter Lohmar as "Husserl's Manuscript A I 35", in G. E. Rosado Haddock (ed.), *Husserl and Analytic Philosophy*, Berlin: de Gruyter, 2016, pp. 289-319.

108 Russell, *Principles of Mathematics*, §489.

109 Claire Ortiz Hill, *Rethinking Identity and Metaphysics, On the Foundations of Analytic Philosophy*, New Haven: Yale University Press, 1997.

110 Husserl, *Formal and Transcendental Logic*, §§ 23, 26.

the work on set theory, Cantor explained in the beginning of his *Mannigfaltigkeitslehre* was absolutely dependent upon the expansion of the concept of real whole numbers beyond the present boundaries and in a direction which, as far as he knew, no one had yet searched. He had, he claimed, burst the confines of the conceptual formation of real whole numbers and broken through into a new realm of transfinite numbers. Initially, he had not been clearly conscious of the fact that these new numbers possessed the same concrete reality that the whole numbers did. He had, however, become persuaded that they did. As strange and daring as his ideas might now seem, he was convinced that they would one day be deemed completely simple, appropriate and natural.[111]

As for Husserl, he would say that it was from Weierstrass that he acquired the ethos of his intellectual endeavors.[112] Late in his career, he would say that he had sought to do for philosophy what Weierstrass had done for mathematics.[113] Impressed by Weierstrass' work to arithmetize analysis and intent upon rigorously deducing all of mathematics from the least number of self-evident principles by first analyzing the concepts and relations that are in themselves simpler and logically prior, then the more complicated, more derivative ones, he embarked upon a project to supply radical foundations for mathematics by submitting the concept of number itself to closer scrutiny. The natural and necessary starting point of any philosophy of mathematics, he initially believed, was the analysis of the concept of whole number.[114] For the still faithful disciple of Weierstrass still believed the "domain of 'positive whole numbers' to be the first and most underivative domain, the sole foundation of all remaining domains of numbers".[115]

However, although in *On the Concept of Number*, Husserl had maintained that all of the more complicated and artificial forms of numbers had their origin and basis in the concept of positive whole numbers and their interrelations and were derivable from them in a strictly logical way,[116] in the *Philosophy of Arithmetic*, he never endorsed Weierstrass' thesis in that

---

111 Cantor, *Grundlagen einer allgemeinen Mannigfaltigkeitslehre*, pp. 165-66.

112 Karl Schuhmann, *Husserl-Chronik*, The Hague: Martinus Nijhoff, 1977, p. 7.

113 Oskar Becker, "The Philosophy of Edmund Husserl", in *The Phenomenology of Husserl, Selected Critical Readings*, Chicago: Quadrangle Books, 1970 (1930), pp. 40-42; Schuhmann, *Husserl-Chronik*, p. 34.

114 Husserl, "On the Concept of Number", pp. 310-11.

115 Edmund Husserl, "The Concept of General Arithmetic" (1890), in his *Early Writings in the Philosophy of Logic and Mathematics*, p. 2.

116 Husserl, "On the Concept of Number", p. 310.

confident way. Rather, we find him explaining that he would provisionally use it as a springboard for his own analyses and warning readers that, although cardinal numbers in a certain way seem to be the basic numbers involved in arithmetic because the signs for them figure in expressions for positive, negative, rational, irrational, real, imaginary, alternative, ideal numbers, quaternions etc., the analyses of the second volume would perhaps show that thesis to be untenable.[117] In the April 1891 preface to the book, he went further to state that the analyses of the second volume would actually show that in no way does a single kind of concept, whether that of cardinal or ordinal numbers, form the basis of general arithmetic.[118] And before the *Philosophy of Arithmetic* was even published, he wrote to Carl Stumpf that the opinion by which had been guided in writing *On the Concept of Number* that the concept of cardinal number formed the foundation of general arithmetic had soon proved to be false, that through no manner of cunning could negative, rational, irrational and the various kinds of complex numbers be derived from the concept of the cardinal number.[119]

Husserl's *Mannigfaltigkeitslehre*

In the foreword to the *Logical Investigations*, Husserl specifically alluded to having been troubled by the theory of manifolds, the *Mannigfaltigkeitslehre*, with its expansion into special forms of numbers and extensions.[120] He always said that it was particularly difficulties that he had experienced in trying to answers questions raised by "imaginary" numbers that arose while trying to complete the *Philosophy of Arithmetic* which had marked the turning point in his thinking. He used the term "imaginary" in a very broad sense to cover negative numbers, negative square roots, fractions and irrational numbers, and so on.[121] He called infinite sets imaginary concepts.[122]

---

117 Husserl, *Philosophy of Arithmetic*, p. 13.
118 *Ibid.*, p. 7.
119 Husserl, "Letter from Edmund Husserl to Carl Stumpf" (1890/91), in his *Early Writings in the Philosophy of Logic and Mathematics*, p. 13.
120 Husserl, *Logical Investigations,* pp. 41-42; his *Introduction to the Logical Investigations*, p. 35.
121 Husserl, "Letter from Edmund Husserl to Carl Stumpf", pp. 13-16; his *Introduction to the Logical Investigations*, p. 33; his *Logical Investigations*, pp. 430-51; his *Formal and Transcendental Logic*, §31; Claire Ortiz Hill, *Word and Object in Husserl, Frege and Russell*, Athens OH: Ohio University Press, 1991, pp. 81-86.
122 Husserl, *Philosophy of Arithmetic*, p. 233.

Now, the kind of work on numbers that Cantor was doing in the late 1880s does make Husserl's quandaries completely understandable. Those were years during which Cantor was particularly engaged in what Grattan-Guinness has called "rather strange work on theory of numbers",[123] producing what Dauben has called "dinosaurs of his mental creation, fantastic creatures whose design was interesting, overwhelming, but impractical to the demands of mathematicians in general".[124]

Husserl ultimately concluded that "the key to the only possible solution of the problem" as to "how in the field of numbers impossible (essenceless) concepts can be methodically treated like real ones" was to be found in the theory of complete manifolds, *definite Mannigfaltigkeiten*, developed during his time in Halle.[125] He concluded that formal constraints banning meaningless expressions, meaningless imaginary concepts, reference to non-existent and impossible objects restrict theoretical, deductive work, but that resorting to the infinity of pure forms and transformations of forms frees us from such conditions and explains why having used imaginaries, what is meaningless, must lead, not to meaningless, but to true results. According to his theory of manifolds, one can operate freely within a manifold with imaginary concepts and be sure that what one deduced is correct when the axiomatic system completely and unequivocally determined the body of all the configurations possible in a domain by a purely analytical procedure.[126]

That solution was compatible with Cantor's conviction that mathematical concepts need only be both non-self-contradictory and stand in systematically determined relations established through definition from the previously formed, proven concepts and that mathematicians are only obliged to provide definitions of the new numbers determinate in this way and, if need be, to establish this relationship to the older numbers.[127] However, no one who has studied Cantor's *Mannigfaltigkeitslehre* could possibly confuse it with Husserl's theory of the same name. Cantor's *Mannigfaltigkeiten* were sets.

---

123 Ivor Grattan-Guinness, "Towards a Biography of Georg Cantor", *Annals of Science* 1971, 27 (4), p. 369.

124 Dauben, *Georg Cantor: His Mathematics and Philosophy of the Infinite*, pp. 158-59.

125 Husserl, *Logical Investigations, Prolegomena*, §70.

126 Husserl, *Introduction to Logic and Theory of Knowledge*, §19; his *Logic and General Theory of Science, 1917/18, with supplementary texts from the first version of 1910/11*, Cham, Switzerland: Springer, 2019, §§56-57 and his *Formal and Transcendental Logic*, §31; Stefania Centrone, *Logic and Philosophy of Mathematics in the Early Husserl*, Dordrecht: Springer, 2010.

127 Cantor, *Grundlagen einer allgemeinen Mannigfaltigkeitslehre*, p. 182.

Husserl's *Mannigfaltigkeiten* were not sets which, as I explain in the next chapter, he located on the second level of pure logic, while *Mannigfaltigkeiten* occupied the third and highest level of pure logic.[128]

Conclusion

I have examined several respects in which Husserl and Cantor might be said to be alike while pointing to dissimilarities between them. Husserl wrote of his time in Halle that it was a "decade of solitary, arduous labor" during which he saw all around him only ambiguously defined problems and profoundly unclear theories. Sick of the confusion and afraid of sinking into an "ocean of endless criticism", for "the sake of philosophical self-preservation", he had felt compelled to set aside his philosophical mathematical investigations and to risk striking out on his own. The course of his development, he wrote in the Foreword to the *Logical Investigations*, had led to his drawing apart from people and writings to whom he owed most of his intellectual training and to his drawing closer to a group of thinkers whose writings he had not been able to evaluate properly and had consulted all too little in the course of his labors.[129]

Initially, Husserl's ideas about mathematics and philosophy, sets, abstraction, and the arithmetization fit in with Cantor's ideas. That may be attributable to Cantor's position on his *Habilitationskommittee* and to the influence Weierstrass had exercised over both men. In 1890, Husserl wrote that with "respect to the starting point and the germinal core of our developments toward the construction of a general arithmetic, we are in agreement with mathematicians that are among the most important and progressive ones of our times: above all with *Weierstrass*, but not less with *Dedekind*, Georg *Cantor* and many others".[130]

In *Concept of Number*, Husserl had expressed his concern that mathematicians had failed to examine the logic of the concepts and methods they introduced and used and called for logical clarification, precise analyses.[131] And, at that point, the naive epistemological theorizing

---

128 Husserl, *Introduction to Logic and Theory of Knowledge*, §§18-19, pp. 434-35; his *Logic and General Theory of Science*, Chapter 11; his *Formal and Transcendental Logic*, §33.

129 Husserl, *Logical Investigations*, p. 43; his *Introduction to the Logical Investigations*, pp. 16-17.

130 Husserl, "The Concept of General Arithmetic", p. 1.

131 Husserl, "On the Concept of Number", p. 310.

in which Cantor was so earnestly engaging while Husserl was grappling with analogous questions could well have seemed to Husserl to be amenable to clarification through Brentano's teachings. He might have thought that Cantor's naïve talk of intuitions and presentations could grow in sophistication through the application of Brentano's ideas about presentation and intentionality; Brentano's collective unification might be what Cantor meant by the "special relationship" binding elements of a set; the objects of thought and intuition of Cantor's sets might be Brentano's intentional objects; Cantor's technique for extracting numbers from reality through abstraction might be a psychological process. Cantor's appeals to inner intuition and talk of things like the fingers of his right hand helping produce or awaken concepts in his mind do sound unabashedly empiricistic or psychologistic. Frege certainly saw them as such as he decried the "psychological and hence empirical turn" in the "Mitteilungen".[132] So, Husserl might have initially hoped that Brentanian analyses could "banish all metaphysical fog and all mysticism" from investigations like Cantor's.

At a later stage, Husserl renounced the psychologism, empiricism, and naturalism that Cantor was renouncing and drew near to the Platonic Idealism he was endorsing. But, the arithmetization that Cantor espoused failed Husserl too, and he confessed to having been troubled by the theory of manifolds, the *Mannigfaltigkeitslehre*, with its expansion into special forms of numbers and extensions. He also said he had been tormented by troubling puzzles about the interrelationship and intrinsic unity of what he called the "incredibly strange" worlds of the purely logical and of actual consciousness that he saw opening up all around him while he was trying to understand the logic of mathematical thought and calculation and to achieve clarity regarding the true meaning of the concepts of set theory and the theory of cardinal numbers in the *Philosophy of Arithmetic.*

However, while it is tempting to think that Husserl's turnabout was conditioned, if not actually induced by Cantor's bold experiments with mathematics and epistemology, and although Cantor's ideas probably did have a hand in unseating Husserl from his earliest convictions by raising a number of unsettling questions, he said that it was Lotze's work that was responsible for his conscious, radical rejection of psychologism, his espousal of Platonism, his newfound comprehension of Bolzano's work on pure

132 Frege, "Review of Georg Cantor, *Zur Lehre vom Transfiniten*", pp. 180, 181.

logic.[133] and, therefore, for his adoption of metaphysical and epistemological views that Brentano had taught him to consider odious and despicable. His rejection of the "blinding prejudices of psychologism", he said, had compelled him to recognize the purely logical ideal and the puzzles involved in the essential relationships between the ideal and actual consciousness at the heart of the dynamic that gave birth to phenomenology.

So, it is fair to say that although his ideas overlapped and crisscrossed with those of Cantor in the various ways discussed here, he figured among the thinkers from whom Husserl parted ways and that Lotze and Bolzano, not he, were among those whose ideas he had not at first appreciated and to whom he drew closer. Husserl said that he had felt intellectually isolated in Halle, that he had encountered confusion, ambiguously defined problems and profoundly unclear theories on all sides and had felt obliged to dare to set out on his own. I know of no evidence that he remained in contact with Cantor once he had left Halle.

---

133 Edmund Husserl, "Review of Melchior Palagyi's *Der Streit der Psychologisten und Formalisten in der modernen Logik*" (1903), in his *Early Writings in the Philosophy of Logic and Mathematics*, pp. 201-02; his *Introduction to the Logical Investigations*, pp. 36-38, 46-49.

4

THE STRANGE WORLDS OF ACTUAL CONSCIOUSNESS AND THE PURELY LOGICAL[1]

Introduction

It was troubling encounters with what he called the "incredibly strange" worlds of the purely logical and that of actual consciousness that he experienced while attempting to achieve clarity regarding the true meaning of the concepts of set theory and the theory of cardinal numbers in the *Philosophy of Arithmetic* that Edmund Husserl said launched him on his phenomenological voyage of discovery.[2]

As he struggled to understand how those two worlds interrelated and formed an intrinsic unity, he found himself facing riddles, tensions, mysteries, paradoxes and "great unsolved puzzles" concerning the very possibility of knowledge in general. He described himself as having been "unsettled – even tormented", powerfully gripped, by the deepest problems and drawn "close to the most obscure parts of the theory of knowledge". He was assailed by questions. If everything purely logical is an in-itself, something ideal having nothing at all to do with acts, subjects or empirical persons belonging to actual reality, then how is symbolic thinking possible? How are objective, mathematical and logical relations constituted in subjectivity? How does one go from mathematics to pure logic elucidated by a theory of knowledge? How can the mathematical-in-itself given to the mind be valid? If scientific knowledge is completely based upon being able to abandon oneself completely to thought that is removed from

---

[1] This was originally a paper given at the International Seminar on Contemporary Readings of Husserl's *Experience and Judgment, Investigations in the Genealogy of Logic,* Lisbon, April 23-27, 2012, organized by Pedro M. S. Alves and Carlos Morujão.

[2] Edmund Husserl, "Personal Notes" (1906-1908), in his *Early Writings in the Philosophy of Logic and Mathematics*, Dordrecht: Kluwer, 1994, pp. 490-92; his *Formal and Transcendental Logic*, The Hague: Martinus Nijhoff, 1969, §§27a, 24 & note; his *Introduction to the Logical Investigations, A Draft of a Preface to the Logical Investigations* (1913), The Hague: Martinus Nijhoff, 1975, pp. 34-35. When I have considered it necessary I have modified the translations of Husserl's writings throughout this text.

intuition, or being able to prefer such thinking over thought more fully in accord with intuition, how is rational insight possible? How does one then arrive at empirically correct results? [3]

Husserl searched until the end of his life for answers to such questions. So it is that in *Experience and Judgment, Investigations in the Genealogy of Logic*, he confronted the challenge of investigating the origin and subjective foundation of traditional Aristotelian formal logic by piercing through the logic of subject and predicates to reach the world of actual consciousness. [4]

Volumes of Husserl's lecture courses[5] first published during the last few decades are now shedding considerable light on many recondite places of his thought and are showing how single-minded he was. In particular, they show how far back the investigations of *Experience and Judgment* reach and provide a clearer idea of what was at stake for Husserl in that book, which echoes numerous passages from those courses. For example, Husserl was already developing the phenomenological method and teaching that all questions concerning the relationship between objectivity and subjectivity were ultimately to be answered by going back to the sources from which logical ideas originate in his *Allgemeine Erkenntnistheorie, Vorlesung 1902/03*.

The publication of this material means that it is now possible to see well what Husserl came to locate in each of the two worlds – and in the different parts of each one – and to have a good understanding of how he envisioned their interrelationship. It is extremely important to see and understand these things because, as Husserl realized, the fact that what belongs in one world, or in another part of one of the worlds, often enjoys

---

[3] Husserl's "Personal Notes", pp. 491-93, his "On the Logic of Signs (Semiotic)" (1890), p. 37 and his "Psychological Studies in the Elements of Logic" (1894), pp. 167-69 in his *Early Writings in the Philosophy of Logic and Mathematics*; Husserl, *Introduction to the Logical Investigations*, pp. 17, 22, 35.

[4] Edmund Husserl, *Experience and Judgment, Investigations in the Genealogy of Logic*, London: Routledge and Kegan Paul, 1973 (1939), §§1, 3, 10, 11.

[5] For example: Husserl's, *Logik, Vorlesung 1896*, Dordrecht: Kluwer, 2001; his *Allgemeine Erkenntnistheorie, Vorlesung 1902/03*, Dordrecht; Kluwer, 2001; his *Logik, Vorlesung 1902/03*, Dordrecht: Kluwer, 2001; his *Introduction to Logic and Theory of Knowledge, Lectures 1906/07*, Dordrecht: Springer, 2008; his *Alte und neue Logik, Vorlesung 1908/09*, Dordrecht: Kluwer, 2003; his *Logic and General Theory of Science, with Supplementary Texts from the First Version of 1910/11*, Cham, Switzerland: Springer, 2019.

the same outward appearance as what belongs in the other world or somewhere else in the same world is often a hard to perceive source of major errors in philosophy.

So, the goal of the following reappraisal of the fundamental tenets of Husserlian phenomenology as exposed in the analyses of the subjective foundations of the part of traditional formal logic to which *Experience and Judgment* is devoted is to take readers on a tour of Husserl's strange worlds, to describe what he found in them and how he saw their interaction. My method is exegetical, because to evaluate the ideas of those who ascribe ideas to Husserl that he did not hold – and against which he strenuously militated with all his intellectual might – it is essential to have, and to maintain, a firm grasp on the theories about what belonged in psychology, phenomenology and pure logic that he persistently and consistently defended.

Psychologism and actual consciousness

Husserl came to divide the world of actual consciousness into the realm of the psychological and that of phenomenological.[6] His journey towards the latter, it is well known, began in the realm of the former. He recalled that when he began the Brentanian psychological analyses of the origins of numbers of the *Philosophy of Arithmetic, Psychological and Logical Investigations*, it was obvious to him that "what mattered most for a philosophy of mathematics was a radical analysis of the 'psychological origin' of the basic mathematical concepts."[7] In *Formal and Transcendental Logic*, he characterized *Philosophy of Arithmetic* as an initial attempt on his part to achieve clarity regarding the authentic meaning of the concepts fundamental to the theory of cardinal numbers and set theory by going back to the spontaneous activities of collecting and counting in which sets and the cardinal numbers are given. He says that that was what he would later come to call a phenomenologico-constitutional investigation.[8]

However, as we have seen, the further he delved into his philosophical investigations into the principles of mathematics, the more he was tormented by doubts as to how to reconcile the objectivity of mathematics and all of science in general with psychological foundations for logic, and

---

[6] Husserl, "Personal Notes", pp. 491-92.
[7] Husserl, *Introduction to the Logical Investigations*, p. 33.
[8] Husserl, *Formal and Transcendental Logic*, §27a.

that led him to engage in critical reflections on the essence of logic and on the relationship between the subjectivity of knowing and the objectivity of the content known.[9] He recalled how his doubts disturbed and even tormented him and then extended to all categorial concepts and ultimately to all concepts of objectivities of any kind whatsoever.[10]

According to Brentano's teachings, the idea of set was to arise out of the unifying consciousness of meaning-together, in the conceiving as one. That could not be physical, so the concept of collection had to arise through psychological reflection upon the act of collecting. But, Husserl realized that the concept of number itself had to be something fundamentally different from that of collecting, which was all that could result from reflection on acts.[11]

When it was a matter of the origin of mathematical presentations, or of the elaboration of practical methods that are actually psychologically determined, he concluded, psychological analyses are appropriate and justified. Mental experiences of knowing have their place in psychology, but what is known is not psychology – not the natural science of mental individuals, their real experiences and experiential mental states – just because it is known in the mental experience of knowing. Out of subjective experiences of perceiving, presenting, we form concepts and we judge and draw conclusions. But, once one tries to go from the psychological connections of thinking to the logical unity of the thought-content, no true continuity and clarity can be established. Scientific investigating and thinking is subjective, as is the relationship between subjective experiences of presenting, judging, deducing, proving, theorizing. But, the experience of presenting is not a concept, judging is not a proposition or truth, theorizing is not a theory. Science in the objective sense, as divorced from the scientifically investigating or learning subject, is a web of theories and so of proofs, conclusions, propositions, concepts, meanings, and none of those are lived experiences, but are certain ideal unities standing in relationship to experiences.[12]

---

[9] Edmund Husserl, *Logical Investigations*, London: Routledge and Kegan Paul, 1970, p. 42.

[10] Husserl, *Introduction to the Logical Investigations*, p. 35.

[11] *Ibid.*, pp. 34-35.

[12] Husserl's *Logical Investigations*, p. 42, his *Allgemeine Erkenntnistheorie*, pp. 16-17 and his *Introduction to Logic and Theory of Knowledge*, §18b.

Mathematicians, Husserl insisted, do not establish laws for subjective acts, but for ideal objects. The concept of number, he observed, like every concept, refers back to a corresponding intuition. A number is only given in actual counting. Someone who had never counted would not know what a number is, just as someone who had never had a sensation of red would not know what red is. But, this does not mean that number is a psychological concept and arithmetic a branch of psychology. Numbers do not concern what happens in mental experiences of experiencing individuals[13] and are not grounded in experience with its actual occurrences. The numbers 1, 2 and so on belong to the series of natural numbers and each such number is a member of the series of cardinal numbers, yet the number 3 is not reproduced if ten people have presentations of 3. Even if thousands of people count 4, the number 4 is a number of the number series.[14]

Arithmetic does not obtain its universal propositions by means of perception and empirical generalizations based on perception and on the substantiation of individual judgments resulting from them. It is not in direct contact with acts of counting, ordering, combining, calculating, collecting. The number 2 is just not an object of possible perception and experience. It "is not a thing, not an event in nature. It has no place and no time. It is just not an object of possible perception and 'experience'. Two apples come into being and pass away, have a place and time. But when the apples are eaten up, the number 2 is not eaten up. The number series of pure arithmetic has not suddenly developed a hole, as if we then had to count 1, 3, 4…." In the world, he pointed out, there are not alongside trees, houses, also things called number 2, number 3. One can perceive 2 apples precisely while one perceives each apple, but one cannot perceive the 2, he pointed out.[15]

Husserl's profound dissatisfaction with his investigations in the psychological realm drove him to its edge and pushed him over the line into transcendental phenomenology. So, once he had secured the objective theoretical scaffolding needed to keep philosophers from falling into the quagmires of psychologism, he began introducing the phenomenological analyses of knowledge that were to yield the general

---

[13] Husserl, *Introduction to Logic and Theory of Knowledge*, §13b.

[14] Husserl, *Allgemeine Erkenntnistheorie*, p. 17.

[15] Husserl, *Allgemeine Erkenntnistheorie*, p. 118 and his *Introduction to Logic and Theory of Knowledge*, §§13c, 18.

concepts of knowledge that he hoped would solve all further problems in theory of knowledge.

The phenomenological realm

Husserl saw that psychology could not solve the epistemological problems he was facing, but he never considered utterly forsaking the world of actual consciousness. He considered that only those, like himself, deeply distressed by the issues in the most intense way,

> compelled by the critical dissolution of the blinding prejudices of psychologism to recognize the purely logical ideal... but... at the same time... compelled by the revealing emphasis upon the essential relationships between the ideal and the psychological... not to abandon by any means the psychological entirely but rather to keep it within view as somehow belonging with the ideal... can also have the insight that such psychological critiques are indispensable for forcing recognition of the ideal as something given prior to all theories.... can realize that the being-in-itself of the ideal sphere in its relation to consciousness brings with it a dimension of puzzles which remain untouched by all such argumentation against psychologism and hence must be solved through special investigations... through phenomenological ones.[16]

The phenomenological analyses of *Experience and Judgment* stand as an example of the science of radical subjectivity that Husserl pursued until the end of his life. The subjectivity in question is a transcendental subjectivity in which knowers go back to the ultimate sources to question all cognitive constructions and to reflect upon themselves and upon knowing. It is more radical than psychological subjectivity can ever be because it is a desconstructing (*Abbau*) of all the deposits of meaning already present in the world of our present experience, a going back to question those deposits of meaning at the subjective sources from which they have arisen.[17]

Thus, it became the particular task of *Experience and Judgment* to elucidate the origin and subjective foundation of traditional Aristotelian formal logic by clarifying the essence of the predicative judgment, because truly philosophical logic requires a radical return to pre-predicative experience, requires that one pierce through the logic of subject and

[16] Husserl, *Introduction to the Logical Investigations*, pp. 21-22.
[17] Husserl, *Experience and Judgment,* §§11, 12.

predicates to the foundations of an underlying, hidden, logic in order to elucidate the origin of predicative judgments. The world in which we live, know and judge, and out of which arises everything that affects us that becomes the substrate of a possible judgment, *Experience and Judgment* explains, is always already given permeated with deposits left by logical operations. From this pregiven world, from this hidden life-world with its deposits of meaning, its science and scientific determination, its veil of ideas, philosophers must think back to the world of experience as immediately pre-given prior to all logical functions. They must re-experience the origination of the operations of idealization from original life-experience. They must think back to the original life-world and the subjective operations out of which it arises. So the task of elucidating the origin of predicative judgments, of establishing their relations to a foundation and of pursuing the origins of pre-predicative self-evidence in that of experience is one of going back to the original life-world as the universal ground of all particular experiences, to the world of immediate intuition and experience, the world in which we already live all the time and which is the basis of all cognitive performance and all scientific determination.[18]

In the truly ultimate, original realm of self-evidence of pre-predicative experience of *Experience and Judgment*, philosophers look upon the world purely as a world of perception. They limit experience to the domain of what is valid only for themselves as reflecting subjects and do so in a manner that excludes all idealization, excludes the presupposition of objectivity, of the validity of judgments for others that oriented traditional logic to the ideal of exact determination in the sense of the definitive scientific validity that is always tacitly presupposed as being an essential part of the act of judgment. Once we disregard others, Husserl acknowledged, there is no question of any validation referring to the cognitive activity of others. There are not yet any deposits of meaning guaranteeing that our world, as far as it is given to us, is always already understood as a world determinable with exactitude and already determined by science in accordance with the idea of definitive validity.[19]

This is the case, according to *Experience and Judgment,* because catching sight of the ultimate origins of logic is at any given time the

18 *Ibid.*, §§10, 11, 12.

19 *Ibid.*, §12.

accomplishment of *a single* subject. Doing so requires me to limit myself to the realm of what is mine at a given time. This means investigating judging as if it is at any given time only for me, the fruits of which are mine only, taking no account of the role it plays in communication and the fact that it already always presupposes prior communication just in the manner in which it has already endowed its objects with meaning. Only then, Husserl thought, does one reach the most primitive building blocks of the logical activity out of which our world is built, which are initially thought of as being not for others, but as objects only for myself, the world as being thought as a world only for myself.[20]

A major part of the job of exploring the worlds of actual consciousness and of the purely logical naturally involves finding the line separating psychology and phenomenology and that separating phenomenology and the objective sciences. And from the time that Husserl first began talking of phenomenology, he was intent upon doing just that. For example, in his 1913 draft of a preface to the *Logical Investigations*, he recalled that in the *Prolegomena to Pure Logic* he had tried to show that efforts to ground logic exclusively on psychology rest on a confusion of distinct classes of problems and on fundamentally mistaken presuppositions about the nature and goals of empirical psychology and pure logic. He wrote:

> The reader of the 'Prolegomena' is made a participant in a conflict between two motifs within the logical sphere which are contrasted in radical sharpness: the one is the psychological, the other the purely logical. The two do not come together by accident as the thought-act on the one side and the thought-meaning on the other. Somehow they necessarily belong together. But they are to be distinguished, namely in this manner: everything 'purely' logical is an 'in itself,' is an 'ideal' which includes in this 'in itself' – in its proper essential content (*Wesengehalt*) – nothing 'mental,' nothing of acts, of subjects, or even of empirically factual persons of actual reality. There corresponds to this unique field of existing objectivities (*Objektivitäten*) a science, a 'pure logic,' which seeks knowledge exclusively related to these ideal objectivities, i.e., which judges on the pure meanings (*Bedeutungen*) and on the meant objectivities as such.... Thereupon follows a task... to determine the natural boundary of the logical-ideal sphere... to grasp the idea of the pure logic in its full scope.[21]

---

[20] *Ibid.*, §§11, 12.

[21] Husserl, *Introduction to the Logical Investigations*, p. 20.

Experience and Judgment stresses that every science has an objective and a subjective side, that even in those cases in which we do not recognize the universal binding force and general applicability of the "exact" methods of natural science and its cognitive ideas, the conviction persists that objects of our experience are determined in themselves and knowing is a matter of discovering those determinations subsisting in themselves and of establishing them objectively, once and for all and for everyone, as they are in themselves. Husserl deemed it necessary to investigate the deposits of meaning in the world of our present experience relative to the subjective sources out of which they had developed and to dismantle everything already pre-existing in those deposits. But he insisted that this was a matter of the subjectivity whose operations of meaning have made the world that is pregiven to us what it is, namely, not a pure world of experience, but a world determined and determinable in itself with exactitude, a world in which any individual entity is given beforehand in an perfectly obvious way as in principle determinable in accordance with the methods of exact science and as being a world in itself in a sense originally deriving from the achievements of the physico-mathematical sciences of nature.[22] He acknowledged that

> our immediate experience.... in its immediacy knows neither exact space nor objective time and causality. And even if it is true that all theoretical scientific determination of existents ultimately refers back to experience and its data, nevertheless experience does not give its objects directly in such a way that the thinking that operates on these objects as it itself experiences them is able to lead by itself... immediately to objects in the sense of true theory, i.e., to objects of science. If we speak of *objects of science*, science being that which as such seeks truth valid for everyone, then these objects... are *not objects of experience*.... 'Judgments of experience,'... which are obtained only from original operations in categorical acts purely on the basis of experience, i.e., sense experience and the experience founded on it of mental reality, are not judgments of definitive validity, are not judgments of science in the precise sense....[23]

In texts dated 1907 and 1908 that were included as appendices to his 1906/07 course on logic and the theory of knowledge, Husserl gave numerous examples of what did and did not belong in phenomenology,

---

[22] Husserl, *Experience and Judgment,* §§3, 10, 11.
[23] *Ibid.,* §10.

either because it fell into the realm of psychology and the natural sciences, or because it belonged to the world of the purely logical. The natural sciences of physical and mental nature, the mathematical sciences, logic, including formal logic, the sciences of value, ethics are not phenomenology, he said.[24] In the case of the formal sciences, he emphasized that in genuine transcendental phenomenology, we have no dealings with *a priori* ontology, formal logic and formal mathematical geometry as *a priori* theory of space, with *a priori* real ontology of any kind. As phenomenology of the constituting consciousness, not a single objective axiom relating to objects that are not consciousness, no *a priori* proposition as truth for objects, as something belonging in the objective science of these objects, or of objects in general in formal universality belongs in transcendental phenomenology. The axioms of geometry do not belong in phenomenology, he explained, because phenomenology is not a theory of the essences of shapes, of spatial objects. Essence-propositions about objects do not belong in the phenomenology of knowledge, insofar are they are objective truths and as truths have their place in a truth-system in general. What is objective belongs to objective science, and what objective science still lacks for completion is its affair to obtain and its alone.[25]

The world of the purely logical

In *Formal and Transcendental Logic*, Husserl explained that his "war against logical psychologism was in fact meant to serve no other end than the supremely important one of making the specific *province* of analytic logic visible in its purity and ideal particularity, freeing it from the psychologizing confusions and misinterpretations in which it had remained enmeshed from the beginning".[26] In his 1913 draft of a preface to the *Logical Investigations*, he had written that he had come to believe that the entire approach whereby phenomenology overthrows psychologism showed that what he had proposed as analyses of immanent consciousness

---

24 Husserl, *Introduction to Logic and Theory of Knowledge*, p. 414.

25 Husserl, *Introduction to Logic and Theory of Knowledge*, pp. 428-29; Claire Ortiz Hill, "Husserl on Axiomatization and Arithmetic", in *Phenomenology and Mathematics*, Dordrecht: Springer, 2010, pp. 47-71, also published in Claire Ortiz Hill and Jairo José da Silva, *The Road Not Taken, On Husserl's Philosophy of Logic and Mathematics*, London: College Publications, 2013.

26 Husserl, *Formal and Transcendental Logic*, §67.

had to be considered as pure a priori analyses of essence.[27] There, he described the world of the purely logical as follows:

> "Pure logic," in its most comprehensive extension characterizes itself by an essential distinction as "*mathesis universalis*." It develops through a step-by-step extension of that particular concept of formal logic which remains as a residue of pure ideal doctrines dealing with 'propositions' and validity after the removal from traditional logic of all the psychological misinterpretations and the normative-practical goal positings (*Zielgebungen*). In its thoroughly proper extension it includes all of the pure "analytical" doctrines of mathematics (arithmetic, number theory, algebra, etc.) and the entire area of formal theories, or rather, speaking in correlative terms, the theory of manifolds (*Mannigfaltigkeitslehre*) in the broadest sense. The newest development of mathematics brings with it that ever new groups of formal-ontological laws are constantly being formulated and mathematically treated which earlier had remained unnoticed. "*Mathesis universalis*" ... includes the sum total of this formal *a priori*. It is... directed toward the entirety of the "categories of meaning" and toward the formal categories for objects correlated to them or, alternatively, the *a priori* laws based upon them. It thus includes the entire *a priori* of what is in the most fundamental sense the "analytic" or "formal sphere"....[28]

In his 1900 abstract for the *Prolegomena to Pure Logic*, Husserl had described pure logic as "the scientific system of ideal laws and theories which are purely grounded in the sense of the ideal categories of meaning; that is, in the fundamental concepts which are common to all sciences because they determine in the most universal way what makes sciences objectively sciences at all: unity of theory. In this sense, pure logic is the science of the ideal 'conditions of the possibility' of science generally, or of the ideal constituents of the idea of theory."[29]

Instead of pure logic, he suggested in the early years of the century, one might speak of analytics or the science of what is analytically knowable in general, the science that establishes and systematically grounds analytic laws. For him, analytically necessary propositions are propositions that are true completely independently of any particular facts about their objects and of any actual matters of fact. He defined analytic laws as

[27] Husserl, *Introduction to the Logical Investigations*, p. 42.
[28] *Ibid.*, pp. 28-29.
[29] *Ibid.*, p. 4.

"unconditionally universal propositions" that include formal concepts lacking all matter or content and free of any explicit or implicit positing of the existence of individuals. As examples of such purely formal concepts, he proposed "something", "one", "object", "property", "relation", "connection", "plurality", "cardinal number", "order", "ordinal number", "whole", "part", "magnitude", which he considered to be fundamentally different in character from concepts like "house", "tree", "color", "sound", "spatial figure", "sensation", "feeling", "smell", "intensity", which express something factual or sensory.[30] He defended analytic logic against charges of being a "useless" spinning out of 'sterile' formalizations", an objection that he considered revelatory of considerable philosophical deficiency, of a lack of understanding of crucial basic issues, and of a disgraceful ignorance of the essence of modern mathematics and the extraordinary significance that the scientifically rigorous, theoretical exploration of forms of pure deduction had acquired for the perfection and most rigorous grounding of the systems of pure mathematics in his day.[31]

In *Allgemeine Erkenntnistheorie* – which he considered presented the methodological and theoretical questions of the theory of knowledge in an incomparably clearer manner than in the *Logical Investigations*[32] –, Husserl taught that all objectivity of thinking was grounded in purely logical forms, that the ultimate meaning and source of all objectivity making it possible for thinking to reach beyond contingent, subjective, human acts and lay hold of objective being in itself was to be found in ideality and in the ideal laws defining it. He presented pure logic as the science of the form concepts to which the objective content of all logical, all scientific thinking in general is subject. He taught that all truly scientific thinking, all proving and theorizing worthy of the name operated in forms corresponding to purely logical laws that included no cognitive material from the individual sciences, but were exclusively made up of concepts like truth, proposition, concept, argument, conclusion, necessity, possibility, object, property, set. Pure logic, he stressed, embraces all the concepts and propositions without which science would not be possible, would not have any sense or validity. For him, any given science was a

---

[30] Husserl, *Logical Investigations*, Investigation III, §§11-12, his *Alte und neue Logik*, p. 244 and his *Experience and Judgment*, §1.

[31] Husserl, *Alte und neue Logik*, p. 39.

[32] Husserl, *Allgemeine Erkenntnistheorie*, p. IX.

web of meanings laying claim to objective validity as a whole and as regards all its individual features.[33]

According to his definition of the purely logical in *Logik, Vorlesung 1902/03*, all concepts relating to objects in general in the most universal ways, or to thought forms in general in which objects are brought to theoretically objective unity, are purely logical. Purely logical concepts, purely formal concepts are not limited to a special field of objects, but are centered on the empty idea of something or of object in general. They not only can and actually do figure in all the sciences, but are common and necessary to all sciences because they belong to what belongs to the ideal essence of science in general. All purely mathematical concepts like unit, multiplicity, cardinal number, order, ordinal number, and manifold are purely logical because they clearly relate in the most universal way to numbers in general and are only made possible out of the most universal concept of object. All purely mathematical theories, purely arithmetical theories, the theory of syllogism are purely logical because their basic concepts express reasoning forms that are free of any cognitive content and cannot be had through sensory abstraction. No epistemological reflection is required.[34]

In his logic courses, Husserl taught that the essence of the mathematical lies in establishing a purely apodictic foundation of the truths of a field from apodictic principles. It is a matter of a rigorously scientific, a priori theory that builds from the bottom up and derives the manifold of possible inferences from the axiomatic foundations a priori in a rigorously deductive way. The mathematical disciplines of the purely logical sphere, he theorized, proceed from given, purely logical basic concepts and axioms that are grounded in the essence of purely logical categories.[35]

For Husserl, the concept of number became the very paradigm of a purely logical concept. According to his theories, arithmetic truths were analytic, grounded in the identical ideal meaning of words independently of matters of fact and had nothing at all to do with experience and induction, but only with concepts. He taught that:

> pure arithmetic investigates what is grounded in the essence of number. It is concerned not with things, not with physical things, not with souls, not

---

33 *Ibid.*, pp. 41, 47, 53, 58, 200, 206.

34 Husserl, *Logik, Vorlesung 1902/03*, pp. 31-43.

35 Husserl, *Logik, Vorlesung 1902/03*, pp. 32-35, 39; Husserl, *Introduction to Logic and Theory of Knowledge*, §§13c, 19d, 25b.

> with real events of a physical and mental nature. It has nothing at all to do with nature. Numbers are not natural objects. The number series is so to speak a world of objectivities of its own, of *ideal* objectivities, *not real* ones.... *The world of the mathematical and purely logical is a world of ideal objects*, a world of "concepts".... *There all truth is nothing other than analysis of essences or concepts.*[36]

The formalness of arithmetic, he explained in *Formal and Transcendental Logic*, lies in its relationship to "anything whatsoever" with empty universality that leaves every material determination indeterminately optional. The theory of cardinal numbers relates to the empty universe, to anything whatsoever with formal universality. The basic concepts are syntactical formations of the empty something that leaves out of consideration any material determination of objects. When the concept of cardinal number is fashioned purely in the broadest universality, the material contents of what is counted must be allowed to vary absolutely freely.[37]

Indeed, from the mid-1890s on, Husserl defended the view, which he attributed to Frege's teacher, Hermann Lotze, that pure arithmetic was basically no more than a branch of logic that had undergone independent development. Eminent thinkers like Lotze, Husserl explained, had correctly recognized cardinal number as a specific differentiation of the concept of multiplicity (*Vielheit*) and multiplicity as the most universal logical concept combining objects in general that splits into the series of different special forms that are the cardinal numbers. The unending profusion of theories that arithmetic develops is already fixed, enfolded in the axioms, and theoretical-systematic deduction effects the unfolding of them following systematic, simple procedures. All of arithmetic is grounded in the arithmetical axioms. Each genuine axiom is a proposition that unfolds the idea of cardinal number from some side or unfolds some of the ideas inseparably connected with the idea of cardinal number. The meaning of cardinal number, he said, is the answer to the question: "How many?" Since each and every thing can be counted as one, he reasoned, to conceive the concept of number, or that of any arbitrarily defined number, we only need the concept of something in general. One is something in general. Anything can be counted as one and out of the units all cardinal numbers are built.[38]

---

36 Husserl, *Introduction to Logic and Theory of Knowledge,* §13c. Husserl's emphasis.

37 Husserl, *Formal and Transcendental Logic*, §§24, 27a.

38 Husserl, *Logik, Vorlesung 1896*, pp. 241-42, 271-72; his *Logik, Vorlesung 1902/03*, pp. 19, 32-35, 39; his *Introduction to Logic and Theory of Knowledge,* §15; Hill, "Husserl on Axiomatization and Arithmetic".

Husserl finds a natural order in the world of formal logic

Husserl's phenomenological elucidation of the origin of the logical showed him that its domain was far more extensive than had been dealt with by traditional logic, and his investigations further led him to detect a natural order in formal logic and to broaden its domain to include two levels above the traditional Aristotelian logic of subject and predicates and states of affairs, the origins of which are so thoroughly studied in *Experience and Judgment.*[39]

These three levels of pure logic are described in *Introduction to Logic and Theory of Knowledge*[40] and Part I of *Formal and Transcendental Logic* is devoted to them. In the introduction to the latter book, Husserl stated that he considered his new understanding of the structure of the world of pure logic – still not fully detected in the *Logical Investigations*, and not yet described in his logical courses of the time – to be of the greatest significance, not only for a genuine understanding of the true sense of logic, but for all of philosophy. He saw it as a matter of a radical clarification of the relationship between formal logic and formal mathematics and as leading to a definitive clarification of the sense of pure formal mathematics as a pure analytics of non-contradiction.[41]

On the first tier of Husserl's hierarchy, the traditional Aristotelian apophantic logic of subject and predicate propositions and states of affairs investigates what can be stated in possible form *a priori* about objects in general from a possible perspective. It deals with the forms of propositions or states of affairs by asking in which forms objects are conceivable as such states of affairs and then which laws for the existence of states of affairs are valid in virtue of their form. He considered that although the concept of predicative judgment stood at the center of formal logic as it had developed historically, it was but a small area of pure logic as a whole.[42]

This explains why numbers, for example, are so conspicuous by their absence in *Experience and Judgment.* According to Husserl's theory of the forms of subject-predicate propositions of the first level, number

---

[39] Husserl, *Introduction to Logic and Theory of Knowledge,* §18c; his *Experience and Judgment, Investigations in the Genealogy of Logic,* §1.

[40] Husserl, *Introduction to Logic and Theory of Knowledge,* §§18-19.

[41] Husserl, *Formal and Transcendental Logic,* p. 11.

[42] Husserl, *Introduction to Logic and Theory of Knowledge,* §18c.

only occurs as form, but not as an object about which something is predicated. He explained that if one says *w* and *x* and *y* and *z* are φ, then one has combined the objects *w*…*z* by 'and'. In that case, the 'and' is form and grounds the unitary form of the plural predication. Corresponding to this is a cardinal number. However, he stressed, that is a new thought configuration, for it is one thing to make statements about objects in which number properties occur as form, and are thereby dependent, and another thing to make statements about numbers as such in such a way that the numbers are the objects. As examples of expressions of the first level in which numbers occur, Husserl gave: '2 men'; '3 houses'.[43]

He emphasized that only the forms of the plural numerical predication about objects as such belong in a simple theory of objects in general and the forms of their states of affairs and that in statements, propositions or state of affairs, forms are dependent. We can make such forms independent, he taught, but then new higher order objects, hypostasizations of forms emerge that are not objects in their own right. Statements about numbers in which numbers are objects have their place on the second level of Husserl's hierarchy, where numbers function in an entirely different way than on this first level.[44]

For Husserl, sets as objects do not occur on the apophantic level any more than numbers do. He observed that,

> in set theory, we make judgments universally about sets that in a certain way are higher order objects. We do not make judgments directly about elements, but about whole totalities of elements and arbitrary elements, and the whole totalities, the sets to be precise, are the objects-about-which. *Corresponding to every plural is a set, but in the theory of proposition forms, or forms of states of affairs, the set does not occur as object.* In it, the objects-about-which are thoroughly indeterminate *A B*…. Rather, only the plural occurs in it, which constitutes a form of predication about arbitrary objects.[45]

So mathematical sets are also conspicuous by their absence in *Experience and Judgment*, which devotes a few pages to a discussion of sets in the non-mathematical sense of objectivities of the understanding. In the pre-predicative world of that book, a "set is an original

[43] *Ibid.*
[44] *Ibid.*
[45] *Ibid.*

objectivity, preconsituted by an activity of colligation which links disjunct objects to one another; the active apprehension of this objectivity consists in a simple reapprehension or laying hold of that which has just been preconstituted". After completing an act of colligating through a retrospective apprehension, a set is given to the ego as an object, as something identifiable. Every set preconstituted in intuition must be conceived a priori as capable of being reduced to ultimate constituents, to particularities which are no longer sets. "As a pure formation of spontaneity, the set represents a pre-eminent form in which thematic objects of every conceivable kind enter as members and with which they can themselves function as members of determining judgments of every kind".[46]

Husserl believed that apophantic logic had to be distinguished and segregated from the formal ontology of the broader sphere of pure logic that included the mathematical disciplines and was immense in range and wealth of content in comparison. According to his theory, the disciplines of the two levels rising above it deal with individual things, but not in the sense of empirical or material entities. These higher ontologies are concerned with purely formally determined higher level object formations like set, cardinal number, quantity, ordinal number, ordered magnitude, that are removed from acts, subjects, or empirical persons of actual reality. In them, it is no longer a question of objects as such about which one might predicate something, but of investigating what is valid for higher order objective constructions that are determined in purely formal terms and deal with objects in indeterminate, general ways.[47]

Husserl conceived of the second level as an expanded, completely developed analytics in which one proceeds in a purely formal manner since every single concept used is analytic. One calculates, reasons deductively, with concepts and propositions. Signs and rules of calculation suffice because each procedure is purely logical. One manipulates signs, which acquire their meaning in the game through the rules of the game. One may proceed mechanically in this way and the result will prove accurate and justified. On the second level of pure logic, Husserl located the basic concepts of mathematics, the theory of cardinal numbers, the theory of ordinals, set theory, mathematical physics, formal pure logic, pure geometry, geometry as *a priori* theory of space, the axioms of geometry as a theory

---

[46] Husserl, *Experience and Judgment,* §61.

[47] Husserl, *Introduction to Logic and Theory of Knowledge,* §18c-d.

of the essences of shapes, of spatial objects, but also the pure theory of meaning and being, *a priori* real ontology of any kind (thing, change), ontology of nature, ontology of minds, natural scientific ontology, the sciences of value, pure ethics, the logic of morality, the ontology of ethical personalities, axiology or the pure logic of values, pure esthetics, ontology of values, the logic of the ideal state or the ideal world government as a system of cooperating ideal nation states, or the science of the ideal state, the ideal of a valuable existence, objective axioms relating to *a priori* propositions as truth for objects, as something belonging in the objective science of these objects, or of objects in general in formal universality, essence-propositions about objects insofar as they are objective truths and as truths have their place in a truth-system in general.[48]

As examples of arithmetical propositions of the second level in which numbers occur as objects, Husserl gave:

1. "Any number can be added to any number".
2. "If *a* is a number and *b* a number, then *a* + *b* is as well".
3. "Any number can be decreased or increased by one".
4. "The numbers form a series continuing from 0 *in infinitum*".[49]

As examples of propositions of the second level in which sets occur as objects, he gave:

1. "2 sets can each be joined into a new set".
2. "2 sets *a b* are each related to one another in such a way that either *a* is part of *b* or *b* is part of *a*, or that they intersect (a set having a part in common), or that it turns out that they are identical, coincide".
3. "The set formed of the elements *A B C* is part of the set formed of the elements *A B C D* containing "more elements".[50]

On the third and highest level of formal logic, Husserl located the theory of manifolds, a new discipline and a new method constituting a new kind of mathematics, the most universal of all. He counted upon it to provide secure foundations for an a priori theory of science. He presented his theory of manifolds in his major published works,[51] but what seems

---

48 Husserl, *Introduction to Logic and Theory of Knowledge*, §§18-19, pp. 434-35; his *Logic and General Theory of Science*, Chapter 11.

49 Husserl, *Introduction to Logic and Theory of Knowledge*, §18c.

50 *Ibid.*

51 Husserl, *Logical Investigations, Prolegomena*, §§69-70; his *Ideas: General Introduction to Pure Phenomenology*, New York: Colliers, 1962, §§71-72; his *Formal and Transcendental Logic*, §33.

inchoate and cryptic there received particularly clear and explicit treatment in the posthumously published lecture courses.

In those courses, Husserl described manifolds as pure forms of possible theories which, like molds, remain totally undetermined as to their content, but to which thought must necessarily conform in order to be thought and known in a theoretical manner. In manifolds, formal logic deals with whole systems of propositions making up possible deductive theories. It is a matter of theorizing about possible fields of knowledge conceived of in a general, undetermined way and purely and simply determined by the fact that the objects stand in certain relations that are themselves subject to certain fundamental laws of such and such determined form.[52] For example, he explained the meaning of the theory of non-Euclidean manifolds as follows,

> Let there be a domain in which the objects are subject to certain forms of relation and connection, for which axioms of such and such a form are valid, then for a domain formally constituted in this way, a mathematics of such and such a form would be valid, there would then result propositions of such and such a form, proofs, theories of such and such a form. There is no *domain. There are no actually given concepts, connections, relations* and *axioms*. One simply says, *if* one had a domain, and *if* axioms of such and such a form obtained for it.[53]

Husserl saw the general theory of manifolds, or science of theory forms, as a field of free, creative investigation made possible once it is discovered that deductions, series of deductions, continue be meaningful and to remain valid when one assigns another meaning to the symbols. No longer restricted to operating in terms of a particular field of knowledge, one is free to reason completely on the level of pure forms. Operating within this sphere of pure forms, one can vary the systems in different ways. Nothing more need be presupposed than the fact that the objects figuring in them are such that, for them, a certain connective supplies new objects and does so in such a way that the form determined is assuredly valid for them. One finds ways of constructing an infinite number of forms of possible disciplines.[54]

---

[52] Husserl, *Introduction to Logic and Theory of Knowledge,* §19; his *Logic and General Theory of Science*, §§54-59.

[53] Husserl, *Introduction to Logic and Theory of Knowledge,* §19c-d.

[54] *Ibid.,* §19.

In the methodology of manifolds, Husserl taught, one speaks of numbers, but does not mean cardinal numbers, quantitative numbers, or anything of that kind, but anything for which formal axioms of the arithmetical prototype hold. If we drop the cardinal number meaning of the letters in the ordinary theory of cardinal numbers and substitute the thought of objects in general for which axioms of the arithmetical form $a+b = b+a$, $a \cdot b = b \cdot a$, are to hold, we no longer have arithmetic, but a purely logical class prototype of theory forms to which, besides innumerably many possible domains, the domain of cardinal numbers is also subject. One may then speak of numbers in the formal sense, but they are not cardinal numbers, but objects indeterminately, universally defined by axiom forms as they are especially actually found for cardinal numbers. Here, as in every theory form or manifold form, the "axioms" are proposition forms that are constituent parts of the definition. For cardinal numbers, $ab = ba$ holds. When constructing a manifold, however, one may just as well stipulate that $ab \neq ba$, for example, $ab = -ba$, and likewise for the other basic principles.[55]

In *Logical Investigations*, Husserl expressed his conviction that his theory of complete manifolds was the key to the only possible solution to the as yet unclarified problem as to how in the realm of numbers, impossible, non-existent, meaningless concepts might be dealt with as real ones.[56] We cannot arbitrarily expand the concept of cardinal number, he explained in posthumous writings on imaginary numbers. But we can abandon it and define a new, pure formal concept of positive whole number with the formal system of definitions and operations valid for cardinal numbers. And, as set out in our definition, this formal concept of positive numbers can be expanded by new definitions while remaining free of contradiction.[57]

In the arithmetic of cardinal numbers, Husserl explained, there are no negative numbers, for the meaning of the axioms is so restrictive as to make subtracting 4 from 3 nonsense. Fractions are meaningless there. So are irrational numbers, $\sqrt{-1}$, and so on. Yet in practice, all the calculations

---

55 *Ibid.*, §19b, d.

56 Husserl, *Logical Investigations*, *Prolegomena*, §70.

57 Edmund Husserl, "Essay III, Double Lecture: On the Transition through the Impossible ('Imaginary') and the Completeness of an Axiom System", in his *Philosophy of Arithmetic, Psychological and Logical Investigations with Supplementary Texts from 1887-1901*, Dordrecht: Kluwer, 2003, p. 415.

of the arithmetic of cardinal numbers can be carried out as if the rules governing the operations were unrestrictedly valid and meaningful. One can disregard the limitations imposed within a narrower domain of deduction and act as if the axiom system were a more extended one.[58] Fractions do not acquire any genuine meaning through our holding onto the concept of cardinal number and assuming that units are divisible, he theorized, but rather through our abandonment of the concept of cardinal number and our reliance on a new concept, that of divisible quantities. That leads to a system which partially coincides with that of cardinal numbers, but part of which is larger – meaning that it includes additional basic elements and axioms. And so in this way, with each new quantity, one also changes arithmetics. The different arithmetics do not have parts in common. They have totally different domains, but have an analogous structure. They have forms of operation that are in part alike, but different concepts of operation.[59]

Understanding the nature of theory forms, Husserl explained in several texts, shows how reference to impossible objects can be justified. According to his theory of manifolds, one could operate freely within a manifold with imaginary concepts and be sure that what one deduced was correct when the axiomatic system completely and unequivocally determined the body of all the configurations possible in a domain by a purely analytical procedure. It was the completeness of the axiomatic system that gave one the right to operate in that free way. A domain was complete, according to Husserl's theory, when each grammatically constructed proposition exclusively using the language of that domain was, from the outset, determined to be true or false in virtue of the axioms, i.e., necessarily followed from the axioms (in which case it is true) or did not (in which case it is false). In that case, calculating with expressions without reference could never lead to contradictions. So, Husserl concluded, it was formal constraints requiring that one not resort to any meaningless expression, no meaningless imaginary concept that were restricting us in our theoretical, deductive work. But what is marvelous, he believed, is that resorting to the infinity of pure forms and transformations of forms frees us from such conditions and at the same time explains to

[58] Husserl, *Logic and General Theory of Science,* §56.
[59] Husserl, "Double Lecture", p. 416.

us why having used imaginaries, what is meaningless, must lead, to what is not meaningless.[60]

Philosophizing on the Borderline

As an investigation of the origin and subjective foundation of traditional Aristotelian formal logic by clarifying the essence of the predicative judgment through an exploration of its origins, Husserl's study of pre-logic in *Experience and Judgment* takes place right on the borderline between transcendental subjectivity and pure, objective logic. So, in reappraising the fundamental tenets of his phenomenology as exposed in the analyses of that book, it is as important to be clear about how he understood the interrelationship of the two interdependent worlds as it is to understand what he found on each side of the border, for the underlying paradox of the science of intentionality that he used to meet the challenge he set for himself in *Experience and Judgment* is that his science of subjectivity was his science of objectivity and vice versa. Indeed, he said that while fighting to separate psychology, the natural sciences, phenomenology, and pure logic, he was wracking his brain trying to put them back together in a new way, trying to understand how the worlds of actual consciousness and the purely logical interrelate and form an intrinsic unity.[61] Now that we have toured both worlds, we are in a position to look at what he found.

To begin with, it is important to remember that for Husserl, the world of actual consciousness always somehow belonged with the ideal world of pure logic. He said that it was his psychological analyses that had compelled him to recognize the ideal as something given prior to all theorizing and impressed upon him the essential interrelationship of the worlds of pure logic and actual consciousness. He specifically tied the breakthrough of phenomenology to investigations aimed at elucidating the cognitive accomplishment of arithmetic and of pure analytical mathematics in general and, above all, to his search to find a theoretical solution to the problem of imaginary quantities. He said that it was that quest that had forced him to engage in general investigations concerning the universal clarification of the meaning, the proper delimitation and

---

[60] Husserl, "Double Lecture", pp. 428-29; his *Logical Investigations, Prolegomena,* §70; his *Introduction to Logic and Theory of Knowledge,* §19; his *Ideas*, §§71-72; his *Formal and Transcendental Logic*, §31; his *Logic and General Theory of Science,* §§54-59.
[61] Husserl, "Personal Notes", p. 492.

unique accomplishment of formal logic and was his chief motivation in developing the theory of manifolds, the pinnacle of pure logic.[62]

In *Allgemeine Erkenntnistheorie*, Husserl portrayed the problems of theory of knowledge as lying between psychology and pure logic, inasmuch as the two disciplines both relate to all of science. He said that he considered logic to be the discipline the very closest to theory of knowledge and stressed the legitimate ties that he saw obtaining between pure, formal, analytic logic and its complement the theory of knowledge. He defined theory of knowledge as the discipline that subjects the concepts and laws secured in pure logic and belonging to the ideal essence of thinking to a clarifying investigation of their meaning and their objective validity and on that basis solves all the problems connected with the validity of knowledge and science or proves that they are pseudo-problems.[63]

He held that every naïve logic constructed in the natural-objective orientation had a corresponding epistemologically and phenomenologically clarified philosophical logic, or one that phenomenologically grounded it from the very beginning.[64] Indeed, *Experience and Judgment* developed out of his conviction that truly philosophical logic requires phenomenologists to pierce through the logic of subject and predicates of the first level of pure logic to reach the world of actual consciousness and expose the foundations of an underlying, hidden, logic.[65] In a 1903 report on German logic that foreshadowed the project of *Experience and Judgment*, Husserl characterized critique of knowledge as:

> the task of rendering "intelligible" the possibility of a knowledge which is delimited by concepts and laws of pure logic, by tracing these back to their 'origin'; the task of resolving, in this way, the profound difficulties which are tied up with the opposition between the subjectivity of the act of knowledge and the objectivity of the content and object of knowledge (or of truth and being). This task does not fall to pure logic itself ....[66]

---

62 Husserl, *Ideas*, §72 and note; his *Introduction to the Logical Investigations*, pp. 21-22, 31, 33.

63 Husserl, *Allgemeine Erkenntnistheorie*, pp. 10, 19, 54.

64 Husserl, *Introduction to the Logical Investigations*, p. 31.

65 Husserl, *Experience and Judgment, Investigations in the Genealogy of Logic*, §§1, 3, 10, 11; his *Formal and Transcendental Logic*, §40.

66 Edmund Husserl, "Report on German Writings in Logic from the Years 1895-1899, Third Article" in his *Early Writings in the Philosophy of Logic and Mathematics*, p. 250.

So, as stressed in *Experience and Judgment*, logic had to have two sides that complement one another, something the tradition had never grasped in a deep way.[67] In *Formal and Transcendental Logic*, Husserl reminded readers that logic turns *both* towards the deeply hidden subjective forms in which reason does its work *and* the objective order, towards ideal objects, towards a world of concepts, where truth is an analysis of essences or concepts, where knowing subjects and the material world play no role.[68] Pure, objective, formal logic had to find its necessary complement in subjective, transcendental logic and the latter had to find its necessary complement in the former.

Husserl always insisted on the primacy of the objective side of logic. In *Experience and Judgment*, the world constituted by transcendental subjectivity is a pregiven world. It is not a pure world of experience, but a world that is determined and determinable in itself with exactitude, a world within which any individual entity is given beforehand in an perfectly obvious way as in principle determinable in accordance with the methods of exact science and as being a world in itself in a sense originally deriving from the achievements of the physico-mathematical sciences of nature.[69] It is knowledge of formal logic, he reminded readers in *Formal and Transcendental Logic*, that supplies the standards by which to measure the extent to which any presumed science meets the criteria of being a genuine science, the extent to which the particular findings of that science constitute genuine knowledge, the extent to which the methods it uses are genuine ones.[70]

In various texts, Husserl explained that theoretical disciplines have a systemic form that belongs to formal logic itself and must be constructed a priori within formal logic itself and within its supreme discipline the theory of manifolds as part of the overall system of forms of deductive systems that are possible a priori. He stressed that all fields of theoretical knowledge are particular instances of manifolds, but he knew that not all sciences are theoretical disciplines that, like mathematical physics, set theory, pure geometry or pure arithmetic, are characterized by the fact that their systemic principle is a purely analytical one. He recognized that sciences like psychology, history, the critique of reason and, notably,

---

[67] Husserl, *Experience and Judgment*, §3.
[68] Husserl, *Formal and Transcendental Logic*, §§7, 8.
[69] Husserl, *Experience and Judgment*, §11.
[70] Husserl, *Formal and Transcendental Logic*, §7.

phenomenology were not purely logical and so obliged philosophers to go beyond the analytico-logical model. When those not purely logical sciences are formalized and philosophers ask what binds the propositional forms into a single system form, they face nothing more than the empty general truth that there is an infinite number of propositions connected in objective ways that are compatible with one another in that they do not contradict each other analytically.

He maintained that since the concepts of geometry, mathematical mechanics and all mathematico-natural scientific disciplines, the natural sciences of physical and mental nature have real content, they belong among the natural sciences and not in phenomenology or in pure logic,[71] but, he wanted to use phenomenology to transform the merely positive sciences into philosophical sciences and to establish new sciences that were philosophical from the very outset.[72] He wanted to see phenomenology transform the naïve physical theory of nature from a mere natural science into a true philosophy of nature, into a philosophical physics that does not begin with vague concepts and then proceed naively, into a physics that has been philosophically deepened and enriched by all the problems concerning the correlation of physical being and cognitive subjectivity, a physics in which the experiencing subject in search of objective knowledge plays an active role and in which the basic concepts and basic propositions are developed from the very beginning in ultimate methodological originality. Philosophical physics would then be a science that understands itself radically and justifies its constitution of meaning and being from the very beginning to the very end.[73]

He stressed that the mathematical sciences, logic, formal logic, the sciences of value, ethics are not phenomenology, because they belong in the world of the purely logical.[74] He considered that if,

> we are not interested in the transcendental task and we remain in pure theory of meaning and being, then we practice logic, natural scientific ontology, pure theory of space, etc. these need not concern themselves at all with cognitive formations, with consciousness. Likewise, if we

---

71 Husserl, *Logic and General Theory of Science*, §54; his *Formal and Transcendental Logic*, §35a; his *Alte und neue Logik*, p. 263; his *Logik, Vorlesung 1902/03*, pp. 31-43, 49.

72 Husserl, *Introduction to the Logical Investigations*, p. 31.

73 *Ibid*, p. 30.

74 Husserl, *Introduction to Logic and Theory of Knowledge*, p. 414.

> practice ethics as pure ethics (or logic of morality), esthetics, or logic of esthetic appreciation, axiology or pure logic of values... the logic of the ideal state or the ideal world government as a system of cooperating ideal nation states (or the science of the ideal state)... the ideal of a valuable existence (ideally valuing and valuable human beings aimed at an ideally valuable nature accommodating their values)... and the logic of this ideal... ideal-esthetic existence, pure esthetics.... ontology of nature, ontology of minds, ontology of ethical personalities, ontology of values, etc.[75]

However, he went on to affirm that "*belonging to all of them are transcendental phenomenologies*" (Husserl's emphasis) that transcendentally investigate the valid objects of different categories, the objects of these ontologies, in relationship to types of consciousness essentially belonging to them.[76]

Indeed, though he believed that only certain of the most general cognitive-formations enter the picture for purposes of phenomenological elucidation in the case of pure logic, of an 'analytics' in the broadest, radical sense of the word,[77] he realized that "even the most trivial analytical knowledge presents big problems and hard problems for critique of knowledge. A puzzle is already present in them: How objectively valid knowledge, knowledge of things existing on their own, is possible vis-à-vis the subjectivity of knowing as a subjective activity".[78]

He acknowledged that, for example, even though ordinary arithmetic, in both its naïve and its technical forms, does not at first have any common cause with theory of knowledge and phenomenology, if it undergoes phenomenological elucidation, and so learns from the sources of phenomenology to solve the great riddles arising from the correlation between pure logic and actual consciousness, and if in so doing it also learns the ultimate formulation of the meaning of concepts and propositions that only phenomenology can provide, then it will have transformed itself into truly philosophical pure logic that is more than a mere coupling of natural-objective *mathesis* with phenomenology of knowledge, but rather is an application of the latter to the former.[79] He

[75] *Ibid.*, pp. 434-35.

[76] *Ibid.*

[77] Husserl, *Introduction to the Logical Investigations*, p. 31.

[78] Husserl, *Introduction to Logic and Theory of Knowledge*, p. 335.

[79] Husserl, *Introduction to the Logical Investigations*, pp. 29-30.

recognized that the critical elucidation of pure arithmetic as knowledge was no arithmetical task.[80]

Although he considered the concept of predicative judgment to be but a small area of pure logic, he reminded readers in *Experience and Judgment* not to forget the importance of understanding the origins and particular legitimacy of the lower levels of logic in elucidating both the path one must take to attain evident knowledge at a higher level and the hidden presuppositions underlying this knowledge, presuppositions that determine and delimit its meaning.[81] For essential reasons, he taught, pure arithmetic and the whole of formal mathematics or theory of manifolds also prove to be intertwined with the logic of assertions, apophantic logic, although in a completely different direction. These disciplines form, as it were, a higher story of apophantics and it is of great philosophical significance to recognize and characterize them in this connection.[82] For example, although he maintained that numbers and sets function in an entirely different way in the apophantic sphere of propositions and states of affairs than in arithmetic and in set theory,[83] he stressed that apophantic logic is intrinsically related to the pure theory of numbers and set theory of the second level, that the *"laws for all these higher order objects form their own branches of pure logic, but branches of the trunk of the one pure logic. The basic trunk is apophantic logic. The branches are, though, united a priori to the basic trunk"* (Husserl's emphasis).[84]

In his theory of manifolds, all purely logical basic concepts are set aside, but they are needed in actually using the theory. It is apophantic logic, he reminded students, that supplies the principles in accordance with which the entire procedure functions, while the higher logic of second order objects supplies basic concepts, like the concept of cardinal number, of ordinal, of combination, and so on, from which one cannot escape in actual thinking about purely hypothetical-formal thought configurations. One can just not think without thinking, without also having and presupposing everything without which thinking of whatever form, or however expressed, would really ever have any meaning. Since

---

80 Husserl, "Report on German Writings in Logic from the Years 1895-1899, Third Article".

81 Husserl, *Experience and Judgment, Investigations in the Genealogy of Logic,* §§10, 11.

82 Husserl, *Logic and General Theory of Science,* §7.

83 Husserl, *Introduction to Logic and Theory of Knowledge,* §18c.

84 *Ibid.,* §18d.

one is making inferences scientifically, since one is thinking (though hypothetically and on the basis of formal specifications), advancing from argument to argument, since one cannot avoid making the inference from *n* to *n*+1, and so on, what is purely logical already proves to be involved in this everywhere, just as the entire theory of manifolds is constructed out of purely logical material.[85]

He considered that all logical formations originate from categorial activity.[86] Every concept of a manifold and of a theory of manifolds is built out of purely categorial concepts.[87] The theory of manifolds is the ultimate culmination of all purely categorial knowledge.[88] He maintained that the formal theory of manifolds, the highest level of pure logic, would be nothing in its own right if it did not draw all its knowledge from the original sources that first make actual science in general possible.[89] He even explicitly wrote of reforming the mathematical theory of manifolds by consciously transforming it into a transcendental theory of manifolds that consciously captures the formal essence of a genuine, constructible totality that consciously analyzes what belongs to the essence of a concept defining a totality, what belongs to the essence of an axiom and axiom system.[90]

---

85 *Ibid.*, §19d.
86 Husserl, *Formal and Transcendental Logic*, §11.
87 Husserl, *Introduction to Logic and Theory of Knowledge,* §18c.
88 Husserl, *Logic and General Theory of Science*, §59.
89 Husserl, *Introduction to Logic and Theory of Knowledge,* §18d.
90 Edmund Husserl, *Ms A 1 35,* untitled, undated manuscript on set theory available at the Husserl Archives in Cologne, Leuven, and Paris, now partially published in German by Carlos Ierna and Dieter Lohmar as "Husserl's Manuscript A I 35", in G. E. Rosado Haddock (ed.), *Husserl and Analytic Philosophy,* Berlin: de Gruyter, 2016, pp. 289-319.

Conclusion

Never able to rest from his experiences in the "strange" worlds of the purely logical and actual consciousness that had opened up to him at the beginning of his philosophical career, Husserl strove until the end of his life to find answers to the very questions about them that launched him on his phenomenological voyage of discovery. His persistent search to fathom and solve the puzzles, mysteries, riddles, enigmas and paradoxes involved in the complex interplay and interdependency between those worlds was at the heart of the dynamic that brought phenomenology into being.

Here, I have tried to show that in reappraising the fundamental tenets of Husserl's phenomenology as exposed in the analyses of the subjective foundations of the part of traditional formal logic to which *Experience and Judgment* is devoted, it is imperative to situate the analyses of that book on the map of the worlds of actual consciousness and the purely logical that can be pieced together from the discoveries about their features that Husserl made during his long, assiduous exploration of those worlds. I have used less well-known, posthumously published texts to piece together the findings about their interrelation and their intrinsic unity that he made during his mental travels in them.

It is imperative to be clear and informed about the answers that Husserl found to his questions about the interrelation and intrinsic unity of the worlds of actual consciousness and the purely logical because, as he himself acknowledged in *Formal and Transcendental Logic*, his theories about what he described as the "two-sidedness of everything logical, in consequence of which the problem-groups become separated and again combined" involve "extraordinary difficulties". He himself recognized that since, according to his theories, the ideal, objective, dimension of logic and the actively constituting, subjective dimension interrelate and overlap, or exist side by side, logical phenomena seem to be suspended between subjectivity and objectivity in a confused way.[91] He even suggested that almost everything concerning the fundamental meaning of logic, the problems it deals with and its method, was laden with misunderstandings owing to the fact that objectivity arises out of subjective activity. Even the ideal objectivity of logical structures and a priori nature of logical doctrines especially pertaining to this objectivity, and the meaning of this a priori are

[91] Husserl, *Formal and Transcendental Logic*, §26c.

afflicted with this lack of clarity, he maintained, since what is ideal appears as located in the subjective sphere and arises from it. He further suggested that it was due to these difficulties that, after centuries and centuries, logic had not attained the secure path of rational development.[92] Presently, the theories of those advocating the naturalization of phenomenology or Brouwerian-type interpretations of Husserl's ideas about mathematics[93] are built upon such misunderstandings, something that, in the case of the latter, I tried to show in my paper "Husserl on Axiomatization and Arithmetic".

By clearly and explicitly outlining what was to be found in each world and how the two worlds interacted, Husserl provided a road map for avoiding confusion in many areas of philosophy. Indeed, if he was right in believing, as I think he was, that his new understanding of the structure of the world of pure logic was of the greatest significance for a genuine understanding of the true sense of logic and all of philosophy and that his radical clarification of the relationship between formal logic and formal mathematics could lead to a definitive clarification of the sense of pure formal mathematics as a pure analytics of non-contradiction,[94] then philosophers need to be particularly lucid about the really important questions that his insights raise for philosophy of logic and mathematics now.

It is, for example, extremely important to see what Husserl came to locate in each of the two worlds and to understand how he envisioned their interaction because what belongs in one world, or in another part of one of the worlds, often enjoys the same outward appearance as what belongs in the other world or somewhere else in the same world. He himself stressed in Logical Investigation IV that identical words often have different types of meanings, that the relations of those words to what they designate can also be of different types and that the failure to realize

[92] *Ibid.*, §8.

[93] For example, for the former see: J.-M. Roy, Jean Petitot, Francisco Varela, Bernard Pachoud (eds.), *Naturalizing Phenomenology, Issues in Contemporary Phenomenology and Cognitive Science*, Stanford CA: Stanford University Press, 1999; for the latter Richard Tieszen, *Mathematical Intuition, Phenomenology and Mathematical Knowledge*, Dordrecht: Kluwer, 1989; Mark van Atten, *Brouwer Meets Husserl. On the Phenomenology of Choice Sequences*, Dordrecht: Springer, 2007; Stathis Livadas, *Contemporary Problems of Epistemology in the Light of Phenomenology, Temporal Consciousness and the Limits of Formal Theories*, London: College Publications, 2012.

[94] Husserl, *Formal and Transcendental Logic*, p. 11.

that fundamental, ultimately inviolable, ontological differences often lie concealed behind inconspicuous linguistic or grammatical distinctions is often a very potent, hard to perceive, source of contradictions, nonsense, confusion, absurdity and error in philosophy,[95] something that I have studied in greater depth elsewhere.[96]

Gottlob Frege and Bertrand Russell also concluded that certain fundamental differences between different kinds of meaning that are concealed behind inconspicuous grammatical distinctions ultimately prove inviolable because they are "founded deep in the nature of things"[97] in such a way that contradictions, paradoxes, antinomies, fallacies, nonsense, confusion, absurdity, inevitably result when they are not respected and that this is a topic of prime importance for the understanding of major issues in twentieth century western philosophy.[98] In several writings, I myself have tried to show how blurring distinctions between dependent and independent meanings by allowing a concept word to be transformed into a proper name and to come to figure in the wrong part of the world of the purely logical opens the door to confusion, contradictions, paradoxes, antinomies, fallacies, nonsense, absurdity, pseudo-objects. Such confusions caused Frege to abandon his logical system and have been the cause of problems that Russell and his successors in the analytic tradition in philosophy have never been able to solve.[99] In *Word and Object in Husserl, Frege and Russell*, I suggested that analytic philosophers have been massively doctoring symptoms of a malady caused by such logical errors grounded in the very insights into logic, language and theory of knowledge that produced the logic they embraced.[100]

---

95 Husserl, *Logical Investigations*, Investigation IV.

96 For example, Claire Ortiz Hill, "Incomplete Symbols, Dependent Meanings, and Paradox", in *Husserl's Logical Investigations*, Daniel Dahlstrom (ed.), Dordrecht: Kluwer, 2003, pp. 69-93; Hill, "On Fundamental Differences between Dependent and Independent Meanings".

97 Gottlob Frege, "Function and Concept", in *Translations from the Philosophical Writings*, Peter Geach and Max Black (eds.), Oxford: Blackwell, 3rd ed., 1980, p. 41.

98 Hill, "Incomplete Symbols, Dependent Meanings, and Paradox"; Hill, "On Fundamental Differences between Dependent and Independent Meanings".

99 Claire Ortiz Hill, *Rethinking Identity and Metaphysics, On the Foundations of Analytic Philosophy*, New Haven CT: Yale University Press, 1997.

100 Claire Ortiz Hill, *Word and Object in Husserl, Frege and Russell, the Roots of Twentieth Century Philosophy*, Athens OH: Ohio University Press, 1991, 2001, p. 165.

Husserl was not philosophizing about logic and mathematics in a vacuum and he was not just extemporizing about the things he liked to believe about those fields. He was as well-versed in them, if not more so, than those who went on to create the theories of logic and philosophy of mathematics that were embraced by the philosophical establishment in the twentieth century and shaped the analytic school philosophy that dominated those fields. If Husserl had been heeded they could have avoided many problems and those fields could have followed a different, less error-ridden course.

5

HUSSERL'S PURELY LOGICAL CHASTITY BELT[1]

Husserl in love

According to the still too popular account of the evolution of Husserl's thought, after a brief romance with anti-psychologistic, Platonic realism following his divorce from empirical psychology during the 1890s, Husserl was unable to resist the charms of subjectivity, espoused psychologism in a different dress and fathered transcendental phenomenology.

There is little that is true in that account. Phenomenology grew out of Husserl's troubling encounters in the 1890s with what he once called the incomprehensibly strange worlds of actual consciousness and the purely logical.[2] He did fall out of love with empirical psychology and he did fall in love with transcendental subjectivity, but he was not the lopsided philosopher generally thought by followers and foes alike to have spent most of his life cogitating only about subjectivity. His phenomenology is not, as is often thought by both those have embraced it and those who have spurned it, in the least an autonomous science of subjectivity.

Stung by his experience with empirical psychology, Husserl spent the rest of his life fighting to avoid naïve psychologizing. He did ultimately throw himself wholeheartedly into really extensive investigations of the realm of transcendental subjectivity, of which he was unmistakably enamored, but his disappointment with empirical psychology had impressed upon him the need to expose the ultimate, objective, a priori, ideal underpinnings of science. So, while he was discovering and courting phenomenology, he devised a strategy to help those enticed by transcendental subjectivity to show self-control and refrain from committing the

---

[1] This was originally a paper presented at the workshop on Constructive Semantics, Meaning in between Phenomenology and Constructivism organized by Christina Weiss held from September 30, 2016-October 1, 2016 at Zeppelin Universität in Friedrichshafen, Germany. My aim was to discuss some things which I believe people interested in constructivism and Husserl's transcendental phenomenology need to keep in mind..

[2] Edmund Husserl, "Personal Notes", in his *Early Writings in the Philosophy of Logic and Mathematics*, Dordrecht: Kluwer, 1994, pp. 491-92.

psychologizing and relativizing sins, the near occasion of which he wanted to make sure were avoided. And he remained faithful to those theories about objective realities until parted from them by death.

What is true about the popular account is that, enthralled by transcendental phenomenology, after a certain point, Husserl no longer desired to pursue pure logic. In 1917, he wrote to Hermann Weyl that despite all the work he had devoted to it, he had not pursued it completely to the end, because it had had to be more important to him to develop his ideas about transcendental phenomenology. In 1930, he confessed to Georg Misch that he had lost all interest in formal logic and all real ontology in the face of a systematic grounding of a theory of transcendental subjectivity.[3] This does not mean, however, that he cast off his purely logical chastity belt or tore up his purely logical safety net. He left them in place, but after a certain point, it was transcendental phenomenology that busied his mind.

The wedding of formal and transcendental logic

The relationship that Husserl saw between transcendental phenomenology and the strictures of the pure logic that was to keep phenomenologists from falling into the temptation to go too far with his science of subjectivity is not well understood and its implications have barely been explored.

One of the main reasons why it has gone all but unstudied is that it is not sufficiently appreciated that for Husserl logic had two sides. Readers of his late work, *Formal and Transcendental Logic*, find him still stressing that logic turns *both* towards the deeply hidden subjective forms in which reason does its work *and* towards the objective order, a world of concepts, ideal objects, where truth is an analysis of essences or concepts and knowing subjects and the material world play no role,[4] that subjective, transcendental logic had to find its complement in pure, objective, a priori formal logic, free from acts, subjects, or empirical persons or objects belonging to actual reality and entirely grounded in conceptual essentialities, and vice versa. His search to comprehend the intercourse

---

[3] Edmund Husserl, *Logik und allgemeine Wissenschaftstheorie, Vorlesungen 1917/18, mit ergänzenden Texten aus der ersten Fassung 1910/11*, Dordrecht: Kluwer, 1996, p. XXIII, nn. 1, 4.

[4] Edmund Husserl, *Formal and Transcendental Logic* (1929), The Hague: Martinus Nijhoff, 1969, §8.

between subjectivity and objectivity was at the heart of the dynamic that brought phenomenology into being.

Science, in the objective sense, he taught, is a web of theories, and so of proofs, propositions, inferences, concepts, meanings, not of experiences.[5] Pure logic, is the science of concepts and relations of concepts, of propositions and relations of propositions, of the possible forms grounded in these concepts and propositions. To further their insight into the essence of pure logic, Husserl once asked students to reflect on the following:

> Scientific reasoning aims for truth. Truth is realized subjectively in judgment and is stated in statements.... *Every scientific theory is a system of statements*.... It is something complete in its own right and, as it is, lays claim to truth and falsehood. The starting propositions lay claim to this directly. The theory, the definitely formed web of propositions, lays claim to substantiating new truth indirectly, step by step. And the system itself lays claim to being true as a system. That means that everywhere one thing is linked to another by logical inference that is also stated, therefore, is also set down as true.[6]

He maintained that the theoretical system of modern pure mathematics was no more than a system of logically combined statement meanings, a system of propositions stating truths about a certain combination of the mathematical facts making up the field of mathematics.[7]

Husserl underscored the primacy of the objective side of logic. Pure logic, he taught, embraces all the concepts and propositions without which science would not be possible, would not have any sense or validity.[8] It supplies the standards by which to measure the extent to which any presumed science meets the criteria of being a genuine science, the extent to which the particular findings of that science constitute genuine knowledge, the extent to which the methods it uses are genuine ones.[9] The world constituted by transcendental subjectivity, he insisted, is a pregiven world, a world determined and determinable in

---

[5] Edmund Husserl, *Introduction to Logic and Theory of Knowledge*, Dordrecht: Springer, 2008, §§11, 17, 19a, b.

[6] *Ibid.*, §11.

[7] *Ibid.*, §§11, 19c.

[8] Edmund Husserl, *Allgemeine Erkennthistheorie, Vorlesung 1902/03*, Dordrecht: Kluwer, 2001, p. 47.

[9] Husserl, *Formal and Transcendental Logic*, §7.

itself with exactitude, a world within which any individual entity is given beforehand as in principle determinable in accordance with the methods of exact science as being a world in itself in a sense originally deriving from the achievements of the physico-mathematical sciences of nature.[10]

Now, having said that, the underlying, undying paradox of Husserl's phenomenology remains that, while he taught that the ultimate meaning and source of all objectivity making it possible for thinking to reach beyond contingent, subjective, human acts and lay hold of objective being-in-itself was to be found in ideality and the ideal laws defining it,[11] he knew that his theories about the "two-sidedness of everything logical, in consequence of which the problem-groups become separated and again combined" involve "extraordinary difficulties". He saw that since, according to his theories, the ideal, objective, dimension of logic and the actively constituting, subjective dimension interrelate and overlap, or exist side by side, logical phenomena seem to be suspended between subjectivity and objectivity in a confused way.[12] He even suggested that almost everything concerning the fundamental meaning of logic, the problems it deals with and its method, was laden with misunderstandings owing to the fact that objectivity arises out of subjective activity. He said that even the ideal objectivity of logical structures and a priori nature of logical doctrines especially pertaining to this objectivity, and the meaning of this a priori were afflicted with a lack of clarity, since what is ideal appears as located in the subjective sphere and arises from it. He further considered that it was due to these difficulties that, after centuries and centuries, logic had not attained the secure path of rational development.[13]

So it is that Husserl's friend and colleague at the University of Göttingen, the mathematician David Hilbert, could write of how Husserl had adopted an a priori method and rejected psychologism, yet conclude that his method was in fact psychological.[14]

---

10 Edmund Husserl, *Experience and Judgment, Investigations in the Genealogy of Logic*, (1939), London: Routledge and Kegan Paul, 1973, §11.

11 Husserl, *Allgemeine Erkennthistheorie*, p. 200.

12 Husserl, *Formal and Transcendental Logic*, §26c.

13 *Ibid.*, §8.

14 David Hilbert, extracts from his *Denkschrift* for Leonard Nelson (undated), published in Claire Ortiz Hill and Jairo José da Silva, 2013, *The Road Not Taken, On Husserl's Philosophy of Logic and Mathematics*. London: College Publications, 2013, p. 386.

Respecting the rules of pure logic

As seen in Chapter 2, Husserl considered that the realm of truth was no disorderly hodgepodge, that truths are connected in systematic ways, governed by consistent laws and theories, that inquiry into truth and its exposition must be systematic and the systematic representation of knowledge must reflect the systematic representation grounded in the things themselves. All invention and discovery, he taught, involves formal patterns, without which there is no testing of given propositions and proofs, no methodical construction of new proofs, theories and whole systems. No blind omnipotent power has heaped together some pile of propositions P, Q, R, strung them together with a proposition S, and then organized the human mind so that the knowledge of the truth of P must unfailingly entail knowledge of S. Not blind chance, but the reason and order of governing laws reigns in argumentation.[15]

According to him, the pure truths of logic were all the ideal laws entirely grounded in the meaning of the concepts that all science had inherited, that is to say, in the meaning, essence or content of the concepts of truth, proposition, object, property, relation, combination, law, fact etc. Such laws must not be violated, not because that would conflict with some truth, but because it would produce *Widersinnigkeiten*, contradictions.[16]

---

15 Edmund Husserl, *Logik, Vorlesung 1896*, Dordrecht: Kluwer, 2001, pp. 9, 13, 16-17.

16 Edmund Husserl, *Logical Investigations* (1900-01), New York: Humanities Press, 1970, *Prolegomena* §37. Hard problems surround the translation of the words '*Widersinn*' and '*widersinnig*', '*Widersinnigkeit*'. Although Husserl used these words in a perfectly normal way, they do not translate neatly into English. The word '*wider*' means against, counter, contrary to, in opposition to. So a very literal translation of these words might be 'countersense' and 'countersensical'. Some have chosen to translate them thus; others have chosen 'absurdity' and 'absurd'. Husserl himself used '*Absurdität*' and '*absurd*' as synonymous with '*Widersinn*', and '*Widersinnig*' (ex. Husserl, *Logical Investigations*, Investigation I §19, Investigation IV, Introduction, §12). '*Widersinn*', '*Widersinnigkeit*' and '*widersinnig*' may, however, be understood in the sense of paradox or contradiction and paradoxical, contradictory, illogical, which better suits our purposes here. In that case, these words fall into the family of '*widersprechen*' (to contradict), '*Widerspruch*' (contradiction), and '*widersprechend*' and '*widerspruchsvoll*, two common German words meaning contradictory. Due to the problems, I have often chosen to leave '*Widersinn*', '*Widersinnigkeit*', and '*widersinnig*' in German.

So, any assertion whose content is at odds with principles rooted in the meaning of truth as such would be self-cancelling or logically *widersinnig*, its particular content in contradiction with what is rooted in the general meaning of its own meaning categories.[17] As an example, he gave the proposition, "Of two contradictory propositions, one is true and one false", which he said is to be viewed as absolutely certain, as simply an "unfolding" of the content of its "concepts", in which it is purely grounded. It cannot be denied without flying in the face of the meaning of those words. Anyone denying it does not know what contradictory means, what true and false mean.[18]

He saw every concrete meaning as being a fitting together of matter and form in conformity with an ideal pattern which could be set forth in formal purity and to which an a priori law of meaning corresponded that governed the formation of coherent meanings out of syntactical materials falling under definite categories having an a priori place in the realm of meanings. So, meanings were governed by a priori laws that regulate the ways in which they could be combined with new meanings, the ways in which they could fit together and constitute a meaningful, coherent whole. They could only do so in antecedently definite ways, while other possibilities of combination were excluded by laws and yielded only a heap of meanings, never a single meaning. For him, this impossibility of combining meanings in certain ways was by no means merely subjective. It was objective, ideal and grounded in the nature, the pure essence, of the realm of meaning. It was an a priori impossibility.[19]

One can freely exchange expressions within a given category, he pointed out. This is true of all meanings whatsoever. The coherent, meaningful expression 'this tree is green' can be formalized to obtain the corresponding pure meaning form 'this *S* is *p*', and so formalized, it can be interpreted in infinitely many ways. Any noun or noun phrase can be put in the place of '*S*', any adjective in the place of '*p*', and a coherent, meaningful meaning and independent proposition of the indicated form will result. Such free exchange of expressions within a given category might yield false, dumb or funny meanings, but it will necessarily yield coherent meanings. On the other hand, mere combinations of words like 'a round or', 'king but or', 'a man and is', 'this reckless is green', 'more

---

[17] *Ibid.*

[18] Husserl, *Introduction to Logic and Theory of Knowledge*, §13c.

[19] Husserl, *Logical Investigations*, Investigation IV, §10.

intensive is round', 'this house is equal' are nonsensical, meaningless, utterly incomprehensible. Substituting the noun 'horse' for the relation word 'similar' in the form '*a* is similar to *b*' yields only a sequence of words in which each word has a meaning. It is completely obvious that so combined no meaning exists, or can possibly exist, for them. They break the laws about what can be meaningful. Meaning itself is missing.[20]

Abstaining from unlawful intercourse with phenomenology

In order to avoid ascribing ideas to Husserl that he did not hold – and against which he strenuously militated – it is very important to realize that Husserl consistently and explicitly stated what one could not do with phenomenology.

The special interest of transcendental phenomenology, he stressed, does not lie in the theoretical concepts and laws to which the sciences are subject. It does not aim at objective being and laying down truths for objective being. It is not an objective science. "What is objective belongs precisely to objective science, and what objective science still lacks for completion is its affair to obtain and its alone. *Transcendental interest, the interest of transcendental phenomenology aims at consciousness as consciousness of objects*". It has no dealings with a priori ontology, none with formal logic and formal mathematics. It is phenomenology of the constituting consciousness, and so not a single objective axiom, meaning one relating to objects that are not consciousness, belongs in it, no a priori proposition as truth for objects, as something belonging in the objective science of these objects, or of objects in general in formal universality.[21]

Husserl's lists of what was purely logical – therefore, not to be approached by phenomenology – included, the theory of gravity, the system of analytic mechanics, the mechanical theory of heat, the theory of metric or projective geometry, which are, he maintained, all entirely made up, not of mental experiences of one person or another, or of states of mind, but of ideal material, of meanings.[22] Not a matter for phenomenology were also the basic concepts of mathematics, the theory of cardinal numbers, the theory of ordinals, set theory, mathematical physics, pure geometry, geometry as a priori theory of space, the axioms of geometry as a theory

---

20 *Ibid.*, §§10, 12.

21 Husserl, *Introduction to Logic and Theory of Knowledge*, p. 432.

22 *Ibid.*, §12.

of the essences of shapes of spatial objects, the pure theory of meaning and being, a priori ontology, a priori real ontology of any kind (thing, change etc.), natural scientific ontology, objective axioms relating to *a priori* propositions as truths for objects, as something belonging in the objective science of these objects, essence-propositions about objects insofar are they are objective truths and as truths have their place in a truth-system in general.[23] He stressed that, if

> *we are not interested in the* transcendental task and we remain in pure theory of meaning and being, then we practice logic, natural scientific ontology, pure theory of space, etc. These need not concern themselves at all with cognitive formations, with consciousness. Likewise, if we practice ethics as pure ethics (or logic of morality), esthetics, or logic of esthetic appreciation, axiology or pure logic of values… the logic of the ideal state or of the ideal world government as a system of cooperating ideal nation states (or the science of the ideal state)… the ideal of a valuable existence (ideally valuing and valuable human beings aimed at an ideally valuable nature accommodating their values)… and the logic of this ideal… ideal-esthetic existence, pure esthetics… Ontology of nature, ontology of minds, ontology of ethical personalities, ontology of values, etc.[24]

However, he went on to affirm that "*belonging to all of them are transcendental phenomenologies*" (Husserl's emphasis) that transcendentally investigate the valid objects of different categories, the objects of these ontologies, in relationship to types of consciousness essentially belonging to them.[25] Indeed, though he believed that only certain of the most general cognitive-formations enter the picture for purposes of phenomenological elucidation in the case of pure logic, of an 'analytics' in the broadest, radical sense of the word,[26] he realized that even "the most trivial analytical knowledge presents big problems and hard problems for critique of knowledge. A puzzle is already present in them: How objectively valid knowledge, knowledge of things existing on their own, is possible vis-à-vis the subjectivity of knowing as a subjective activity".[27]

---

23 Husserl, *Introduction to Logic and Theory of Knowledge*, §§18-19; his *Logic and General Theory of Science 1917/18*, Cham, Switzerland: Springer, 2019, chapter 11.

24 Husserl, *Introduction to Logic and Theory of Knowledge*, pp. 434-35.

25 *Ibid.*, p. 435.

26 Edmund Husserl, *Introduction to the Logical Investigations, A Draft of a Preface to the Logical Investigations*, The Hague: Martinus Nijhoff, 1975, p. 31.

27 Husserl, *Introduction to Logic and Theory of Knowledge*, p. 335.

And, he recognized that although all fields of *theoretical* knowledge have a systemic form that belongs to formal logic itself, not all sciences are theoretical disciplines that, like mathematical physics, set theory, pure geometry or pure arithmetic, are characterized by the fact that their systemic principle is a purely analytical one based on the meanings of their concepts. For him, sciences like psychology, history, the critique of reason and, notably, phenomenology, were not purely logical and so obliged philosophers to go beyond the analytico-logical model. When those not purely logical sciences were formalized and philosophers asked what binds the propositional forms into a single system form, they faced nothing more than the empty general truth that there is an infinite number of propositions connected in objective ways that are compatible with one another in that they did not contradict one another analytically.[28]

For example, pure arithmetic

As a mathematician by training who had long kept company with the most outstanding mathematicians of his time, Husserl often used examples from mathematics to illustrate the points he wanted to drive in.

He insisted that mathematical propositions were a priori, that there, all truth was nothing other than the analysis of essences or concepts,[29] that the original mathematical disciplines were disciplines of the purely logical sphere that had proceeded from given, purely logical basic concepts and axioms and directly perspicuous laws grounded in the essence of purely logical categories and had thus yielded the concept of cardinal number, the primitive laws of number given as directly perspicuous truths and the dependent laws of number based on them.[30] He taught that,

> If one ascends to a purely theoretical and a priori discipline.... to all the concepts that determine the objective meaning of science in general and are inseparable from it, then it is clear without further ado that all of pure mathematics belongs in this sphere, that all purely mathematical disciplines... are encompassed by pure logic as naturally conceived.... all concepts belong in pure logic that are not to be assigned to a particular science limited to

[28] Husserl, *Logic and General Theory of Science*, §54; his *Formal and Transcendental Logic*, §35a; his *Logik, Vorlesung 1902/03*, Dordrecht: Kluwer, 2001, pp. 31-43, 49.
[29] Husserl, *Introduction to Logic and Theory of Knowledge*, §13c.
[30] *Ibid.*, §19d.

> particular domains of objects, but to all sciences in general and are necessarily common to them, all concepts, therefore, that have this reference to objects in general in the most universal way.... The concept of cardinal number is such a concept, and every numerically determined cardinal number belongs among these concepts. One is something in general. Anything, no matter what it is, can be posited as one.... And all numbers are built upon units....[31]

Pure arithmetic, he held, explores what is grounded in the essence of number. It has nothing at all to do with nature. It is not concerned with physical things, souls, real occurrences of a physical or mental nature, does not acquire its universal propositions by perception and empirical generalizations on the basis of the perception and the substantiation of the resulting individual judgments. Insofar as they are really purely mathematical, all mathematical propositions express something about the essence of what is mathematical, about the meaning of what belongs to it. Their denial is consequently an absurdity. When I say that 2×2 is not 4, but 5, I am saying something "unthinkable", absurd, something nullifying the meaning of the words. Mathematicians do not state $a + 1 = 1 + a$ as a hypothesis to be established as true in further experience or inductively in conformity with the methods of the natural sciences. Rather, they start with $a+1 = 1+a$ as something unconditionally valid and certain, for it is obviously part of the meaning of the term "cardinal number" that each thing can be increased by one. To say that a cardinal number cannot be increased amounts to being in conflict with the meaning of "cardinal number". It amounts to not knowing what one is talking about.[32]

However, he acknowledged that, even though ordinary arithmetic, in both its naive and its technical forms, does not at first have any common cause with theory of knowledge and phenomenology, if it undergoes phenomenological elucidation, and so learns from the sources of phenomenology to solve the great riddles arising from the correlation between pure logic and actual consciousness, and if in so doing it also learns the ultimate formulation of the meaning of concepts and propositions that only phenomenology can provide, then it will have transformed itself into truly philosophical pure logic that is more than a mere coupling of natural-objective *mathesis* with phenomenology of knowledge, but rather is an application of the latter to the former.[33]

---

[31] Husserl, *Logik, Vorlesung 1902/03*, p. 35.

[32] Husserl, *Introduction to Logic and Theory of Knowledge*, §13c.

[33] Husserl, *Introduction to the Logical Investigations*, pp. 29-30.

Chastity as personal integrity, purity in conduct and intention

Besides abstention from unlawful intercourse with, for instance, phenomenology, chastity can be defined as personal integrity and purity in conduct and intention. For Husserl, his commitment to the ideal realm was a matter of integrity. He knew that what he was claiming about it was "very hotly combated as being mysticism and scholasticism".[34] Indeed, on December 29, 1916, the Social Democratic philosopher Leonard Nelson wrote to Hilbert that Husserl,

> admittedly also originally came from the mathematical school, but... bit by bit turned more and more away from it and turned towards a school of mystical vision, whereby he also deadened the feel in his school for the demands and value of a specifically scientific method. He even goes so far, after his own lack of success with it, as to see a danger in methodological thinking and thinks that it would ruin philosophers for whom the truth only reveals itself in mystical vision. Even though Husserl himself remains protected by certain inhibitions from mystical degeneracy by virtue of strong ties to mathematics that he has not been able to cast off, one must unfortunately nonetheless note with horror that after the school as such had torn down the bridges to mathematics behind them, how unrestrainedly his students lapsed into every excess of Neo-platonic mysticism, the prevalence of which is all the more dangerous since Husserl's scientific past will unjustifiably carry over to the school the assurance that it is willing to do scientific philosophy in earnest and is capable of this. Here I fundamentally part company with Husserl's circle. For me philosophy is not a matter of mystical vision, but one of the most sober, driest thinking....[35]

Husserl, though, wanted it understood that he was "far from any mystico-metaphysical exploitation of 'Ideas', ideal possibilities and such"[36] and he considered this a matter of integrity. He did not believe that he was according the word 'idea' any sort of mystical meaning. He taught that, as regards its essential, theoretical makeup, science is a system of ideal meanings,[37] but that ideal entities had not been artificially devised by

---

[34] Husserl, *Logic and General Theory of Science*, §4.

[35] Extracts from Leonard Nelson's letter to David Hilbert (1916), published in Hill & da Silva, pp. 390-91.

[36] Edmund Husserl, "Husserl an Brentano, 27. III. 1905", in his *Briefwechsel, Die Brentanoschule I*, Dordrecht: Kluwer, 1994, p. 39.

[37] Husserl, *Introduction to Logic and Theory of Knowledge*, §12.

him or anyone else; they were given beforehand by the meaning of the universal talk of propositions and truths indispensable in all the sciences. This indubitable fact, he stressed, was the starting point of all logic.[38]

He defended himself saying that he had not embraced Ideas and classes of idealities because he prided himself on his own intellectual intuition and wanted to penetrate into a mystical transcendental world by means of it, or because he was looking down his nose at vile empiricism and psychologism, or because they made it easier for him to devise a "nobler" sort of philosophy that brought him a reputation of being a noble soul. He said he embraced them for the same mundane reason that he embraced things, just because he saw them and in looking at them grasped them himself.

The world of the purely logical, he explained, is a world of ideal objects, a world of concepts.[39] The constant talk of propositions, of true and false means something identical and atemporal. No more is meant by ideality than that it is a matter of a kind of possible objects of knowledge, whose particular characteristics can, and in scientific investigation must, be determined, while they are just not objects in the sense of real objects.[40] He considered the recognition of ideal objects, or Ideas, with a capital I, as atemporal, supraempirical objects to be the pivotal point of all theory of knowledge and decisive for all further considerations. He taught that it was imperative for people to concede once and for all that they are genuine, actual objects, new kinds of objects.[41]

Ideal objects, he said, were not anything particularly lofty, but were what was the very most ordinary, like ordinary stones on the road. All people know them in a certain naïve way since they talk of numbers and do so on in ideal ways. Only philosophers do not wish to know them. They dismiss them as Platonic Ideas. However, he argued, if one recognizes givens like the series of natural numbers as objectivities, one can only describe them in the way Plato did in his theory of Ideas, as eternal, selfsame, non-temporal and non-spatial, unmoved, unchangeable, etc. But, he complained, people trained in traditional philosophy then instantly think Platonic Ideas. Such Platonic realism becomes associated with mysticism and Neo-Platonism with a magical view of nature as far

---

38 Edmund Husserl, *Alte und neue Logik, Vorlesung 1908/09*, Dordrecht: Kluwer, 2003, p. 45.

39 Husserl *Introduction to Logic and Theory of Knowledge*, §13c.

40 Husserl, *Alte und neue Logik, Vorlesung*, p. 47.

41 Husserl, *Logic and General Theory of Science*, §8.

removed as can be from genuine natural science. Philosophers recall how this merged into scholastic realism during the Middle Ages. Anyone advocating giving ideal objects their due is open to charges of being a mystic, reactionary, scholastic, the latter two being the strongest scientific terms of abuse of his time, in which formal logic was vilified as being empty scholasticism, and espousing idealism for a pure logic undefended.[42]

He said that if someone wants to know what Ideas are, one need only point to the self-evident givens like the cardinal number series, or to absolutely self-evident statements about members of the number series. He stressed that one knows what it is being talked about when one speaks of the numbers 1, 2, 3. One knows that one is not talking about nothing, but always about an unreal-existing something.... It is absolutely clear that 2 is 1 + 1. One thereby grasps it, has it itself, so that any doubt as to its existence would be entirely absurd. The important thing is that it is something to be had, something one can grasp, and about which self-evident statements can be made. It is an absolute, indubitable truth that 2 < 3, that in the cardinal number series, 2 has its place between 1 and 3, etc. If absolute truths hold for 2, then 2 is precisely something as subject of these truths themselves, or it is an object, because that implies absolutely the same thing. Consequently, there are objects of insightful givenness that are not things and not existential moments in the spatio-temporal world, but are Ideas or ideal objects. Each time, one makes a self-evident statement about numbers of the number series and thus grasps an objectively valid truth, precisely these numbers, and not something else, are the objects to which the truth refers. They are therefore objects. They are not things and not moments of things. They do not exist in space and time, etc. They are precisely what they give themselves to be.[43]

Each cardinal number occurs only once in the number series. Infinitely many possible empirical sets can be counted: cardinal numbers of horses, of carrots, etc., but those empirical cardinal numbers come into being and pass away, start and stop, etc. That does not, however, affect the pure cardinal numbers. If no concrete cardinal number n existed in the real world from a certain point in time on, then that would not mean there was a hole in the pure number series between $n - 1$ and $n + 1$.[44] The number 2 is not an object of perception and experience. Two apples come into

42 *Ibid.*, §§5a, 19a.

43 *Ibid.*, §8.

44 *Ibid.*

being and pass away, have a place and time, but if they are eaten up, the number 2 is not eaten up. The number series of pure arithmetic has not suddenly then acquired a hole, as if we were to have to count 1, 3, 4.[45]

To give another, non-mathematical, example, Husserl speculated that belonging to individual human beings and the individual mind is an a priori Idea implying a whole wealth of a priori Ideas regarding all the multiple forms of consciousness and their interweaving, as well as the pure Ideas of ego, personality, character traits etc. A priori, one can surely say that a subject is conceivable without relation to other subjects. But, if we conceive of it as it really is experientially, woven into the societal context, and a co-bearer of the societal consciousness and its cultural correlates, then we see that new Ideas arise, above all, the Idea of the collective mind with all related Ideas. So, a field of a priori considerations opens up. An ontology of the collective mind, an a priori essence-theory prior to all the empirical human sciences precedes here, the way the a priori of nature does the natural sciences. This essence-theory builds itself up above the essence-theory of the individual mind, is therefore not independent of the former – just as the collective mind is a higher-order objectivity grounded in the objectivities we call individual minds. But, he saw this Idea of an a priori analysis of the collective life of the mind and its objective correlates as being so far from the thoughts of sociologists that they were liable to dismiss the mere suggestion that there might be anything of the kind and that it might be the necessary epistemological basis of all genuine social science as mysticism or scholasticism.[46]

Husserl defended himself against such charges by saying that he was requiring nothing more than the intellectual integrity to allow the things that are prior to any theory because they are the most evident of all evident facts to count as being precisely what they proclaim themselves to be.[47] He said that if this was enough to have him called a scholastic, then that was all fine and good. He asked whether it was preferable to have integrity and be called a scholastic or to lack integrity and be a modern empiricist. He said that he was pleading in favor of integrity and did not fall flat on his face when he was called a scholastic. "Integrity stands the test of time", he reminded.[48]

---

45 Husserl, *Introduction to Logic and Theory of Knowledge*, §13c.
46 Husserl, *Logic and General Theory of Science*, §64.
47 *Ibid.*, §4.
48 *Ibid.*, §8.

6

ON LIMNING THE TRUE AND ULTIMATE STRUCTURE OF REALITY[1]

Introduction

Of Franz Brentano's theory of intentionality, Willard Quine, the pre-eminent American, analytic philosopher of the last half of the twentieth century, wrote in his chef d'oeuvre *Word and Object*, that one,

> may accept the Brentano thesis either as showing the indispensability of intentional idioms and the importance of an autonomous science of intention, or as showing the baselessness of intentional idioms and the emptiness of a science of intention. My attitude, unlike Brentano's, is the second.... If we are limning the true and ultimate structure of reality, the canonical scheme for us is the austere scheme that knows... no propositional attitudes.... If we are venturing to formulate the fundamental laws of a branch of science, however tentatively, this austere idiom is again likely to be the one that suits.[2]

Quine also considered that modern empiricism had to a large extent been conditioned by an ill-founded belief in a fundamental cleavage made by Kant between analytic truths grounded in meaning independently of matters of fact and synthetic truths grounded in fact. In "Two Dogmas of Empiricism", he famously argued that it was a folly to look for such a boundary and that the idea that there was such distinction to be drawn at all was "an unempirical dogma of empiricists, a metaphysical article of faith".[3]

Indeed, Quine made exposing and bewailing any suspicion of connivance with metaphysics one of the main planks of his philosophical program. He counselled philosophers to shun what he called curiously idealistic ontologies that repudiated material objects and he conjured up

---

[1] This essay was originally written for *Mereologies, Ontologies, and Facets: The Categorial Structure of Reality*, Paul Hackett (ed.), Lanham MD: Lexington Books, 2018.

[2] Willard Quine, *Word and Object*, Cambridge MA: M.I.T. Press, 1960, p. 221.

[3] Willard Quine, "Two Dogmas of Empiricism", *From a Logical Point of View* (2nd ed. rev.), New York: Harper & Row, 1961 (1953), p. 37.

nightmare visions of the ontological crisis that would ensue were logicians to disobey his strictures and begin a retreat back into essentialism[4]. Quine's views were extremely influential and held sway for decades. Where Fregeo-Russello-Quineo (FRQ, pronounced "freak") philosophy and logic prevailed it was long professionally necessary to philosophize within the power of them and few dared to contradict what seemed false in them.

Now, it is not well known that Brentano's most famous student Edmund Husserl also elaborated an austere scheme to limn the true and ultimate structure of reality. However, he did so in a perfectly un-Quinean way. He eschewed empiricism and made essences and a fundamental, but anti-Kantian, cleavage between analytic and synthetic truths integral parts of his endeavor. Moreover, he wedded all this to his own non-autonomous science of intention. In short, he devised a plan to achieve what Quine and like-minded philosophers aspired to achieve by embracing everything they excoriated and wanted to wipe out.

However, for a number of reasons, Husserl's strategy for keeping knowledge of reality from collapsing into a formless blob of facts – or breaking apart into, for example, Quinean rabbit bits and pieces[5] – became buried in all the excitement, both positive and negative, generated by his science of intentionality, and so its implications for logic and philosophy nowadays have barely been explored, if at all. Fortunately though, since the 1980s, the Husserl Archives has been publishing the material needed to recuperate the map of the underlying objective structure of reality that he drew. Here I use that material to outline his austere scheme for finding clarity with respect to the central traits of reality. In particular, I seek to dig up the parts and members of the categorial skeleton that he limned to uphold knowledge in a manner that stands in sharp contrast to the logical point of view that has propped up analytic philosophy, of which Quine was a preeminent exponent.

---

[4] Willard Quine, "The Problem of Interpreting Modal Logic", *Journal of Symbolic Logic* 12, 2 (June 1947), pp. 43, 47; his, "Quantifiers and Propositional Attitudes", *Journal of Philosophy*, 53 (1956), p. 185; his *Word and Object*, Chapter 6; Claire Ortiz Hill, *Rethinking Identity and Metaphysics, On the Foundations of Analytic Philosophy*, New Haven CT: Yale University Press, 1997, Chapter 11; her "Cantor's Paradise, Metaphysics and Husserlian Logic", *Categories of Being, Essays on Metaphysics and Logic*, Leila Haaparanta and Heikki Koskinen (eds.), Oxford: Oxford University Press, 2012, Chapter 10.

[5] Quine, *Word and Object*, §12; his "Ontological Relativity", *Ontological Relativity and Other Essays*, New York: Columbia University Press, 1969, pp. 34-35, 48, 50.

No mere wallowing in an orgy of subjectivity

One of the main reasons why Husserl's austere scheme has gone all but unstudied is that it is not sufficiently appreciated that for him logic had two sides. Subjective, transcendental logic had to find its necessary complement in pure, objective, formal logic, and the latter find its necessary complement in the former. For example, in *Formal and Transcendental Logic*, he tried to impress upon readers that logic turns *both* towards the deeply hidden subjective forms in which reason does its work *and* towards the objective order, towards ideal objects, towards a world of concepts, where truth is an analysis of essences or concepts and knowing subjects and the material world play no role.[6]

Husserl definitely abandoned Brentano's empirical psychology, but he held fast to his teacher's theory of intentionality, out of which he developed the science of subjectivity that he called transcendental phenomenology, which is generally seen by both those have embraced it and those who have rejected it as being precisely the sort of autonomous science of intention that Quine and like-minded philosophers have so adamantly decried. However, Husserl's science of intention was not autonomous, and he was not the lopsided philosopher generally thought by followers and foes alike to have spent most of his career cogitating only about subjectivity.

Philosophy as Husserl conceived it was not the wallowing in an orgy of subjectivity that his detractors have imagined it to be. Once he abandoned empirical psychology, he spent the rest of his career fighting to overturn naive psychologizing. He did ultimately throw himself wholeheartedly into extensive Cartesian-inspired investigations of the realm of transcendental subjectivity, of which he was unmistakably enamored, but in so doing he himself never lost sight of objective realities and strove to expose the ultimate, objective, structure of reality in a way that he hoped would keep explorers of the world of transcendental subjectivity from falling into the psychologizing errors he was determined to stamp out.

Husserl in fact underscored the primacy of the objective side of logic. It is knowledge of formal logic, he stressed in *Formal and Transcendental Logic*, that supplies the standards by which to measure the extent to which any presumed science meets the criteria of being a genuine science, the extent to which the particular findings of that science constitute genuine

---

[6] Edmund Husserl, *Formal and Transcendental Logic*, The Hague: Martinus Nijhoff, 1969 (1929) §8.

knowledge, the extent to which the methods it uses are genuine ones.[7] The world constituted by transcendental subjectivity is a pre-given world, he explained in *Experience and Judgement.* It is a world that is determined and determinable in itself with exactitude, a world within which any individual entity is given beforehand as in principle determinable in accordance with the methods of exact science as being a world in itself in a sense originally deriving from the achievements of the physico-mathematical sciences of nature.[8]

The realm of truth, we found him teaching students attending his 1896 lectures on logic, is no disorderly hodgepodge. Truths are connected in systematic ways, governed by consistent laws and theories, and so the inquiry into truth and its exposition must be systematic. The systematic representation of knowledge must to a certain degree reflect the systematic representation grounded in the things themselves. All invention and discovery involves formal patterns without which there is no testing of given propositions and proofs, no methodical construction of new proofs, no methodical building of theories and whole systems. No blind omnipotent power has heaped together some pile of propositions P, Q, R, strung them together with a proposition S, and then organized the human mind so that the knowledge of the truth of P unfailingly must entail knowledge of S. Not blind chance, but the reason and order of governing laws reigns in argumentation.[9]

In his lecture courses *Allgemeine Erkenntnistheorie 1902/03* and *Logik 1902/03*, we found him teaching that objectivity of thinking is grounded in purely logical forms. Pure logic, he told students, is the science of concepts and relations of concepts, of propositions and relations of propositions, of the possible forms grounded in these concepts and propositions. It defines the form-concepts to which the objective content of all logical and all scientific thinking in general is subject and on whose basis they develop the laws of validity grounded in those form concepts. Science, in the objective sense, is a web of theories, and so of proofs, propositions, inferences, concepts, meanings, not of experiences.[10]

---

[7] *Ibid.*, §7.

[8] Edmund Husserl, *Experience and Judgment*, London: Routledge and Kegan Paul, 1973 (1939), §11.

[9] Edmund Husserl, *Logik, Vorlesung 1896*, Dordrecht: Kluwer, 2001, pp. 9, 13, 16-17.

[10] Edmund Husserl, *Allgemeine Erkenntnistheorie, Vorlesung 1902/03*, Dordrecht: Kluwer, 2001; his *Logik, Vorlesung 1902/03*, Dordrecht: Kluwer, 2001.

Purely logical, we further found him teaching, were the basic concepts of mathematics, the theory of cardinal numbers, the theory of ordinals, mathematical physics, set theory, formal pure logic, pure geometry, geometry as *a priori* theory of space, the axioms of geometry as a theory of the essences of shapes, of spatial objects, but also the pure theory of meaning and being, *a priori* real ontology of any kind (thing, change, etc.), the ontology of nature, the ontology of minds, natural scientific ontology, the sciences of value, pure ethics, the logic of morality, the ontology of ethical personalities, axiology or the pure logic of values, pure esthetics, the ontology of values, the logic of the ideal state or the ideal world government as a system of cooperating ideal nation states, or the science of the ideal state, the ideal of a valuable existence, objective axioms (relating to *a priori* propositions as truth for objects, as something belonging in the objective science of these objects, or of objects in general in formal universality, essence-propositions about objects insofar are they are objective truths and as truths have their place in a truth-system in general.[11]

So, though Husserl's science of subjectivity ultimately all but totally eclipsed his philosophy of objectivity, the latter is still there to be uncovered, and if we really want to understand Husserl's contribution to FRQ logic and philosophy and how it may provide solutions to the still unsolved problems undermining it, it is really imperative to do so. In what follows, I want to do justice to his philosophy of objectivity, especially as spelled out in the lecture courses that have been published by the Husserl Archives since the 1980s.

Husserl pins down the concept of category

Fundamental to Husserl's philosophy of objectivity were his theories about categories. As an example of how a science dealing with a pre-established, determinate, categorial, field is constituted, he gave the original mathematical disciplines of the purely logical sphere which, according to him, had proceeded from given, purely logical basic concepts and axioms and directly perspicuous laws grounded in the essence of purely logical categories and thus, for instance, yielded the concept of cardinal number,

---

[11] Edmund Husserl, *Introduction to Logic and Theory of Knowledge, Lectures* 1906/1907, Dordrecht: Springer, 2008, §§18-19, pp. 434-35; his *Logic and General Theory of Science 1917/18*, with supplementary texts from the first version of 1910/11, Cham, Switzerland: Springer, 2019, Chapter 11.

the primitive laws of number given as directly perspicuous truths, and the dependent laws of number based on them.[12]

So it is imperative to sort through his various uses of the term 'category' and to come to clarity about how he distinguished between the various concepts of categories that he juggled with as he labored to expose the structure of reality. A good place to begin is with his statement in Logical Investigation VI that one might "try to pin down the concept of category by saying that *it comprises all objective form arising out of the forms, and not out of the matters, of conceptual interpretation*".[13] Later, in *Introduction to Logic and Theory of Knowledge*, he acknowledged that in the earlier work, he had essentially spoken only about the logical forms, which he had called categorial forms, but that if categories were to be the basic forms of objectivity without regard to its changing matter, one was then obliged to distinguish between the *logical* categories and the *metaphysical* categories, i.e., the categories of thingness that investigate the categories and principles expressing the essence of what is real in general. Wherever it is a question of reality, in life and in all empirical sciences, he taught in that lecture course, we apply concepts seeming to belong necessarily to the idea of a reality. As examples of such concepts, he cited thing, real property, real relation between things, real whole, real part, cause and effect, real genus and species, state, process, coming into being and passing away, space and time, the basic categories in which what is real as such is to be understood in terms of its essence.[14]

With respect to these essential categories of reality, he taught that reality as objectivity was subject to all forms and laws belonging to the essence of objectivity in general and that the theory of every real objectivity was necessarily subject to the laws belonging to the theory in general of any objectivity whatsoever. Of the a priori pertaining to the idea of reality as such, he considered all the totality of truths relating to the essential categories of reality to be a foundation and prerequisite for any further knowledge of reality, a necessary, common resource for the sciences of reality. Understood in that sense, he said, logic would encompass the whole of formal logic and could also be called a theory of science of the real. Formal logic, he maintained, would therefore be the science of this first a priori.[15]

---

12 Husserl, *Introduction to Logic and Theory of Knowledge*, §19d.

13 Edmund Husserl, *Logical Investigations*, London: Routledge & Kegan Paul, 1970 (1900-01), Investigation VI, §58.

14 Husserl, *Introduction to Logic and Theory of Knowledge*, §§21, 22, 23, 46.

15 *Ibid.*, §§22, 23, p. 46.

However, although he saw that a priori connections ran from the formal domain into the domain of the real, he did not believe that metaphysical categories should be placed on a par with the purely logical categories, because purely logical concepts and principles abstracted from all cognitive material, and it was owing to that abstraction, owing to their fully undetermined universality as concerns matter, that they could relate to every possible field of knowledge, every possible science. Formal logic was to reach as far as the realm of matter-free – therefore, formal, and in the purest sense, mathematical – concepts as far as there was talk of things and objects in general, but only insofar as they were thought through the simple thinking forms. Metaphysics, even *a priori* metaphysics, could therefore not have any place there and was not to be constructed as a single science with formal logic. A strict line of demarcation had to be drawn between it and the sphere of formal logic, which was necessarily a distinct, strictly separate, discipline.[16]

He explained that the concept of formal logic as the most fundamental concept of logic of all had in fact been acquired by adopting the perspective of the idea of science in general, therefore, by accepting all the sciences as equivalent and declining to distinguish between them. In doing so, he said, sciences were found that specifically related to the different spheres of reality and other sciences, even completely formed and highly developed sciences such as pure mathematics, that wholly excluded any relationship to any specific sphere of reality. What they had in common was pure form.[17] He regarded the formal character of logical analysis as consisting in the fact that it never deals with the material constitution of something, that it considers only the categorial form that it assumes in the judgment (subject form, predicate form, and so on), but in other respects remains completely indeterminate, just designated symbolically by *S*, by *p*, which only denote empty places that can be filled any way at all.[18] He further illustrated what he meant as follows,

> If one ascends to a purely theoretical and a priori discipline having reference to… logical categories, therefore to all the concepts that determine the objective meaning of science in general and are inseparable from it, then it is clear without further ado that all of pure mathematics belongs in this sphere, that all purely mathematical disciplines, aside from the syllogistics

---

16 *Ibid.*

17 *Ibid.*, §23.

18 Husserl, *Experience and Judgment*, §5c.

traditionally dealt with in logic, are encompassed by pure logic as naturally conceived.... all concepts belong in pure logic that are not to be assigned to a particular science limited to particular domains of objects, but to all sciences in general and are necessarily common to them, all concepts, therefore, that have this reference to objects in general in the most universal way.... The concept of cardinal number is such a concept, and every numerically determined cardinal number belongs among these concepts. One is something in general. Anything, no matter what it is, can posited as one.... And all numbers are built upon units....[19]

It was precisely the *logical* categories that were to be used to put together the skeleton for upholding science. Within them, Husserl made an extremely important distinction between the concepts and laws of the formal logical or meaning categories and those of the formal ontological categories. He explained that one of the jobs of formal logic was first to single out the constituent concepts belonging to the essence of a theory as such, something that leads to the group of concepts designated as *meaning* categories, namely, such concepts as that of proposition, judgment, concept, and generally all the concepts concerning the structure of judgments, simple and complex, and naturally also to the concept of truth, and so on.[20] Closely connected with the categories of meaning, and wedded to them by ideal laws were, to Husserl's mind, the correlative concepts of the formal *object* categories, the formal ontological concepts under which every object of every imaginable sphere of objects could in principle be brought and which included such concepts as object, state-of-affairs, quality, property, genus, multiplicity, conjunction, cardinal number, magnitude, relation, plurality, unit, existence, all of them kept free of cognitive material. "Object" was the master concept of formal ontology. It was the concept that determined the formal system of axioms and thus the system of formal categories.[21]

As, Husserl said over and over, all the categorial concepts of formal logic, those of both the meaning categories and the formal ontological categories, were particularly characterized by the fact that they are independent of the particularity of any material of knowledge. For example,

---

19 Husserl, *Logik, Vorlesung 1902/03*, pp. 34-35.

20 Husserl, *Formal and Transcendental Logic*, §27b.

21 Husserl, *Logical Investigations, Prolegomena*, §67; his *Ideas, General Introduction to Pure Phenomenology*, New York: Collier Books, 1962 (1913), §16; his *Formal and Transcendental Logic*, §27.

in *Introduction to Logic and Theory of Knowledge*, he stressed that, whereas matter and form are inseparable in the sphere of intuition and the actual givenness of objectivities, the

> possibility of considering formal relationships in their own right and of logical reflection upon them is, however, intellectually and meaningfully feasible precisely by positing what is material as undetermined and universal in thought. And, it is with this intellectual exclusion of matter, which is nothing other than *formalization or mathematical universalization, that formal logic* is constituted. It is operative in the sphere of pure determinations of form and of the laws pertaining to it. It deals with propositions in general, or proposition forms in general, inference forms in general, correlatively with states of affairs in general, with objects in general, with sets in general, with numbers in general, etc.[22]

Categoriality, whole and parts

Husserl's theory of wholes and parts is a theory of what is dependent and what is independent.[23] In Logical Investigation IV, he very importantly maintained that the study of wholes and parts, therefore of what is dependent and independent, reveals the meaning categories.[24] Independent, to his mind, were substantives, objects, particulars, parts, arguments, members. Dependent were predicates, properties, concepts, functions, universals, forms, sets, wholes. Predicates need subjects. Concepts need objects. Functions need arguments. Universals need particulars. Properties must be properties of something. Sets need members. Forms are incomplete, meaningless, unless they are forms of something. They need matter to make up a complete whole. And, for Husserl, categories were forms.

He stressed that all knowledge presupposes both form and matter. Were all matter of knowledge imagined to be non-existent, he taught, then the categorial would not make any sense, for logical form a priori points to matter to be formed, logicized, rationalized. Indeterminately universal, everything logical points beyond itself to something extra-logical to be grasped logically, which must first be there for logical grasping to find something to grasp. All talk of objects in general would lose its meaning if

---

22 Husserl, *Introduction to Logic and Theory of Knowledge*, §23.

23 *Ibid.*, §22.

24 Husserl, *Logical Investigations*, Investigation IV, §10.

objects were never really to be given at any time. The formal logic ultimately structuring the universe is pure form, but all form ultimately *a priori* refers back to some kind of matter – be it itself of a formal logical nature, such as multiplicities and numbers in mathematical universality – to be given form by means of it. Behind everything formal is the thought – however vague – of absolute particulars, therefore, of real particulars, and likewise of genera and species, of properties and relations of real particulars. Every proposition has both predicative forms expressed in form words and terms indicating what it is that is being spoken of. The terms may be categorial concepts (as is the case in every proposition of purely logical content), therefore, designate simple objectifications of forms and thus indicate only relative matter. However, the objectifications in question ultimately point back to original forms and to possible propositions in which those forms join terms that are no longer solely categorial in nature and so contain matter in the absolute sense.[25]

According to Husserl's theories, any instance of dependent meaning is accompanied by an essential law governing its need for completion by other meanings and establishing the ways in which they might be connected together that rules out other possible combinations that would yield a jumble of meanings instead of one meaning. This impossibility of combining meanings in certain ways is not merely subjective, he insisted. It does not merely lie in our actual incapacity to achieve unity. It is objective, ideal and grounded in the nature, the pure essence, of the realm of meaning. A priori insight into laws shows that certain combinations are ruled out by the very nature of the constituents of the pure patterns in question, that such constituents can only enter into definitely constituted meaning-patterns. Meanings, he repeated over and over, are governed by *a priori* laws that regulate the ways in which they can be combined with new meanings, the ways in which they can fit together and constitute a meaningful, coherent whole.[26]

It is an analytic truth, he explained, that the forms in a whole cannot function as its matter or vice-versa and this fact clearly carries over into the sphere of meanings. The pure elements of form in a concrete unit of meaning can never change places with the elements to which they give form and which also give the meaning its relation to things. For him, every concrete meaning is a fitting together of materials and forms and every

---

25 Husserl, *Introduction to Logic and Theory of Knowledge*, §22.

26 Husserl, *Logical Investigations*, Investigation IV, §10.

such meaning falls under an ideal pattern that can be set forth in formal purity, and to every such pattern an a priori law of meaning corresponds. This law governs the forming of coherent meanings out of syntactical materials falling under definite categories having an a priori place in the realm of meanings. This takes place in accordance with syntactical forms which are likewise fixed a priori and constitute a fixed system of forms.[27]

Bertrand Russell's description of a propositional function standing on its own as "a mere schema, a mere shell, an empty receptacle for meaning, not something already significant"[28] might well be used to describe forms as Husserl saw them. Following him, one might compare, albeit imperfectly, dependent meanings to a wineglass. Unless a wineglass contains wine it is just an empty receptacle. The wine and the glass go together to make the glass of wine. The role of the wineglass is such that it can only be replaced by another receptacle, never by the wine. By its very nature, the receptacle, the wineglass, as such cannot play the part of the wine. It cannot be a glass of wine and it obviously cannot be converted into wine. The wine is just as obviously dependent on a receptacle. If the latter is broken, the wine will come to be in a place not intended for it.

Categoriality, nonsense, *Widersinnigkeit*...[29]

Frege, Russell, and Husserl, the inventors of twentieth century western philosophy, all concluded, that the fundamental differences between dependent and independent meanings ultimately prove inviolable because they are "founded deep in the nature of things"[30] in such a way that contradictions, paradoxes, antinomies, fallacies, nonsense, confusion, absurdity are bound to result when they are not respected.[31]

---

27 *Ibid.*

28 Bertrand Russell, *Introduction to Mathematical Philosophy*, London: Allen & Unwin, 1919, p. 157.

29 See p. 93 n. 16 regarding the difficulties surrounding the translation of the words '*Widersinn*' and '*widersinnig*', '*Widersinnigkeit*' into English and, therefore, my choice to use the German words in this paper

30 Gottlob Frege, "Function and Concept" (1891), in *Translations from the Philosophical Writings*, Peter Geach and Max Black (eds.), Oxford: Blackwell, 3rd ed., 1980, p. 41.

31 Claire Ortiz Hill, "On Fundamental Differences Between Dependent and Independent Meanings", *Axiomathes, An International Journal in Ontology and Cognitive Systems* 20: 2-3, online since May 29, 2010, 313-32, anthologized in Hill & da Silva.

In Logical Investigation IV, Husserl maintained that it was the primitive, essential distinction between dependent and independent meanings that formed the necessary basis for discovering the essential categories of meaning in which were grounded essential laws of meaning whose business it was to distinguish sense from nonsense by determining the *a priori* forms in accordance with which the meanings of the different meaning categories might combine into one meaning instead of producing chaotic nonsense.[32]

We can freely exchange expressions within a given category, he explained. Where nominal material stands, any nominal material can stand, but not adjectival, not relational, not completed propositional material. This is true of all meanings whatsoever. To illustrate this, he took the coherent, meaningful expression 'this tree is green' and proposed formalizing the given meaning, the independent logical statement, to obtain the corresponding pure meaning form: 'this *S* is *p*'. It is clear, he pointed out, that formalized in that way it could be interpreted in infinitely many ways. The statement 'this tree is green' could be transformed. Any noun or noun phrase could be put in the place of '*S*' and any adjective in the place of '*p*' and a coherent, meaningful meaning and an independent proposition of the form indicated would be obtained. Such free exchange of expressions within a given category might yield false, dumb, or funny meanings, but it would necessarily yield coherent meanings.[33]

However, Husserl emphasized, we are not in free in the way we bind meanings to meanings. Not just any meaning can be substituted for *S* or for *p*. Once we transgress the bounds of categories of our meaning, material, coherent meaning vanishes. Mere combinations of words like 'a round or', 'king but or', 'a man and is', 'this reckless is green', 'more intensive is round', 'this house is equal' are nonsensical, meaningless, utterly incomprehensible. One can, he noted, substitute 'horse' for 'similar' in the relational form '*a* is similar to *b*', but then one obtains only a sequence of words, in which each word has a meaning, but their meanings do not combine to give a coherent meaning to the whole expression. It is completely obvious that so combined, no meaning exists or can possibly exist, for them. They break the laws about what can be meaningful. Meaning itself is missing. When dependent meanings come to be in the places for independent meanings, the

32 Husserl, *Logical Investigations*, Investigation IV, Introduction, §10.

33 *Ibid.*

fundamental structure grounded in the differences between the two is broken, like the broken wineglass.[34]

In his course on *Introduction to Logic and Theory of Knowledge*, Husserl taught that since, when proposition forms are arranged in a purely grammatical manner, the meaning components are assembled in specific ways, and it is clear that it is not some arbitrary rearrangement of the components that is yielding yet another proposition, by the same token, the proposition forms express laws. The meaning components, or the components of the proposition categories, constitute a matter that can only be put and fit together in certain specific ways, or else no unitary whole can emerge, no coherent meaning result. So it is that one sees that a purely grammatical pattern of separating unitary meaning from nonsense, which is independent of truth and falsehood, prevails in the meaning sphere.[35] He explained that,

> we cannot juggle with the elements of a significantly given, connected unity at will. Meanings only fit together in antecedently definite ways, composing other significantly unified meanings, while other possibilities of combination are excluded by laws, and yield only a heap of meanings, never a single meaning. The impossibility of their combination rests on a law of essence, and is by no means merely subjective. It is not our mere factual incapacity, the compulsion of our mental make-up, which puts it beyond us to realize such a unity. In the cases we here have in mind, the impossibility is rather objective, ideal, rooted in the pure essence of the meaning-realm.... The impossibility attaches, to be more precise, not to what is singular in the meanings to be combined, but to the essential *kinds*, the *semantic categories* that they fall under.... Wherever, therefore, we see the impossibility of combining given meanings, this impossibility points to an unconditionally general law to the effect that meanings belonging to corresponding meaning-categories, and conforming to the same pure forms, should lack a unified result. We have in short an a priori impossibility. What we have said holds of course of the possibility of significant combinations as it holds of their impossibility.[36]

He considered that the job of a science of meanings is to construct meanings in accordance with essential laws, to discover the laws of combining meanings and transforming them, and to trace them back to a

---

[34] *Ibid.*, §§10, 12.

[35] Husserl, *Introduction to Logic and Theory of Knowledge*, §18b.

[36] Husserl, *Logical Investigations*, §10.

minimal number of independently elementary laws. It would be necessary first to identify the primitive meaning formations and to investigate their inner structure in order to identify the pure meaning categories that define the meaning and extension of what is indeterminate in the laws.[37]

He further maintained that the laws of meaning then provide logic with possible coherent, meaningful meaning forms whose formal truth or falsehood, reference to objects, *Widersinnigkeit* or lack thereof, is determined by logical laws.[38] So it is that for him, the "sphere of the *genuinely logical laws* is based upon the purely grammatical sphere. In the sphere of meaningful (therefore purely grammatically established) forms, they separate those propositions that produce or do not produce possible truth according to their form, and also those <that> are valid and not valid *a priori* and purely on the basis of form".[39]

In the *Prolegomena to Pure Logic*, he explained that the pure truths of logic were all the ideal laws having their entire foundation in the meaning of the concepts that all science has inherited and that represent the categories of constituents out of which science is essentially constituted, that is to say that they are entirely founded in the meaning, essence, or content of the concepts of truth, proposition, object, property, relation, combination, law, fact, and so forth. Such laws are not to be violated, not because they would be false – be in conflict with some truth – but because they would produce *Widersinnigkeiten.* Any assertion whose content is at odds with principles rooted in the meaning of truth as such is self-cancelling or logically *widersinnig*, which means that its particular content, sense, meaning is in contradiction with the general exigencies of its own meaning categories, is in contradiction with what is rooted in the general meaning of those categories.[40]

I have elsewhere tried to make certain of Frege's, Russell's and Husserl's ideas about the inviolability of logical form more tangible by describing some intertwined, problems that creep into reasoning when differences between dependent and independent meanings are not respected, namely, insidious problems with pseudo-objects, inference, substitutivity of identicals, existential generalization, semantical paradoxes, type ambiguities of the kind Russell tried to evade through his theory of types, in other

---

[37] *Ibid.*, §13.

[38] *Ibid.*, Investigation IV, Introduction, §10.

[39] Husserl, *Introduction to Logic and Theory of Knowledge*, §18b.

[40] Husserl, *Logical Investigations*, *Prolegomena,* §37.

words, much of what FRQ philosophers have been battling since Frege's time.[41]

Russell's contradictions

The importance of Husserl's insights into the inviolable differences between what is dependent and independent has for FRQ philosophy and logic can be illustrated by taking a look at some issues involved in Husserl's ideas about sets and what is commonly called Russell's paradox.

Husserl viewed set theory as a mathematical discipline of the purely logical sphere. It was a matter of a rigorously scientific, a priori theory proceeding from purely logical concepts and axioms grounded in purely logical categories.[42] For him, a set was a kind of whole and so was subject to the formal rules governing wholes and parts that stipulate that a whole cannot be its own part. So, viewed from the angle of his ideas about the differences between dependent and independent meanings, Russell's contradiction about the set of all sets that are not members of themselves is just faithfully telling us that the set X of x's is not a member of what it is a set of; what is predicated of an object is of a different logical type from the object itself; a concept is not an object; a function is not an argument; a whole is not a part; what is dependent is not independent... In short, logic is doing what logic is supposed to do.[43]

Husserl reasoned that it is part of the idea of set to be a unit, a whole, comprising certain members as parts in such a way that it is something new that is first formed by them. It belongs essentially to the concept of whole that no whole can contain itself as a part. So, as a kind of whole, a set is subject to the formal rules governing wholes and parts that stipulate that a whole cannot, without contradiction, be its own part. So no set can contain itself as a member. Sets are *a priori* different from their members.[44]

---

41 Hill, "On Fundamental Differences Between Dependent and Independent Meanings".

42 Husserl, *Introduction to Logic and Theory of Knowledge*, §18d.

43 Hill, *Rethinking Identity and Metaphysics*, p. 80.

44 Edmund Husserl, Ms A I 35, untitled, undated manuscript on set theory available at the Husserl Archives in Cologne, Leuven, and Paris, now partially published in German by Carlos Ierna and Dieter Lohmar as "Husserl's Manuscript A I 35", in *Husserl and Analytic Philosophy*, Guillermo Rosado-Haddock (ed.), Berlin: de Gruyter, 2016, pp. 289-319.

And he repeatedly relegated the set-theoretical paradoxes to the category of *Widersinnigkeiten.* For him, a set that contains itself as an element was *widersinnig.* By saying that the set of all sets that were not members of themselves is a *Widersinnigkeit*, he explicitly put it into the same category as the round square, the golden mountain, and the present emperor of France. The formal logical construction "set of all sets that do not contain themselves as parts", he argued, may not be presupposed to be about something that already exists. Just as it is contradictory for a whole to be its own part at the same time, so it is contradictory for a set to be its own member. It proceeds from the paradox that a set that contains itself as an element or a set that does not must be a *Widersinn.*

The contradictions to which Frege's logic leads illustrate Husserl's points about sets and the non-substitutivity of what is dependent and what is independent. Remember that Russell wrote to Frege in 1903 that,

> On functions in particular (sect. 9 of your *Conceptual Notation*) I have been led independently to the same views even in detail. I have encountered a difficulty only on one point. You assert (p. 17) that a function could also constitute the indefinite element. This is what I used to believe, but this view now seems to me to be dubious because of the following contradiction: Let *w* be the predicate of being a predicate which cannot be predicated of itself. Can *w* be predicated of itself? From either answer follows its contradictory. We must therefore conclude that *w* is not a predicate.[45]

True to his convictions that the fundamental differences between predicates and objects were inviolable and founded in the deep nature of things, Frege replied to Russell that "A predicate is predicated of itself" did not seem exact to him. A predicate, he explained, was as a rule a first-level function which requires an object as argument and cannot therefore have itself as argument.[46] When, late in his life, he was asked about the causes of the paradoxes of set theory, Frege answered that the essence of the procedure leading into a thicket of contradictions consisted in regarding the objects falling under F as a whole, as an object designated by the name 'set of Fs', 'extension of 'F', or 'class of Fs'.[47]

---

[45] Gottlob Frege, *Philosophical and Mathematical Correspondence*, Oxford: Blackwell, 1980, pp. 130-31.

[46] *Ibid.*, pp. 132-33.

[47] Gottlob Frege, "On Concept and Object" (1892), in *Translations from the Philosophical Writings*, pp. 54-55.

Russell acknowledged that the contradiction about the classes that are not members of themselves had shown him that classes must be something radically different from individuals.[48] He came to believe that if one assumes that the class is an entity, one cannot escape the contradiction. As he explained, "if you think for a moment that classes are things in the same sense in which things are things, you will then have to say that the class consisting of all the things in the world is itself a thing in the world, and that therefore this class is a member of itself".[49]

Early in his search for ways to evade (his choice of verb) the problem of the contradiction about the class of all classes that are not members of themselves, Russell thought that "the key to the whole mystery" was to be found by inventing (his choice of verb) a hierarchy of types. He said that it had become clear to him that the contradiction about the classes that are not members of themselves could only be avoided by realizing that no class either is or is not a member of itself, that the entire question as to whether a class is or is not a member of itself is nonsense. So, he invented a hierarchy of classes according to which the first type of classes would be made up of classes made up entirely of particulars, the second type made up of classes whose members are classes of the first type, the third type composed of classes whose members are classes of the second type, and so on. The types would be mutually exclusive, thus making the notion of a class being a member of itself meaningless.[50] His hierarchy of types was to perform "the single, though essential, service of justifying us in refraining from entering on trains of reasoning which lead to contradictory conclusions. The justification is that what seem to be propositions are really nonsense".[51]

Indeed, the contradictions that in Russell's words had "infected logic and set theory" and "troubled students of symbolic logic and set theory" and that he had expended so much energy to "avoid"[52] were derived using a concept of set that allows one to form the expression "a set may be a

---

[48] Bertrand Russell, *Logic and Knowledge, Essays 1901-1950*, London: Allen & Unwin, 1956, p. 81.

[49] Russell, *Logic and Knowledge*, pp. 81, 261; his *Essays in Analysis*, London: Allen & Unwin, 1973, p. 171.

[50] Russell, *Essays in Analysis*, p. 201; his *Principles of Mathematics*, London: Norton, 1903, §§104-105; his *Logic and Knowledge*, pp. 261-64.

[51] Bertrand Russell and Alfred North Whitehead, *Principia Mathematica to *56*, Cambridge UK: Cambridge University Press, 2nd ed. 1964 (1927), p. 24.

[52] *Ibid.*, pp. vii, 1.

member of itself', which Husserl judged to be *widersinnig*. In contrast, Husserl would derive set theory analytically from the concept of set which, according to his theories, if it is to be mathematical would have to have a "set essence" in view. This set essence would be expressed in the relation between a set itself and its elements. He reasoned that an essence relation makes it impossible for the members of the relation to be identical. So it belongs essentially to the concept of set that no set can contain itself as an element without contradiction. Reasoning appealing to the notion of sets that do not contain themselves as members would therefore be entirely untenable.

Blurring distinctions by allowing sets as dependent forms to be transformed into proper names breaks logical structure, which smooths the way for things to come into places not intended for them. Once logical structure is broken and meaning categories are violated trouble lies ahead in the form of failures of inference, something I cannot go into further here, but have examined from various different angles in *Rethinking Identity and Metaphysics,* "On Fundamental Differences Between Dependent and Independent Meanings", "Incomplete Symbols, Dependent Meanings, and Paradox", "Reference and Paradox", cited in this text, and in the upcoming chapters: "Husserlian Sets or Fregean Sets" and in "Husserl's Way Out of Frege's Jungle".

Categoriality and analyticity

Husserl (not to mention Bernard Bolzano, Karl Weierstrass, Georg Cantor, Brentano, Frege, or Johnny-come-lately Quine in his famous "Two Dogmas of Empiricism") rejected the way in which Kant distinguished between analytic and synthetic truths. For instance, in *Introduction to Logic and Theory of Knowledge,* Husserl reminded students that he had repeatedly said that no matter how proud Kant had been of the manner in which he had defined the concept of analyticity, it was altogether inadequate and really fundamentally wrong-headed.[53] In *Ideas I,* he maintained that it was the purely logical, as he himself defined it that determines the concept of the analytical as opposed to the synthetic.[54] In *Logic and General Theory of Science,*

[53] Husserl, *Introduction to Logic and Theory of Knowledge*, §23; Claire Ortiz Hill, "One Dogma of Empiricism", *Experience and Analysis, Erfahrung und Analyse,* M. E. Reicher and J. C. Marek (eds), Vienna: ÖBV&HPT Verlag, 2005, pp. 30-38, anthologized in Hill & da Silva.

[54] Husserl, *Ideas, General Introduction to Pure Phenomenology*, §10.

he explained that by analytic truths in the broadest sense, he understood "analytic concept-truths, therefore all pure categorial truths, therefore, the entire pure mathesis, pure logic, then however, also their a priori and empirical individuations, therefore, the analytic necessities". He saw the pure categorial concept-truths as a whole as essentially belonging together and forming a single system of scientific disciplines to be dealt with under the broadest heading of formal logic, or analytics, or the *mathesis universalis* in Leibniz' sense. He specified that in carrying the analytic and synthetic distinction over to deductive theories and disciplines, one obtains analytic (or categorial) and non-categorial or synthetic theories and disciplines, the latter breaking down into synthetic a priori ones and a posteriori ones. He maintained that all the analytic disciplines – which he defined as disciplines bringing all the laws to ultimate theoretical unity – belonging to the formal categories form a homogeneous unit, namely, analytics in a broader sense. So it is that Husserl identified analyticity and categoriality.[55] This means that the categorial scaffolding he wanted have buttress scientific knowledge of reality was analytic.

In the *Logical Investigations,* he defined analytic laws as unconditionally universal propositions that were free of any assertion, implicit or explicit, of individual existence and were grounded solely in formal categories, thereby unaffected by any material knowledge. They were composed exclusively of formal concepts and primitive or basic laws containing only formal categories and they were completely formalizable. As an example of such an analytic law, he proposed the analytic proposition that the existence of this house includes that of its roof, its walls and its other parts, for which the analytic formula holds that the existence of a whole W (A, B, C…) generally includes that of its parts A, B, C….[56]

To the question as to what was the essential line of demarcation within pure laws by which analytic laws set themselves apart from all other laws, Husserl once replied that the distinction permitting one to draw that line clearly was that between the material and the analytic-categorial, according to which meanings, propositions, judgments split into ones only containing formal-categorial terms and ones also containing material terms.[57]

So it is that he further divided pure concept-truths not exclusively containing what he called "that remarkable group of pure concepts… called

---

[55] Husserl, *Logic and General Theory of Science*, §§45b, 47e, 50.
[56] Husserl, *Logical Investigations*, Investigation III, §12.
[57] Husserl, *Logic and General Theory of Science*, Appendix XV.

the formal categories" into those that do not remain truths when their material concepts are replaced by pure categories and those that do. As examples of pure concept-truths falling into the first group, Husserl gave geometrical and kinematic axioms, which according to his theories were synthetic or synthetic a priori concept-truths, not analytic necessities. Into the second group he placed all a priori individuations of pure laws of meaning. As examples of these, he proposed: "Two colors the same as a third, are the same as one another", as a particular instance of "Two objects the same as one and the same third one are the same as one another", a real proposition such as, for example, "If something is red, then it is not not-red", which is an extra-essential material truth corresponding to the formal law that, "If something is a, then it is not not-a, which is not essentially bound to the concept "red", but holds for the property "red", because it holds for arbitrary properties of arbitrary objects", and the truth that "If one spatial distance is greater than a second one, then the latter is smaller than the former", which is a particular instance of a universal principle holding not only for spatial distances, but for any magnitude, the concept of which is a categorial.[58] Every formal-logically valid inference as such, he added, is also characterized by the fact that it changes into a categorial law-truth when its material terms are replaced by indefinite terms of the corresponding categories. As an example, he gave, "If all humans are mortal and Socrates is a human, then Socrates is mortal", which is merely a particular instance of the formal-logical law, "If All A are α, and x is an A, then x is also α". Every such inference, he concluded, is therefore an analytic necessity.[59]

The proposition category as the highest logical category

Husserl thought that *"the logical categories form precisely the source of all science as such,* therefore, of all science in terms of its theoretical form". And he maintained that those logical categories, the primitive concepts of pure logic, were grouped around the proposition category as the highest logical category.[60]

Adopting the Aristotelian word for proposition, *apophansis,* he called the sphere of the proposition categories apophantic categories.[61] As he explained to his students,

---

[58] *Ibid.,* §45b.
[59] *Ibid.,* Appendix XV.
[60] Husserl, *Introduction to Logic and Theory of Knowledge,* §§18a, 19d.
[61] *Ibid.,* §18a.

> From the standpoint that we adopted for the definition of apophantic logic, the idea of proposition was the basic category. In more common parlance, we could also say the idea of statement, of predication, and this insofar as it is a statement that something is or is not, the idea of a claim to validity or truth. What is grounded in the essence of the proposition as unit of validity is to be investigated. In certain ways, therefore, it is a matter of a logic of truth. Truth is simply true proposition. If we want to investigate what is grounded in the essence of truth, then we must go back to the propositional forms to be distinguished in essential ways. We therefore need a theory of forms of proposition. And based upon this as a higher level at which it is genuinely aimed, is the logical theory of laws: the laws of validity and non-validity grounded in the essence of these forms.[62]

The basic trunk of the one pure logic, he stressed, is apophantic logic, by which he understood all the laws of essence pertaining to the idea of proposition. For him, this was a matter of laws making up the most universal, clearly indispensable basis for establishing norms for thinking, laws without which it would be meaningless to talk of truth and falsehood, attribution or non-attribution, assuming and inferring, therefore of yes and no, if and then, either, or, and so on.[63]

He saw the proposition category as separating into a series of separate categories of propositions differing in terms of their formal constitution where various formal elements occur which, conceptually differentiated, produce a series of related categories of formal constituents of propositions. As examples of such constituents, he gave subject, predicate, attribute, is, not, if, then, and, either, or, plural, singular, all, some, a, etc. Out of this are built, the propositional categories, existential proposition, categorical, hypothetical, disjunctive proposition, conjunctive proposition etc.[64]

Every proposition as such, he explained, declares that something is or is not and in so doing lays claim to validity. However, this covers, a variety of particular cases which are expressed in different forms and grounded in the universal nature of the proposition as a unit positing an objectivity. So it is that propositions declare that something exists or does not exist, that a given property φ is or is not attributable to an object, that if φ is attributable to it, then another property ψ is or is not also attributable to it, or is not

[62] *Ibid.*, §18c.
[63] *Ibid.*, §18a, d.
[64] *Ibid.*, §18a.

attributable to it because either one property or the other is attributable to it, if property φ is attributable to an *S*, property ψ must also be attributable to a *Q*, etc. Laws grounded in the nature of these forms, laws of validity or lack of validity on the basis of mere form then pertain to these propositional forms and to the forms of their involvement in compound propositions. These form concepts and the laws accompanying them must be absolutely universal. These forms occur *in concreto* and the accompanying laws of validity are therefore applicable wherever propositions are stated, wherever they figure in theoretical structures, inferences, proofs, theories.[65]

Concepts such as proposition, valid and invalid proposition, truth and falsehood, Husserl pointed out, clearly have to be applicable always and everywhere. Concepts expressing the possible constituents of propositions in formal universality, for example, subject and predicate, universality and particularity, singular and plural naturally belong there, as well as, in general, all forms of propositions and possible systems of propositions that, irrespective of specific cognitive content, involve possibilities lying in the universal nature of the proposition of capturing arbitrarily determined contents in propositional form, therefore, of capturing them in meaning units that by their very nature lay claim to validity or truth. In contrast, however, concepts such as whole and part, relation and order, set, cardinal number, combination do not express essential forms of propositions, and the laws pertaining to them are not laws for truths grounded in the essence of the proposition in general. Rather, they *a priori* express possible object prototypes and what is grounded in their formal essence. They therefore must take a backseat to the concept of propositions.[66]

Importantly, Husserl considered that owing to the correlation of the concepts of proposition and state of affairs, concept and object, apophantic logic also in certain ways contains a formal ontology which, inseparably connected with the apophantic a priori – that of statement meanings –, is the a priori of formal ontology. So, for example, if in virtue of this correlation between meaning and objectivity, one changed standpoints and adopted the standpoint on the side of objectivity, then corresponding to the theory of forms of propositions would be a theory of forms of the corresponding states of affairs.[67]

---

65 *Ibid.*

66 *Ibid.*

67 *Ibid.*, §18c

Every science's entire theoretical content, he told students, is totally composed of meanings, is made up of propositions as units of meaning and validity that are complete in themselves.[68] A theory, he wrote in the *Prolegomena*, is a certain deductive combination of propositions which are themselves certain combinations of given concepts, among them the concepts of concept, proposition, truth, etc.[69] To further their insight into the essence of pure logic, Husserl asked his students to reflect on the following:

> Scientific reasoning aims for truth. Truth is realized subjectively in judgment and is stated in statements.... *Every scientific theory is a system of statements*.... It is something complete in its own right and, as it is, lays claim to truth and falsehood. The starting propositions lay claim to this directly. The theory, the definitely formed web of propositions, lays claim to substantiating new truth indirectly, step by step. And the system itself lays claim to being true as a system. That means that everywhere one thing is linked to another by logical inference that is also stated, therefore, is also set down as true.[70]

As was his wont, to illustrate the role of propositions in a theoretical system, he asked his students to consider that of modern pure mathematics. As regards its essence, he explained to them, it

> is no more than a system of logically combined statement meanings, *a system of propositions*. This system states truths about a certain combination of facts, namely that of the mathematical facts making up the field of mathematics. This field is not given to us externally and apart from knowledge, but only in and by means of knowledge. And, it is scientifically given and known as far as it has been dealt with theoretically, as far as the subjects of the propositions refer, say, to numbers, the predicates to properties of numbers, or to relations between numbers, the combinations of propositions to combinations of properties and relations as regards cause and effect, as regards compatibility and incompatibility, etc.[71]

Once the ideal of constituting a system of propositions in a field as basic principles is realized, then all the theoretical work is done. The

---

68 *Ibid.*, §18a.

69 Husserl, *Logical Investigations*, *Prolegomena*, §67.

70 Husserl, *Introduction to Logic and Theory of Knowledge*, §11.

71 *Ibid.*

propositions would be expressed algebraically. One could look at the form and say that it yields a deductive theory falling within the scope of a given mathematical prototype. All its possible formal consequences in formal universality have already been theoretically derived. It need only be applied.[72]

The entire categorial form of the edifice of science

As we have seen, Husserl's search for answers that he did not believe Brentano's empirical psychology could provide led him to espouse metaphysical, epistemological, and logical views that Brentano – and Quine – deemed odious and despicable. But, disenchanted with his teacher's ideas, Husserl grew convinced that knowledge of the world of the natural sciences could not be definitive knowledge of reality, that although many worthwhile findings had been made through advances in the natural sciences, they did not provide definitive, ultimate, conclusive knowledge of the essence of nature and lacked the critical insight into the meaning of the fundamental concepts and fundamental principles needed to be clear about the sense in which their findings could be taken as expressions of ultimate Being. The empirical sciences, he came to teach, are not creations of a purely theoretical mind, not based on absolutely scrupulously lain foundations in accordance with a rigorous logical method.[73]

He had come to hold that from the point of view of their form, all propositions, inferences, proofs, theories in the sciences are structured in a regular way and that that regularity is purely logical, so that, if the purely logical sphere has been developed to the proper extent, its concepts and laws make it possible in advance – and irrespective of actual scientific fields and any actual theories about them – to construct *a priori* forms of possible theories and possible sciences and subsequently make use of those theory forms and the regularity of their relations for actual theorizing about any a priori or empirical fields of knowledge defined step by step in the actual investigating of the world and awaiting theorization.[74]

Lifting out the elementary concepts belonging to the essence of the theoretical content of science in general and investigating the systems of

---

[72] *Ibid.*, §19c.

[73] Husserl, *Introduction to Logic and Theory of Knowledge*, §20; his "Aus der Einleitung der Vorlesung 'Erkenntnistheorie und Hauptpunkte der Metaphysik 1898/99'", in his *Allgemeine Erkenntnistheorie*, p. 233.

[74] Husserl, *Introduction to Logic and Theory of Knowledge*, §19c.

laws grounded in them, one can obtain a group of disciplines embodying the direct and indirect conditions of the possibility of a theory and, in this regard, of a science in general. This is a matter of basic laws and disciplines developing out of them that all sciences can use in like measure and that no science can and may ever violate, because embodied there is precisely what is either directly constitutive of the science or is a pure consequence of it.[75]

Persuaded that belonging to the essence of science in general is the form of the theory, he went on to conclude that there must be a most universal theory of science of all, a theory of theory in general, a science of what is ultimately grounded in the essence of statements claiming validity, in the essence of the apophansis.[76] It was certain, he maintained, that the formal disciplines make up a self-contained unit and that taken all together they constitute a science of everything that with respect to its form belongs *a priori* to the essence of theory in general and can be developed scientifically there, or they constitute a theory of science, in so far as science must, by essence, contain theory, science being really only completed science in so far as it provides theory.[77]

To build an ideal *mathesis universalis* as Husserl envisioned it, one must obtain a comprehensive set of completely direct axioms that are formally independent of one another and state all the direct law-truths pertaining to all the formal categories, both apophantic and formal ontological. The categories themselves being intertwined, their interconnections would have to be kept track of systematically and the axioms laid down step by step. But, since mere axioms are not theories, the consequences would therefore have to be systematically deduced from the axioms. Each step of indirect thinking taken would have to be directly perspicuous, would only be valid if its law was valid and that law would have to occur among the axioms, therefore, be directly warranted in and of itself.[78]

All possible proof and theory forms *a priori* being thus outlined, Husserl envisioned the very same procedure as extending to the entire categorial form of the edifice of science. He was "ultimately striving after the ideal of an all-embracing theory of theories, of a science of all possible forms

---

75 *Ibid.*

76 *Ibid.*, §23.

77 *Ibid.*, §§22, 23.

78 Husserl, *Logic and General Theory of Science*, §59.

of deductive disciplines, or at least of a differentiation of main prototypes and of systematic, separate development of prototypes within a main prototype" which, if carried out with such completeness of the deductions that each possible form of a theoretical discipline falling within the scope of the main prototypes is already established and fully developed in advance, would yield all theories before we even know the fields in which they will formulate and solve their problems.[79] He described the goal of this modern "supramathematics" as being:

> to obtain the disciplines belonging to the categories of proposition, concept, cardinal number, relation, equality, quantity etc. and to all possible spheres of theories in an entirely new, unique way. Instead of everywhere purely holding on to the concepts and setting up for their own sake the axioms and out of them the mathematics pertaining to each sphere, it proves vastly more advantageous and infinitely more fruitful to set up a universal, and thereby hypothetical, theory of theories that defines the main prototypes of theories and constructs them completely in terms of their form, so that this mathematics itself is not to be effected anew for every preestablished purely logical or extralogical domain that in general admits of a mathematics, but is to be obtained by simple subsumption under the corresponding theory form.[80]

This all-embracing theory of theories, of a science of all possible forms of deductive disciplines that Husserl was intent upon devising was his theory of manifolds, which he saw as the ultimate consummation of all purely categorial knowledge.[81]

The ultimate consummation of all purely categorial knowledge

So, for Husserl, all purely categorial knowledge culminated, in his words, in a "theory of theories, in a rational morphology and physiology of theories possible *a priori*, or correlatively speaking, in a rational discipline of the manifolds, of scientific fields that are exclusively defined by the form of their theoretical connections", which therefore yields "a perfectly complete unit directly characterized by the fact that everything having to do with content is excluded on principle".[82]

---

[79] Husserl, *Introduction to Logic and Theory of Knowledge*, §19c.
[80] *Ibid.*, §19d.
[81] Husserl, *Logic and General Theory of Science*, §59.
[82] Husserl, *Introduction to Logic and Theory of Knowledge*, §23.

He stressed that "every concept of a manifold and of a theory of manifolds is entirely built out of *purely categorial concepts*". As to what he meant by "manifold", he replied that to begin with, it was,

> nothing more than an "aggregate" or a "class" of objects conceived in complete indeterminacy and universality. Now, those are, though, purely and simply categorial concepts. Furthermore, when we say we are stipulating of these objects of the presently fully undetermined class that there are certain connectives ±, etc. for them for which $a+b = b+a$, etc. then hold, then the concepts "certain" relation, sameness when changing the order of the relation, etc. in turn occur. Purely and simply logico-categorial concepts. Here, the sign "±" only means a sign for an indeterminately conceived relation and not, for example, for a relationship of quantities, or any other specific thing. Therefore, nothing leading outside the categorial sphere enters in here through the sign. We construct, therefore, purely logical concepts of possible objectivities.[83]

He conceived of manifolds as pure forms of possible theories which, like molds, remain totally undetermined as to their content, but to which thought must necessarily conform in order to be thought and known in a theoretical manner. In manifolds, he explained, formal logic deals with whole systems of propositions making up possible deductive theories. It is a matter of theorizing about possible fields of knowledge conceived of in a general, undetermined way and purely and simply determined by the fact that the objects stand in certain relations that are themselves subject to certain fundamental laws of such and such determined form.[84] Universally speaking, he explained, the meaning of a theory of manifolds is,

> Let there be a domain in which the objects are subject to certain forms of relation and connection, for which axioms of such and such a form are valid, then for a domain formally constituted in this way, a mathematics of such and such a form would be valid, there would then result propositions of such and such a form, proofs, theories of such and such a form. Here, one does *not actually have a domain, does not have actually given concepts, does not have actually given connections and relations, and finally does not have actual axioms*, but is simply saying, *if* one had a domain, and *if* axioms of such and such a form obtained for it. The so-called axioms of such a mathematics calling

[83] *Ibid.*, §19c.

[84] Husserl, *Introduction to Logic and Theory of Knowledge*, §19; his *Logic and General Theory of Science*, §§54-59.

> itself axiomatic are, therefore, not actual axioms, actual propositions entitled to be validating truths. They are axiom forms that are to actual axioms precisely what proposition forms are to actual propositions.
>
> The thought *S* is *P* is not a proposition, but a thought that universally presents a proposition and presents it as having a certain formal prototype. If we say: Let there be a domain in which axioms of such and such a form hold, for example, an axiom of the form $a+b = b+a$, then I do not have an axiom, but am simply saying, let there be something such that for objects of the domain and for an unknown connective called +, commutativity applies. No truth is, therefore, advanced there. And, so the whole dependent theory is also simply the form of a theory. It really only says: From axioms of such a form (if axioms having such a form can be produced), theories would develop of such and such a codetermined form. If one actually finds a field of knowledge somewhere for which principles have the form required, then application to this field produces an actual mathematics forthwith: *instead of a hypothetical science form, a true and actual science.* [85]

Husserl saw the general theory of manifolds, or science of theory forms, as a field of free, creative investigation made possible once one realizes that deductions, series of deductions, continue to be meaningful and to remain valid when one assigns another meaning to the symbols. No longer restricted to operating in terms of a particular field of knowledge, one is free to reason completely on the level of pure forms. Operating within this sphere of pure forms, one can vary the systems in different ways. Nothing more need be presupposed than the fact that the objects figuring in them are such that, for them, a certain connective supplies new objects and does so in such a way that the form determined is assuredly valid for them. One finds ways of constructing an infinite number of forms of possible disciplines.[86] In his course on *Logic and General Theory of Science,* he explained:

> All actual theories, therefore, also the analytic theories, can precisely be formalized in the sense of the theory of theories. Even syllogistic logic is not to be made an exception here. In its case, formalization even leads to a theory-form that can be understood as a special case of the formal genus-type "arithmetic". All the well-known algebraic propositions ab = ba, the laws of association, distribution, hold, and the brilliant *Boole* saw

[85] Husserl, *Introduction to Logic and Theory of Knowledge,* §19d.
[86] *Ibid.,* §19.

> that two closed domains of ordinary syllogistic logic can be dealt with as if it were an arithmetic, only that the number series reduces to the numbers 0 and 1. All arithmetical laws are valid there if we but add the fact that 1 + 1 does not = 2, but = 1. If one knows nothing about the theory of theories that seems to be perfect nonsense, and it then seems absolutely strange when one hears of machines, of a kind of piano, that analogously permits one to resolve complex webs of syllogisms by means of a mechanical game, the way one can randomly mechanically carry out additions, multiplications, divisions, and so forth with calculating machines. However, the matter is no more miraculous there than here, and in syllogistic logic, the 0 and <the> 1 are signs that have very little to do with the arithmetical 0 and <the arithmetical> 1. They are only selected, just as the signs +, ×, = are, in order to allow certain formal analogies to come to the fore and in further consequence to make perceptible the fact that the theory-form agrees to the extent indicated with that of an arithmetic.[87]

So, in the methodology of manifolds, one speaks of numbers, but one does not speak, for example, of cardinal numbers, but anything for which formal axioms of the arithmetical prototype hold. If, Husserl taught, we drop the cardinal number meaning of the letters in the ordinary theory of cardinal numbers and substitute the thought of objects in general for which axioms of the arithmetical form $a+b = b+a$, $a \cdot b = b \cdot a$, etc. are to hold, we no longer have arithmetic, but a purely logical class prototype of theory forms to which, like innumerably many possible domains, the domain of cardinal numbers is also subject. In this case, it is no longer a matter of arithmetic, but of a class prototype of possible mathematics. One may speak of numbers in the formal sense, but they are not cardinal numbers, but objects indeterminately, universally defined by axiom forms as they are especially actually found for cardinal numbers. Here, as in every theory form or manifold form, the "axioms" are proposition forms that are constituent parts of the definition. For cardinal numbers, $ab = ba$ holds. In constructing a manifold, though, one may just as well stipulate that $ab \neq ba$, for example, $ab = -ba$, and likewise for the other basic principles.[88]

This procedure, Husserl enthused, has proven "splendidly effective" and it was only owing to it that mathematics had become "a magnificent

---

[87] Husserl, *Logic and General Theory of Science*, §58.

[88] Husserl, *Introduction to Logic and Theory of Knowledge*, §19b, d.

tool for investigating nature". One can everywhere go back to the form and derive the whole system of consequences, or rather consequence forms, on the basis of the form, something which is very helpful since the same theory forms recur in different fields.[89] However, in spite of all its advantages, Husserl realized that, because the theory of manifolds itself proceeds deductively, because it is based on pure analytic categories, and because its every step is subject to analytic laws that are not merely forms, thinking within the hypothetical reflection of theory-forms cannot be exhaustive, the formal theory of manifolds cannot confirm all of analytics or the special domains of analytics we call arithmetics. In drawing an inference, some laws of inference belong to the inference. If it weighs the possibilities combinatorially when solving problems, it makes use of propositions for cardinal number and combination, and so on.[90]

He further realized that although all fields of theoretical knowledge have a systemic form that belongs to formal logic itself, and so are particular instances of manifolds, not all sciences are theoretical disciplines that, like mathematical physics, set theory, pure geometry or pure arithmetic, are characterized by the fact that their systemic principle is a purely analytical one. He recognized that sciences like psychology, history, the critique of reason and, notably, phenomenology were not purely logical and so obliged philosophers to go beyond the analytico-logical model. When those not purely logical sciences were formalized and philosophers asked what binds the propositional forms into a single system form, they faced nothing more than the empty general truth that there is an infinite number of propositions connected in objective ways that are compatible with one another in that they do not contradict one another analytically.[91]

Conclusion

With this account of Husserl's theory of manifolds as "the ultimate consummation of all purely categorial knowledge", I have sought to expose what might be viewed as the backbone of the true and ultimate skeleton that Husserl held up to philosophers to uphold truly scientific knowledge

89 *Ibid.*, §19c, d.

90 Husserl, *Logic and General Theory of Science*, §58.

91 Husserl, *Logic and General Theory of Science*, §54; his *Formal and Transcendental Logic*, §35a; his, *Alte und neue Logik, Vorlesung 1908/09*, Dordrecht: Kluwer, 2003, p. 263; his *Logik, Vorlesung 1902/03*, pp. 31-43, 49.

of reality. I have tried to show that the father of the science of intentionality also elaborated a formal logic that is as austere and free from acts, subjects, or empirical persons or objects belonging to actual reality as Quinean logic is, and that he manufactured it out of everything that Quine and those of his mind reviled and conspired to have ignored. He made essences, a fundamental cleavage between analytic truths and synthetic truths, metaphysics, integral parts of this endeavor. He renounced empiricism and espoused an idealistic ontology that repudiated material objects and surely would have fled Quine's ontologies of rabbit parts, stages, and fusions, and river stages and kinship, person stages, where physical and mathematical objects, where are but myths relative to an epistemological view.[92]

However, seduced by the siren of transcendental phenomenology, Husserl did not to pursue the issues, implications and consequences of his ideas about formal logic as far as he could have. In 1917, he confessed to Hermann Weyl that despite of all the work he had devoted to the theory of functional judgments, of judgments with empty places, to distinguishing the different modes of the empty something, to implementing the fundamental distinctions between formal and factual ways of judgment, between proposition form and proposition or judgment, proof- and theory-form and theory and the objective correlates associated with them, to his concept of complete manifolds, he had not pursued that train of thought completely to the end, because it had had to be more important to him to develop his ideas about transcendental phenomenology.[93] In 1930, he wrote to Georg Misch that he had lost all the interest that formal logic and all real ontology had held for him in the face of a systematic grounding of a theory of transcendental subjectivity.[94]

As a result of Husserl's manifest love for transcendental phenomenology, his pioneering, prophetic work in the field of formal logic was never furthered in a way that ever made much of an impact on FRQ, or even on his own followers. Nonetheless, the awareness that there is

---

92 Willard Quine, "On What There Is" (1948), in his *From a Logical Point of View*, p. 19; "Identity, Ostension, and Hypothesis" (1950), also published in his *From a Logical Point of View*, pp. 68, 70-71; his *Word and Object*, §12; his "Ontological Relativity", pp. 34-35, 48, 50.

93 Edmund Husserl, *Logik und allgemeine Wissenschaftstheorie, Vorlesungen 1917/18, mit ergänzenden Texten aus der ersten Fassung 1910/11*, Ursula Panzer (ed.), Dordrecht: Kluwer, 1996, p. XXIII nn. 1 & 4.

94 *Ibid.*, n. 4.

something about reality that cannot be manipulated at will, that for example, logic must be rooted in the ways in which being is structured or it will turn out illogical, may one day prove to be one of the principal lessons of twentieth century analytic philosophy and phenomenology both. So, once the pieces of his theory about the categorial structure of reality are reassembled, philosophers can, and should, experiment with it as an alternative to FRQ philosophy and logic, which unsuccessfully tried to wipe out the very differences that he deemed revelatory of categoriality.[95] It will surely one day prove to be one of the ironies of the history of philosophy that it is the study of the failings of phenomenology's rival that has provided the key to understanding the importance of Husserl's more lucid alternative.

---

[95] My *Rethinking Identity and Metaphysics* and my "Reference and Paradox", *Synthese*, 138, 2, January 2004, 207-32, anthologized in Hill & da Silva.

7

HUSSERL, FREGE AND 'THE PARADOX'[1]

Introduction

Careful readers of Gottlob Frege's philosophical and mathematical correspondence are bound to notice the intriguing fact that in letters that he and Edmund Husserl exchanged during late 1906 and early 1907 Husserl "expressed his views about the 'paradox'" and that by this he "might have meant Russell's paradox".[2] Conscientious scholars will also further note that those letters were exchanged during the very year in which it is now thought that Frege definitively abandoned his attempts to solve what, because of the preeminent role that Bertrand Russell played in publicizing Frege's errors and in bringing the point home to him, is known as Russell's paradox.[3]

This merits elucidation. However, even the most diligent scholar might be forgiven for believing that there could be little to say on the matter. It is only through some suggestive notes once penned by the German logician Heinrich Scholz about the contents of the letters that we even know that

---

[1] This was originally written for *Manuscrito, Revista Internacional de Filosofia* 23, 2, October 2000.

[2] It is important to note here that according to Heinrich Scholz, who collected the letters, Husserl wrote about 'the paradox' and not 'the paradoxes'. The note to the English edition informs readers that one of Husserl's letters dealt with 'the paradoxes', possibly Russell's paradox and that another contained remarks on 'the paradoxes' (Gottlob Frege, *Philosophical and Mathematical Correspondence*, Oxford: Blackwell, 1980, p. 70 n.). However, in the German editions the word 'paradox' is in the singular with the definite article (see Gottlob Frege, *Wissenschaftlicher Briefwechsel*, Hamburg: Meiner, 1976, pp. 101-07 and *Gottlob Freges Briefwechsel mit D. Hilbert, E. Husserl, B. Russell, sowie ausgewählte Einzelbriefe Freges*, Hamburg: Meiner, 1980, pp. 44-46). The English edition of Frege's correspondence was abridged by Brian McGuinness and contains a number of really unpardonable errors. See Claire Ortiz Hill, "Frege's Letters", in *From Dedekind to Gödel,* Jaakko Hintikka (ed.), Dordrecht: Kluwer, 1995, pp. 97-118, also published in Claire Ortiz Hill and Guillermo Rosado Haddock, *Husserl or Frege, Meaning, Objectivity and Mathematics,* La Salle IL: Open Court, 2000. One wonders why readers of English were only offered an abridged edition in the first place.

[3] Michael Dummett, *The Interpretation of Frege's Philosophy*, Cambridge MA: Harvard University Press, 1981, pp. 21-22; Michael Dummett, *Frege, Philosophy of Mathematics*, Cambridge MA: Harvard University Press, 1991, pp. 5-6.

Husserl ever wrote to Frege about a paradox that might have been Russell's paradox. Although copies of two letters that Frege wrote to Husserl between October 30 and December 9, 1906 have been retrieved and published, the three letters that Husserl is known to have written to Frege between November 10, 1906 and January 13, 1907 seem irretrievably lost.[4]

Nevertheless, philosophers need not resign themselves to the idea that Scholz' intriguing remarks are all that can possibly be known about the matter. Even though we may never know exactly what Husserl wrote to Frege at that juncture, that does not mean that nothing significant can be ascertained about the content of that obscure interchange at that important time between those two giants of twentieth century philosophy. Facts can be gathered that allow us to combine what Frege wrote in those letters with his cogitations on Russell's paradox and to connect the result with the ideas of Husserl, whose struggle to come to terms with paradoxical consequences courted when reasoning with symbols played a significant role in the development of the ideas that went into the making of the *Logical Investigations.*

Here I study three paradox courting practices that Frege adopted, but Husserl made a point of eschewing. I do so in support of the presupposition that Husserl makes in the *Logical Investigations* that "one does not wish to be satisfied with developing pure logic merely after the fashion of our mathematical disciplines as an expanding system of propositions with naive objective validity, but that one strives for philosophical clarity with respect to these propositions, i.e., for insight into the essence of the ways of knowing involved in the implementation and ideally possible applications of such propositions and into the accompanying essentially constituting conferrals of sense and objective forms of validity".[5]

---

[4] Frege, *Philosophical and Mathematical Correspondence*, pp. 66-71; Heinrich Scholz, "Briefe an Husserl 8. III 1936", in Husserl's *Briefwechsel vol. VI, Philosophenbriefe,* Dordrecht: Kluwer, 1994, pp. 379-80; Albert Veraart, "Geschichte des wissenschaftlichen Nachlasses Gottlob Freges und seiner Edition. Mit einen Katalog des ursprünglichen Bestands der nachgelassenen Schriften Freges", in *Studies on Frege*, Matthias Schirn (ed.), vol. 1, Stuttgart Bad Cannstatt: Frommann-Holzboog Verlag, 1976, p. 104. In addition, there seems to be no sign of a copy that Husserl asked Scholz to send him in 1936, or of Scholz' letters to Husserl at that time. This appears to have gone unnoticed. I wish to thank Dr. Sebastian Luft for inquiring into this for me at the Husserl Archives in Leuven, Belgium.

[5] Edmund Husserl, *Logical Investigations*, London: Routledge and Kegan Paul, 1970 (1900/01), "Introduction", Volume II, §1, my translation.

The letters and Frege's *Nachlass*

As a first step in our study of Husserl, Frege and 'the paradox', we need to look at the exchange that took place between him and Frege within the broader context of Frege's ill-starred *Nachlass*. A close study of Frege's epistolary exchanges and other writings of his *Nachlass* that have survived and of what we can know about what did not survive actually proves more revealing than one might expect.[6]

Of particular interest here is the unfortunate fact that once one begins looking for information on Frege's ideas about Russell's paradox, the causes of it and potential remedies for it, one finds that practically all the lost letters and many of the other lost writings were written after Russell's discovery of the paradox and broadly concerned Frege's views on what the problem was and why he found the solutions that his contemporaries were proposing unacceptable. These subjects were: the paradoxes of set theory and possible solutions to them; extensionality and classes; the Basic Law V that he blamed for the downfall of his project; the differences between concepts and objects; identity; and Frege's opinion of the work of his contemporaries. Moreover, since Frege published so little after Russell's discovery, that never published material was one of the only sources of evidence about the evolution of his ideas on these important matters.[7] However, as I have said, all is not lost and much can still to be pieced together from the available remnants.

The year 1906

For instance, Michael Dummett has argued that Frege's "posthumous papers allow us with high probability to date almost exactly Frege's disillusionment over the attempt, to which he had devoted his life, to derive arithmetic from logic".[8] During 1906, Dummett has observed, Frege had begun to write "On Schoenflies: *Die logischen Paradoxien der Mengenlehre*",[9] an article on the paradoxes of set theory and the inadequacy of the solutions proposed for them by Arthur Schoenflies in a January 1906 article and by Alwin Korselt in a March-April 1906 article.

---

[6] Hill, "Frege's Letters".

[7] See the "Smart Bombs" section of my "Frege's Letters", pp. 106-15.

[8] Dummett, *The Interpretation of Frege's Philosophy*, p. 21.

[9] Gottlob Frege, *Posthumous Writings*, Oxford: Blackwell, 1979, pp. 176-83.

"The article was never completed and never submitted", Dummett explained, "but his plan for it contains an item showing clearly that, when he drew it up, he still believed in his solution to the contradiction: 'Russell's contradiction cannot be eliminated in Schoenflies's way. Concepts which coincide in their extension although this extension falls under the one but not under the other'".[10] In that surviving plan for the article Frege plainly stated that set theory was "in ruins".[11]

An incomplete draft of the article has also survived. In it Frege discussed Russell's paradox and problems with extensions and Basic Law V. At one point, Frege alludes to the shock that the law had sustained from Russell's paradox, but suggests that readers put their doubts temporarily aside and carry out the operation that the problematic law would prescribe.[12] "Tantalizingly little of the article survives", Dummett writes, concluding that it "very probably represents the very moment at which Frege came to realize that the attempt was hopeless".[13] Dummett next draws attention to "a tiny fragment, dated 5 August 1906" called "What may I regard as the outcome of my work?" that has survived too. Frege's answer to his own question begins with the affirmation that it is almost entirely tied up with the *Begriffsschrift*[14] and includes what Dummett has called "the apologetic remark, 'the extension of a concept or the class is not for me the first thing'".[15]

Dummett concludes that Frege must have been moved to ask himself what his work had achieved at that particular time "because he had finally come to recognize that his ambition to set beyond doubt the derivation of arithmetic from logic had irrevocably failed. Instead of completing the project, he had to acknowledge that it could not be accomplished; and he wanted to take stock of what survived from the disaster, what truths he had nevertheless established".[16] "His task now", Dummett writes, "was to salvage from the wreck whichever of his ideas remained undamaged, those, namely, not dependent on the notion of a

[10] Dummett, *Frege, Philosophy of Mathematics*, p. 5.
[11] Frege, *Posthumous Writings*, p. 176.
[12] *Ibid.*, pp. 181-82.
[13] Dummett, *The Interpretation of Frege's Philosophy*, p. 22.
[14] Frege, *Posthumous Writings*, p. 184.
[15] Dummett, *The Interpretation of Frege's Philosophy*, p. 22.
[16] *Ibid.*

class or extension of a concept.... We may thus set the date of his discovery that his solution of Russell's contradiction would not work...."[17]

In addition to the above mentioned writings dated 1906, an "Introduction to Logic"[18] of August 1906 and the kindred "A Brief Survey of my Logical Doctrines"[19] have survived.[20] However, with the exception of the incomplete draft of the article about Schoenflies and another incomplete draft of a 1924/5 article,[21] all Frege's unpublished writings after 1906 in which he wrote about Schoenflies, Korselt, extensions, identity and Russell's paradox are lost. Missing are Frege's offprint of Schoenflies' 1906 article with critical remarks that Frege made, notes on Russell's paradox, set theory, identity, extensions; a 35 column supplement to *Basic Laws* called "Basic Law V replaced by (Basic Law) V'"; two versions ("58 columns, 18 columns and 70 pages") of a piece from about 1906 about constructing concepts and extensions of concepts called "On Two Odd Concepts" and directly related to that solution to Russell's paradox that Frege proposed in the appendix to *Basic Laws II*; and an undated piece about the impossibility of predicating a predicate of itself.

---

[17] Dummett, *Frege, Philosophy of Mathematics*, p. 6. Hans Sluga also has concluded that by 1906 Frege "was beginning to think that the theory of sets was undermined by the contradiction. He concluded that there was no use for sets or classes anymore", Hans Sluga, *Gottlob Frege*, London: Routledge & Kegan Paul, 1980, pp. 169-70.

[18] Frege, *Posthumous Writings*, pp. 185-96.

[19] *Ibid.*, pp. 197-202.

[20] There is confusion about the date of "17 Key Sentences on Logic" (Frege *Posthumous Writings*, pp. 174-75). The editor of Frege's *Schriften zur Logik und Sprachphilosophie aus dem Nachlass* dates it before 1892 (2nd ed. rev., Hamburg: Meiner, 1978, p. 174 n. 1). Frege's *Nachgelassene Schriften* (Hamburg: Meiner, 1969) and the English edition of them give "1906 or earlier" because according "to a note of Heinrich Scholz the manuscript should be dated around 1906" (Frege, *Posthumous Writings*, p. 174 and note), but remarks that it could have been written earlier. However, according to Scholz' note as reproduced by Veraart in his "Geschichte des wissenschaftlichen Nachlasses Gottlob Freges", p. 89, it dates from about the same time as "My Basic Logical Insights", which, in accordance with a note by Scholz, the English edition dates 1915 (Frege, *Posthumous Writings*, p. 251 and note). Veraart ("Geschichte des wissenschaftlichen Nachlasses Gottlob Freges", p. 89) reproduces Scholz' note for that piece as reading "from the war years". Be that as it may, the piece shows no kinship with Frege's other writings of 1906, which cling to certain specific themes. 1906 might have been a typographical error for 1916, a war year.

[21] Frege, *Posthumous Writings*, pp. 267-74.

Of particular interest to the present investigation is the loss of materials dealing with the subjects discussed in Frege's 1906 letters to Husserl. Missing are remarks by Frege on a lecture given by Hugh Mc Coll on "The Calculus of Equivalent Statements and Integration Limits" published in 1901; a lecture on the *Begriffsschrift*; a draft for a brief overview of his logical teachings on thoughts, equipollent propositions, coloring or illumination, disassociating assertoric force from the predicate, negation and the hypothetical mode of sentence composition,[22] apparently covering much the same material as that dealt with in the surviving, posthumously published texts from 1906 on the subject;[23] and, of course, Husserl's letters themselves.

Husserl's 1906-1907 correspondence with Frege

Husserl initiated this exchange of letters by sending Frege a copy of "A Report on German Writings in Logic from the Years 1895-1899, Fifth Article",[24] a review by Husserl of a long 1895 article about propositions without subjects and the relationship of grammar to logic and psychology by Anton Marty,[25] a prominent member of Franz Brentano's school. There is no indication of an accompanying letter.

Frege replied in a letter dated October 30 to November 1, 1906[26] that he did not have the time to go into Husserl's review thoroughly, but would make some observations that had occurred to him in reading it. Echoing remarks made in the above-mentioned "Introduction to Logic" and "A Brief Survey of my Logical Doctrines", Frege begins his observations by complaining that logicians needlessly complicate matters by not heeding his writings and then he goes on to discourse about the

---

22 Veraart, "Geschichte des wissenschaftlichen Nachlasses Gottlob Freges", pp. 89, 94, 97-101. Heinrich Scholz and Friedrich Bachmann, "Der wissenschaftliche Nachlass von Frege", in *Actes du congrès international de philosophie scientifique*, vol. VIII, *Histoire de la logique et de la philosophie scientifique*, Paris: Hermann, 1936, p. 28.

23 Frege, *Posthumous Writings*, pp. 185-96, 197-202.

24 Edmund Husserl, "Report on German Writings in Logic from the Years 1895-1899, Fifth Article" (1904), in his *Early Writings in the Philosophy of Logic and Mathematics*, Dordrecht: Kluwer, 1994, pp. 280-302.

25 Anton Marty, "Über subjektlose Sätze und das Verhältnis der Grammatik zur Logik und Psychologie", *Vierteljahrsschrift für wissenschaftliche Philosophie* 19 (1895): 19-87, pp. 263-334.

26 Frege, *Philosophical and Mathematical Correspondence*, pp. 66-70.

need to divorce logic from psychology and from language and grammar, leitmotifs that recur as he writes on.

The last three quarters of his letter is devoted to a discussion of equipollent propositions. Logicians, he stresses, must engage in proper logical analyses for which equipollent propositions differ only with regard to form. Equipollent propositions, he maintains, have something in common in their content, what he calls the thought that they express. It alone is of concern to logic. The rest is "the coloring" and "the illumination" of the thought. In proper logical analysis a single standard proposition for each system of equipollent propositions is all that is needed and any thought could be communicated by such a standard proposition. Given a standard proposition everyone would then have the whole system of equipollent propositions and could make the transition to any one of them.

He then turns to the question as to whether 'If *A* then *B*' is really equipollent to 'It is not the case that *A* without *B*', something that Husserl had disputed in his review of Marty. The answer, Frege claims, is to be found in his *Begriffsschrift* without further ado. It must be understood, he explains, that hypothetical constructions are generally composed of improper propositions such that each proposition is only an "indicative component, and each proposition indicates the other", so that neither the antecedent alone, nor the consequent alone expresses a thought, but the whole propositional complex. Taking the letters '*A*' and '*B*' to stand for proper propositions, we have four combinations: *A* is true and *B* is true; *A* is true and *B* is false; *A* is false and *B* is true; *A* is false and *B* is false, of which the first, third and fourth, but not the second, are compatible with the proposition 'If *A* then *B*'. By negation, Frege concludes, we obtain: *A* is true and *B* is false, or: *A* holds without *B* holding, just as on the right-hand side.

Frege then goes on to say that replacing '*A*' and '*B*' by the propositions '$\Phi(a)$' and '$\Psi(b)$', 'If $\Phi(a)$ then $\Psi(a)$' acquires generality of content, and its negation cancels this generality and says that there is an object (say Δ) such that and $\Psi(\Delta)$ is false. The proposition '$\Phi(a)$ does not hold without $\Psi(a)$ holding' is now understood to read: 'In general, whatever *a* may be, '$\Phi(a)$' does not hold without '$\Psi(a)$'. By negation we obtain: 'It is not in general so that, whatever *a* may be, '$\Phi(a)$' does not hold without '$\Psi(a)$'. In other words: 'There is at least one object (say Δ) such that $\Phi(\Delta)$ is true while $\Psi(\Delta)$ is false'. We get the same as on the left-hand side. So in each case we therefore have an equipollence, he concludes.

Scholz' notes tell us that in the lost November 10th response to Frege's letter, Husserl referred to Bolzano and expressed his views on equipollent propositions and coloring, as well as on logic. A continuation of that letter followed on November 16th. It was in this lost letter, according to Scholz' notes, that Husserl first expressed his views on 'the paradox', by which Scholz thought that he might have meant Russell's paradox.[27]

In a letter dated December 9th,[28] in which there is no mention of Bolzano or 'the paradox' and half of which is about equipollency, Frege writes that Husserl's second letter had prompted him to reply that it seemed to him that for logical analysis to be possible an objective criterion was necessary for recognizing a thought again as the same. Frege said that he considered the only possible means of deciding whether proposition *A* expressed the same thought as proposition *B* to be that if by using only purely logical laws it could be established, without knowing whether the content of *A* or *B* was true or false, that *both* the assumption that the content of *A* was false *and* that of *B* true and the assumption that the content of *A* was true and that of *B* false led to a logical contradiction, then nothing could belong to the content of *A* as far as it was capable of being judged true or false, which did not also belong to the content of *B*. For, there would be no reason at all for any such surplus in the content of *B* and such a surplus would not be logically self-evident either. In the same way, nothing could belong to the content of *B*, as far as it was capable of being judged true or false, except what also belonged to the content of *A*. Thus, Frege concluded, what may be judged true or false in the contents of *A* and *B* was identical, and this alone, the thought expressed by both *A* and *B*, was of concern to logic. This, Frege maintained, was the only means of judging when two propositions express the same thought, or what part of the content of a proposition is subject to logic.[29]

---

27 This mention of Bolzano is found in German editions of Frege's correspondence, but not in the abridged English edition. See *Gottlob Freges Briefwechsel mit D. Hilbert, E. Husserl, B. Russell, sowie ausgewählte Einzelbriefe Freges*, p. 71 n.

28 Frege, *Philosophical and Mathematical Correspondence*, pp. 70-71.

29 In the last long paragraph of his letter, Frege comments on Husserl's statement in his letter that "the form containing 'all' is normally so understood that the existence of objects falling under the subject and predicate concepts is part of what is meant and is presupposed as having been admitted". Now the word 'all', the presupposition of existence and Russell's paradox of the set of all sets that is not a member of itself is one of the themes of Husserl's unpublished writings on sets and Russell's paradox. Unfortunately, though, entering into this here would take us much too far afield.

In reply, Husserl wrote another two-part letter, dated December 21, 1906 - January 13, 1907. According to Scholz, the first part was a continuation of his previous letter in which he expressed his views about hypothetical constructions and brought up the 'paradox' once again; the second part was a reply to Frege's letter. There is no indication that Frege ever replied.

Now, it is quite telling that in these letters Frege has only referred to theories that he developed in his *Begriffsschrift* of 1879. Indeed, it is important to cogitate on this, for it lends support to Dummett's interpretation of Frege's writings of that year. Not only are neither *The Foundations of Arithmetic* nor *The Basic Laws of Arithmetic* ever mentioned in these letters, but there is no mention of such characteristically post-*Begriffsschrift* theories as the famous semantical distinction between sense and reference that had figured so prominently in his 1891 correspondence with Husserl, or Basic Law V and the extensions that in 1894 he had castigated Husserl so severely for eschewing and that Frege later came to blame for undermining the foundations of his logical edifice.[30] Frege certainly does appear to be in full retreat.

Husserl and a paradox of material implication

In the letter to Husserl, Frege affirmed the equivalence of 'If A then B' and material implication because of objections that Husserl had voiced regarding Marty's and Brentano's conviction that 'If *A* then *B*' equaled 'No *A* (or *A* is not true) unless *B*'. "There is not even equivalence (or equipollence) here", Husserl had complained in his review of Marty, "and the test of negation, which surely must yield propositions that once again are of the same truth value, rejects it. Negation of the left-hand side yields: *A can* be true without *B* being true; and of the right: *A is* true without *B* being true". It is only a predisposition to think that belief signifies acknowledgment or denial of existence and is appropriately expressed by the existential "is" or "is not", Husserl argues, that makes it seem that every hypothetical judgment is also purely and simply an existential judgment and can therefore be expressed as an existential proposition without undergoing a change in meaning. There are only a few cases, in which the transition to equipollent existential propositions so approaches

[30] Gottlob Frege, *Translations from the Philosophical Writings of Gottlob Frege,* 3rd ed. Oxford: Blackwell, 1980, p. 214.

natural thinking that the temptation to confuse *logical analysis* (analysis of what is logically contained in the sense of the proposition and is to be logically deduced from it) with *genuine signification analysis* (analysis of what is actually contained in the sense) proves favorable for the existential interpretations, he maintains.[31]

In a note, Husserl wrote of an "interesting and significant paradox" that he had chanced upon about ten years earlier and had led him to undertake a thorough study of hypothetical judgments. He formulates this paradox in the following way: "From the proposition, If *A* then *B*, there obviously follows, No *A* (or *A* is not true) unless *B*. It is also Evident that from the second proposition the first follows. Thus it is totally certain that the propositions are equivalent. But the test of negation on both sides... proves, again with Evidence, that the two propositions are *not* equivalent: a complete contradiction". He then adds: "Now *A* and *B* can signify propositions, but also concepts. Thus we perhaps more precisely read: If the proposition *A* is true, so is the proposition *B*; or, If something is A, then it is B; or If A exists, then B exists...."[32]

In another note to the expression "*genuine signification analysis*" that he has used, Husserl informs readers that by this he means "the purely grammatical" in the sense of his concept of "pure grammar" of Logical Investigation IV.[33] In that investigation about the distinction between independent and non-independent meanings and the idea of pure grammar, Husserl particularly stresses the importance of drawing the line between *meaning analysis*, which distinguishes what is meaningful and intelligible from what is nonsensical, and *logical analysis*, which it is a matter of purely formal, objective compatibility. The latter distinguishes what is formally consistent from what is formally inconsistent, or logically

---

31 Husserl, "Report on German Writings in Logic from the Years 1895-1899, Fifth Article", pp. 299-300.

32 *Ibid.*, p. 299 n. Objections like Husserl's can come of no surprise to modern logicians because such discrepancies between material implication and 'if' are still a subject of controversy today. As Susan Haack has noted, it "seems pretty much agreed" that if 'If A then B' is true, then 'A → B' is true, and though some may hold that 'If A then B' is derivable from 'A→ B', so that 'A→ B' and 'If A then B' are interderivable, if not synonymous, it is highly controversial whether, if 'A→ B' is true, 'If A then B' is true'. See her *Philosophy of Logics*, Cambridge UK: Cambridge University Press, 1978, pp. 36-37.

33 Husserl, *Logical Investigations*, pp. 493-529.

contradictory or paradoxical. For Husserl, *logical* laws were inviolable, analytic laws that showed what held for objects in general, what could be said of the objective validity of meanings purely on the basis of their form alone.

To illustrate his point, he gave examples of meaningless combinations of words like: "a round or". In comparison, "round square" has meaning, but as a logical contradiction fails the logic test.[34] His main point concerning Marty and material implication would then be that, although a hypothetical construction could be *meaningfully* translated into a material implication, that would still run counter to the laws of *logic*, and so court paradox.

This difference between what was meaningful and what was logically admissible was no minor issue for Husserl. The gap between the two had already been impressed upon him as he tried to complete his *Philosophy of Arithmetic* at a time when he maintained close personal and professional ties with Georg Cantor, who was hard at work investigating the paradoxical world of transfinite numbers. Although in the review of Marty it was a matter of meaningful combinations of symbols leading to logical paradox, during the 1890s Husserl had struggled particularly hard with the opposite question of how in mathematical contexts formalization yielded combinations of symbols, like$\sqrt{2}$ or $\sqrt{-1}$, that arithmetically speaking were nonsensical, but could nevertheless be used in calculations without engendering logical contradiction. By 1891, Husserl was already rejecting Frege's answer that such signs or combinations of signs were unfit for scientific use and should be rejected outright.[35]

Frege on grasping logical objects and recognizing them as the same again in a purely logical manner

Now "Husserl's" paradox of material implication may well be 'the paradox' of the missing letters and it is perfectly possible that Husserl was only writing to Frege about it and not at all about anything as dramatic as Russell's paradox. However, for Frege, 'the' paradox was Russell's paradox and, though unmentioned in these letters, it is present just below the surface, for it and equipollency were very much on Frege's mind that year. So it is worthwhile to inquire further into links between Russell's paradox

---

[34] Husserl, *Logical Investigations*, p. 517.

[35] *Ibid.*, pp. 182-85.

and what Frege and Husserl had to say to one another about what is ostensibly the main topic of the letters, equipollency.

The bridge between Frege's 1906 ideas about equipollency and Russell's paradox is to be found by examining the evolution of Frege's ideas about Basic Law V. And study of Frege's December 9th letter actually turns up an important clue as to how to his ideas about equipollency and Basic Law V are connected. There Frege wrote: "an objective criterion is necessary for recognizing a thought as the same, for without it logical analysis is impossible".[36] And he concluded that there was not "any other means of judging what part of the content of a proposition is subject to logic, or when two propositions express the same thought" than through the application of his equipollency test.[37]

Frege had placed the need to apprehend logical objects and to recognize them as the same again at the very heart of his plan to derive arithmetic from logic in *Foundations*. And it was this need that had inspired the leap of faith in extensions that had led him to mandate the paradox producing Basic Law V. Let us take a closer look at his reasoning. In *Foundations*, he defined the problem as follows:

> Since it is only in the context of a proposition that words have any meaning, our problem becomes this: To define the sense of a proposition in which a number word occurs... we have already settled that number words are to be understood as standing for self-subsistent objects. And that is enough to give us a class of propositions which must have a sense, namely those which express our recognition of a number as the same again. If we are to use the symbol *a* to signify an object, we must have a criterion for deciding in all cases whether *b* is the same as *a*.... In our present case, we have to define the sense of the proposition "the number which belongs to the concept *F* is the same as that which belongs to the concept *G*".[38]

Reasoning on, Frege adopted a modified version of Leibniz' principle of substitutivity of identicals as his definition of identity. He recognized, however, that this definition would only afford a means of recognizing an object again in case it should crop up in some other guise, but did not provide for all cases (§66). Adopting this way, he

---

36 Frege, *Philosophical and Mathematical Correspondence*, p. 70.
37 *Ibid.*, p. 71.
38 Gottlob Frege, *The Foundations of Arithmetic*, Oxford: Blackwell, 1980 (1884), §62.

acknowledged, required presupposing that an object can only be given in a single way. But were that so, he realized, all identities would merely amount to a statement that whatever is given to us in the same way is to be reckoned as the same, which is a principle so obvious and so sterile as not to be worth stating. No conclusion could in fact be drawn from it which was not the same as one of the premises. However, if we are able to make use of identities in such diverse fields, he realized, it is surely because we can recognize something as the same again even though it is given in a different way.[39]

So, lucidly recognizing the inadequacy of theories that he had tested up to that point, Frege felt pushed to introduce the extensions[40] that became an indispensable part of the logic of *Basic Laws*.[41] It was Basic Law V that was to guarantee the needed passage from concepts to their extensions. Part Va of that law asserts that if two functions always have the same value for the same argument, then they have the same graph; whatever falls under either one of the two concepts will fall under both. So they are equal in extension. According to Vb, two functions having the same graph, always have the same value for the same arguments; if concepts are equal in extension then whatever falls under one falls under the other.[42]

It was this law that Frege ultimately blamed for Russell's paradox.[43] In his 1903 appendix about it, Frege defines the question raised by Russell's finding as being: "Can we always infer from one concept's coinciding in extension with another concept that any object that falls

---

[39] *Ibid.*, §§65-67.

[40] It is impossible to review here all the steps in Frege's reasoning leading up his introduction of extensions, but I have that elsewhere, notably in my *Rethinking Identity and Metaphysics, Foundations of Analytic Philosophy*, New Haven CT: Yale University Press, 1997, or in "Husserl and Frege on Substitutivity" and "The Varied Sorrows of Logical Abstraction", both in Hill & Rosado Haddock.

[41] Gottlob Frege, *The Basic Laws of Arithmetic I*, Berkeley: University of California Press, 1963 (1893), pp. ix-x.

[42] Frege, *Translations from the Philosophical Writings*, pp. 159-60, 218 n. F; Frege, *The Basic Laws of Arithmetic I*, §§9, 21.

[43] Frege, *Philosophical and Mathematical Correspondence*, pp. 130-31; Frege, *Translations from the Philosophical Writings*, pp. 214-24.

under one falls under the other likewise?".[44] And he answers himself writing:

> If in general, for any first-level concept, we may speak of its extension, then the case arises of concepts having the same extension, although not all objects that fall under one fall under the other as well.
>
> This, however, really abolishes the extension of the concept, in the sense we have given the word. We may not say that in general the expression 'the extension of one concept coincides with that of another' means the same thing as the expression 'all objects that fall under the one concept fall under the other as well, and conversely.'[45]

The only place where the mistake could lie, Frege had found, was in his law Vb, which must therefore be false. Along with Vb, V itself collapses, but not Va.[46]

In the 1906 article on Schoenflies and the logical paradoxes of set theory, Frege explained how in sentences of the form 'If something is a Φ, then it is a Ψ and if something is a Ψ then it is a Φ, we designate mutual subordination which has strong affinities with the first level relation of identity-equality. And this, he further contended, almost ineluctably compels us to transform a sentence in which this mutual subordination is asserted of concepts into a sentence expressing an equality. However, he was aware that it would be necessary to assume an unprovable law authorizing the desired transformation. And he realized that such a law was not as self-evident as is desirable for a law of logic. "And if it was possible for there to be doubts previously", he then confessed, "these doubts have been reinforced by the shock the law has sustained from Russell's paradox".[47]

No longer defending the transformation and his law, in notes published in a 1912 article by Phillip Jourdain, Frege acknowledged that:

---

[44] *Ibid.*, p. 214. Regarding this, in 1904, David Hilbert wrote of Frege and the paradoxes: "he accepts among other things the fundamental principle that a concept (a set) is defined and immediately usable if only it is determined for every object whether the object is subsumed under the concept or not, and here he imposes no restriction on the notion 'every'; he thus exposes himself to precisely the set-theoretic paradoxes that are contained, for example, in the notion of the set of all sets...." David Hilbert, "On the Foundations of Logic and Arithmetic", in *From Frege to Gödel*, Jean van Heijenoort (ed.), Cambridge MA: Harvard University Press, 1967, p. 130.

[45] Frege, *Translations from the Philosophical Writings*, p. 221.

[46] *Ibid.*, p. 219.

[47] Frege, *Posthumous Writings*, pp. 180-81.

> when classes are introduced, a difficulty (Russell's contradiction) arises. In my fashion of regarding concepts as functions, we can treat the principal parts of Logic without speaking of classes, as I have done in my *Begriffsschrift*.... Only with difficulty did I resolve to introduce classes (or extents of concepts) because the matter did not appear to me quite secure – and rightly so, as it turned out. The laws of numbers are to be developed in a purely logical manner. But numbers are objects, and in logic we have only two objects, in the first place: the two truth-values. Our first aim, then, was to obtain objects out of concepts, namely, extents of concepts or classes. By this I was constrained to overcome my resistance and to admit the passage from concepts to their extents. I fell into the error of letting go too easily my initial doubts....[48]

"The prime problem of arithmetic", Frege had concluded in his study of Russell's paradox in the 1903 appendix to *Basic Laws II*, "may be taken to be the problem: How do we apprehend logical objects, in particular numbers? What justifies us in recognizing numbers as objects?"[49] "And even now", he had agonized in the beginning of the appendix, "I do not see how arithmetic can be scientifically established; how numbers can be apprehended as logical objects, and brought under review; unless we are permitted – at least conditionally – to pass from a concept to its extension".[50]

In his 1906 letter to Husserl, Frege is still wrestling with the problem of how to grasp logical objects and to recognize them as the same again in a *purely logical manner*. This is evident in his theories about equipollent propositions, material implication, in the importance that he is still placing on using logic alone to recognize a thought as the same again. Bitten by paradox he has abandoned the course of reasoning adopted in *Foundations* and *Basic Laws* and retreated to the seemingly safer ground of the *Begriffsschrift*.

Husserl on pure logic and actual consciousness

Grasping logical objects and recognizing them as the same again was also one of Husserl's lifelong concerns. But his most basic philosophical convictions had never allowed him to be seduced by the paradox producing line of reasoning that led Frege to embrace extensions and to try to legitimate his involvement with them through Basic Law V. Of the

[48] Philip Jourdain, "Gottlob Frege" (1912), in Frege's *Philosophical and Mathematical Correspondence*, p. 191 n. 29.

[49] Frege, *Translations from the Philosophical Writings*, pp. 224.

[50] *Ibid.*, p. 214.

direction that Frege's thought had taken in *Foundations*, Husserl bluntly stated in *Philosophy of Arithmetic* that he could not see how it might signify an advance in logic and that it was such as to make one wonder how anyone would could hold them as true but in passing.[51]

Husserl's conception of pure logic was substantially different from Frege's. What Frege deemed purely logical analyses, Husserl considered a blind manipulation of symbols. He was firm in the conviction that "logic must not be a mere formal (mathematical) theory… but requires phenomenological and epistemological elucidations in virtue of which we not merely are completely certain of the validity of its concepts and theories, but also truly understand them".[52] His phenomenology would "afford access to the 'sources' from which the fundamental concepts and ideal laws of pure logic proceed and back to which they must be traced in order to procure the necessary clarity and distinctness for a critical epistemological understanding of logic".[53] So Husserl would not have found the ideas about pure logical analysis, equipollency and recognizing when two propositions express the same thought that Frege outlined in his letter any more convincing than his ideas about material implication and equipollency.

Late September 1906 actually found Husserl calling for "a new and large work" to analyze, in connection with the phenomenological theory of judgment, "the essences of the various forms of propositions, which belong, from another viewpoint to the domain of pure grammar". Listed are investigations "concerning pure logic (and pure grammar), the logical calculus… the essence of the categorical propositions well as the existential" and a "comprehensive work on hypothetical judgments and hypothetical inferences",[54] all themes of the correspondence with Frege initiated a month later.

As we have seen, late September 1906 also found Husserl reminiscing about how, while working on the logic of mathematical thought and mathematical calculation in the 1890s, he had been "tormented by those incredibly strange realms: the world of the purely logical and the world

51 Edmund Husserl, *Philosophy of Arithmetic, Psychological and Logical Investigations with Supplementary Texts from 1887-1901*, Dordrecht: Kluwer, 2003, p. 128.
52 Edmund Husserl, "Report on German Writings in Logic from the Years 1895-1899, First Article" (1903), in his *Early Writings in the Philosophy of Logic and Mathematics*, p. 215.
53 Husserl, *Logical Investigations,* "Introduction", Volume II, §1, my translation.
54 Edmund Husserl, "Personal Notes" (1906-1908), in his *Early Writings in the Philosophy of Logic and Mathematics*, p. 495.

of actual consciousness – or… the phenomenological and also the psychological". He had had no idea of how to unite them, he recalled, and yet believed that they had to interrelate and form an intrinsic unity. So he had wracked his "brain concerning, on the one hand the essence of representation and judgment, the theory of relations and so on, and, on the other hand, concerning the elucidation of the interrelationships between the formalism of mathematics and logic". The extension of his efforts to the whole domain of the purely logical, he said, had been occasioned by his work on the logical calculus during the winter of 1890.[55]

In an article of that year, "On the Logic of Signs (Semiotic)", we find him inquiring into the logical justification of symbolic reasoning. It begins with the question: "How is it that one can speak of 'concepts' which one, nevertheless, does not authentically (*eigentlich*) possess, and how is it not absurd that the most certain of all the sciences, arithmetic, is to be based upon such concepts?" He wanted to know "by what *right* do we operate in our practice of judging…, using symbols instead of the true concepts?" He complained that one might "search logical works in vain for light on what really makes such mechanical operations, with mere written characters or word signs, capable of vastly expanding our actual knowledge concerning the number concepts…."[56] His painful struggle to understand and come to terms with paradoxical or seemingly paradoxical results of blindly reasoning with symbols was really the crucible in which many of the most important ideas of the *Logical Investigations* became purified.

Hints of Husserl's answer that logic must not be a mere formal theory, but requires phenomenological and epistemological elucidations in virtue of which we truly understand its concepts and theories[57] were already evident in his interesting reaction to Ernst Schröder's attempt to show in *Vorlesungen über die Algebra der Logik* that bringing all possible objects of thought into a class gives rise to contradictions. In his 1891 review of that work, he argued that it was the *blind* reasoning with the symbols that left one vulnerable to contradiction. He lucidly stressed that:

> in the cases where we simultaneously have, besides certain classes, also classes *of* those classes, the calculus may not be blindly applied. In the sense

---

[55] *Ibid.*, pp. 490-91.

[56] Edmund Husserl, "On the Logic of Signs (Semiotic) 1890)", in his *Early Writings in the Philosophy of Logic and Mathematics*, pp. 20, 37, 50.

[57] Husserl, "Report on German Writings in Logic from the Years 1895-1899, First Article" (1903), p. 215.

> of the calculus of sets as such, any set ceases to have the status of a set as soon as it is considered as an element of another set; and this latter in turn has the status of a set only in relation to its primary and authentic elements, but not in relation to whatever elements *of* those elements there may be. If one does not keep this in mind, then actual errors in inference can arise.[58]

For Husserl, logicians could only submit to a logic which they had thought through and thought through with insight. An epistemology of pure logic had to be developed. On this note, let us turn to our last area of divergence between Frege and Husserl on the matter of equipollency.

Frege on equipollency and Basic Law V

Guillermo Rosado Haddock has made some thought provoking observations about Husserl's and Frege's semantics, equipollency and Basic Law V that illustrate some of the main theses of this paper. Remember that in his letters to Husserl, Frege maintained that if it could be established, without knowing whether the content of *A* or *B* was true or false, that *both* the assumption that the content of *A* was false *and* that of *B* true, and the assumption that the content of *A* was true and that of *B* false, led to a logical contradiction, then nothing could belong to the content of *A* as far as it could be judged true or false, which did not also belong to the content of *B*, and nothing could belong to the content of *B*, as far as it could be judged true or false, except what also belonged to the content of *A*. That meant, Frege believed, that what could be judged true or false in the contents of *A* and *B* was identical.

Now Rosado Haddock has used the fact that Frege's distressing Basic Law V, or Principle V, is an identity statement between statements, and thus a dramatic illustration of Frege's 1906 ideas about equipollency, to show how Frege's semantics of sense and reference proves inadequate with respect to that law. Husserl's semantics of sense and reference, Rosado Haddock maintains, is more fruitful, more detailed than Frege's and can serve to explain some confusions incurred by him.[59] Let us first

---

[58] Edmund Husserl, "Review of Ernst Schröder's *Vorlesungen über die Algebra der Logik*" (1891), in his *Early Writings in the Philosophy of Logic and Mathematics*, pp. 84-85.
[59] See his "On Husserl's Two Notions of Sense", *History and Philosophy of Logic* 7, 1, 1986, pp. 31-41 and "To be a Fregean or to be a Husserlian: That is the Question for Platonists", *Advances in Contemporary Logic and Computer Science*, W. Carnielli and

apply Frege's ideas on equipollency to Basic Law V before turning to Rosado Haddock's ideas about Husserlian and Fregean semantics.

Since readers are familiar with the content of Basic Law V as discussed above, and since for Frege equipollency should be decided independently of the content of the statements anyway, for the purposes of this discussion we can abbreviate the law to read Va = Vb. Now for Frege, the reference of a statement was a truth value, and according to the equipollency test in his letter to Husserl, Va and Vb would only prove equipollent were both true or both false. For Basic Law V to be the true law that it would have had to have been for Frege's system to work, both the reference of Va and the reference of Vb would obviously have to be T. If that could have been so, then Basic Law V would also pass Frege's equipollency test.

However, Frege ultimately concluded that although the truth value of Va was T, the truth value of Vb was F. This being so, then the assumption that the content of Va is false and that of Vb true leads to a logical contradiction, but the assumption that the content of Va is true and that of Vb false does not. So, according to Frege's theory, something belongs to the content of Va as far as it is capable of being judged true or false that does not also belong to the content of Vb, and something may belong to the content of Vb, as far as it is capable of being judged true or false that does not belong to the content of Va.

Frege would thus be obliged to conclude that what may be judged true or false in the contents of Va and Vb was not identical and his law failed his equipollency test. Since in his letter to Husserl, Frege says that he thinks that his equipollency test is the only possible means of judging what part of the content of a proposition is subject to logic, or when two propositions express the same thought, and that without such an objective criterion logical analysis is impossible, he is once more tacitly confessing that Basic Law V could not fulfil the role that it was designed to fulfil.

Husserl on states of affairs and situations of affairs

Now, in a number of articles, Rosado Haddock has argued that the official Fregean semantics of sense and reference according to which the sense of a statement is the thought that it expresses and its referent is a truth value cannot adequately deal with certain important semantical

---

I. D'Ottaviano (eds.), American Mathematical Society, 1999, cited as found in Hill & Rosado Haddock, pp. 58, 202, 213-15.

issues. To make his point, he has drawn attention to Husserl's semantical distinction between state of affairs (*Sachverhalt*) and situation of affairs (*Sachlage*).[60] He attributes certain ambiguities present in Frege's theory of sense to "the fact that – contrary to Husserl – he lacked the notion of a state of affairs, which… lies between the thought and the situation of affairs and prevents them from collapsing into each other".[61]

In the *Logical Investigations*, Rosado Haddock explains, Husserl, like Frege, distinguished between the sense and the reference of statements. But for Husserl the referent of a statement was

> not a truth value, but a state of affairs (*Sachverhalt*). Although it is true that the predicates 'is true' and 'is false' apply to thoughts, this does not make them, according to Husserl, the reference of assertive sentences. Thus, the sentence 'The earth is round' refers to the state of affairs that the earth is round. Different sentences can refer to the same state of affairs by means of different propositions (thoughts).[62]

Rosado Haddock takes Frege's well known example of 'The morning star is a planet' and 'The evening star is a planet' to illustrate Husserl's point. For Frege, these statements express different thoughts, and when a proper name is substituted for another in a statement, only the truth value remains invariant. For Husserl, however, the referent of both statements is the state of affairs that Venus is a planet, which also remains invariant when going from one of the statements to the other.[63]

In addition, though, Rosado Haddock explains, Husserl came to teach "that there are important invariance relations between sentences that are not adequately described either as relations of invariance of states of affairs, or as relations of invariance of truth value, nor as relations of invariance of thought".[64] Using an example from arithmetic, $5 + 3 > 6 + 1$,

---

[60] Husserl began alluding to this distinction in his *Logical Investigations*, Investigation IV §11. Other references are to his *Vorlesungen über Bedeutungslehre Sommersemester 1908*, Dordrecht: Kluwer, 1987, §§ 7, 30b and his *Experience and Judgment*, London: Routledge and Kegan Paul, 1973 (1939), §59.

[61] Hill & Rosado Haddock, p. 215.

[62] Guillermo Rosado Haddock, "Remarks on Sense and Reference in Frege and Husserl", *Kant-Studien* 73, Heft 4 December, 1982, pp. 425-39, Hill & Rosado Haddock, p. 34.

[63] Hill & Rosado Haddock, pp. 34, 209.

[64] *Ibid.*, p. 61.

Rosado Haddock points out that the state of affairs referred to in this case is that number 8 is greater than the number 7 and that it remains invariant if we substitute the expression '9 – 1' for the expression '5 + 3' or the expression '3 + 4' for the expression '6 + 1'. He then looks at 6 + 1 < 5 + 3, which is not obtained from 5 + 3 > 6 +1 by mere substitution of an expression for another expression differing in sense but having the same referent. Here '<' and '>' do not refer to the same state of affairs. But apart from the truth value, which they share with any other true statement whatsoever, Husserl has pointed out, these statements have in common the *abstract* situation of affairs, a certain proto-relation of which they are categorizations that also remains invariant under transformations of statements in which expressions are substituted for expressions with different sense but the same reference.[65]

Thus Husserl, Rosado Haddock emphasizes, has proposed an invariance principle stronger than Frege's.[66] For the state of affairs and the situation of affairs remain invariant under substitutions that affect only the senses but not the reference.[67] It is unprovable, Rosado Haddock points out in support of Husserl's new distinction, "that by transforming statements into statements by way of substituting expressions for expressions with different senses but the same reference only the truth value remains invariant".[68] And it is easy, "to imagine sorts of transformations of sentences that affect the state of affairs and the situation of affairs without affecting the truth value of the sentence".[69]

Moreover, the situation of affairs is a sort of referential basis of the state of affairs that even remains invariant under transformations of statements that could change the state of affairs referred to by the statement.[70] When we say that we have the same physical law expressed in two different but equivalent ways, what we mean according to Husserl,[71] Rosado Haddock points out, is that the situation of affairs is the same, even though the states of affairs that the two expressions refer to may

65 *Ibid.*, p. 209.
66 *Ibid.*, p. 37.
67 *Ibid.*, p. 35.
68 *Ibid.*, p. 211.
69 *Ibid.*, p. 36.
70 *Ibid.*, p. 209.
71 Husserl, *Vorlesungen über Bedeutungslehre Sommersemester 1908*, §30b.

vary.[72] It seems unavoidable, Rosado Haddock deems, "for an adequate semantic analysis of mathematics to distinguish the abstract situation of affairs of mathematical statements both from the state of affairs referred to by them and from their truth value".[73]

Looking at Frege's highly problematic Basic Law V,[74] Rosado Haddock observes that, in spite of what some scholars have conjectured, the "statements at either side of the identity sign of Principle V have different senses. Moreover, none is obtained from the substitution of an expression for another expression having different sense but the same referent. Thus they do not even refer to the same state of affairs. But if Principle V were true, its two sides would have in common not only the truth value – which they would have in common with denumerably many statements expressible in conceptual notations – but also the situation of affairs".[75]

Rosado Haddock's conclusion? Frege's lack of the notion of a state of affairs lying between the thought and the situation of affairs and preventing them from collapsing one into the other contributed to the semantical confusion that contaminated Basic Law V.[76] Comparing Husserl's and Frege's choices, Rosado Haddock finds that "Frege's candidate has the advantage of simplicity. Actually, it is the simplest possible choice. But it has the disadvantage of not being very informative, since it obviates important semantic relations between sentences not reducible to sameness or difference of truth value (in the actual world). Both of Husserl's candidates are informative and nontrivial".[77] "Thus, after all," Rosado Haddock finds, "also as a semanticist Frege fell short of being a Husserlian".[78]

Conclusion

The paradox of Husserl's lost letters and Scholz' notes is probably only the paradox of material implication that Husserl discusses in his article on Marty. Husserl's use of the definite article and the singular form of the noun (in spite of what the English translation says) indicates that

---

[72] Hill & Rosado Haddock, p. 210.
[73] *Ibid.*, p. 63.
[74] *Ibid.*, pp. 58-60; 208-15.
[75] *Ibid.*, p. 214.
[76] *Ibid.*, p. 215.
[77] *Ibid.*, pp. 37-38.
[78] *Ibid.*, p. 215.

he was referring to a specific paradox and that Frege knew which one this was. The fact remains, though, that for philosophers and mathematicians in 1906 (including Husserl, as his unpublished writings on Russell's paradox show), *the* paradox was Russell's paradox and the topics that Frege chose to address in the extant letters are plainly connected with his ruminations about the paradox derived within his own system.

Here I have discussed three deep-rooted and longstanding differences between Husserl's and Frege's basic approaches to pure logic that are present beneath the surface of what is said in the letters that we have. These differences concern Husserl's ideas about avoiding paradoxical consequences by shunning three potentially paradox-producing practices that Frege espoused. Specifically, Husserl saw the need for: 1) correctly drawing the line between meaning analyses and logical analyses; 2) an epistemology of pure logic; 3) a subtler understanding of the semantics of statements than Frege ever proposed.

My study is part of a larger, ongoing project to lend insight into the questions that Russell's paradox raises for logic and epistemology once signaled by Kurt Gödel,[79] a secret admirer of Husserl's work.[80] Like Husserl, Gödel believed that the certainty of mathematics was to be secured not by the manipulation of physical symbols, but by acquiring a deeper understanding of the abstract concepts that lead to the setting up of these systems and by seeking insight into the solvability and actual methods of solving all meaningful mathematical problems. He saw phenomenology as "a procedure or technique that should produce in us a new state of consciousness in which we describe in detail the basic concepts we use in our thought, or grasp other basic concepts hitherto unknown to us".[81] He believed that Husserl's theories could "safeguard for mathematics the certainty of its knowledge" and "uphold the belief that for clear questions posed by reason, reason can also find clear answers".[82]

---

[79] Kurt Gödel, "What is Cantor's continuum problem", in his *Collected Works* II, New York: Oxford University Press, 1990 (1964), p. 258.

[80] See Hao Wang's books: *Beyond Analytic Philosophy*, Cambridge MA: M.I.T. Press, 1986; his *Reflections on Kurt Gödel*, Cambridge MA: M.I.T. Press, 1987; and his *A Logical Journey, From Gödel to Philosophy*, Cambridge MA: M.I.T. Press, 1996.

[81] Kurt Gödel, "The Modern Development of the Foundations of Mathematics in the Light of Philosophy", in his *Collected Works* III, New York: Oxford University Press, 1995, p. 383.

[82] *Ibid.*, p. 381.

The judgment that David Hilbert passed on Frege's efforts can help set some of Husserl's ideas into perspective. Explicitly contrasting his own views with those of Frege, on more than one occasion, Hilbert stressed that Frege's efforts were bound to fail because:

> No more than any other science can mathematics be founded by logic alone; rather, as a condition for the use of logical inferences and the performance of logical operations, something must already be given to us in our faculty of representation [*in der Vorstellung*], certain extralogical concrete objects that are intuitively [*anschaulich*] present as immediate experience prior to all thought. If logical inference is to be reliable, it must be possible to survey these objects completely in all their parts, and the fact that they occur, that they differ from one another, and that they follow each other, or are concatenated, is immediately given intuitively, together with the objects, as something that neither can be reduced to anything else nor requires reduction.[83]

Frege's entire line of reasoning regarding pure logic always ran counter to Husserl's deepest convictions that philosophical logicians could not be satisfied with developing pure logic as a mere formal, mathematical theory, as an expanding system of propositions with naive objective validity, but that they had to go further and strive for philosophical clarity with respect to their propositions and objective forms of validity. They needed insight into the essence of the ways of knowing involved in the use and application of these propositions and into the way logicians interacted with both the objective structures of formal logic and mathematics and those of extralogical reality. From a Husserlian perspective, failure to investigate these matters would and did leave Frege vulnerable to paradoxical consequences that he could not have overcome and still hold fast to his views about pure logic. For Husserl, Frege's ideas about pure logic were shortsighted, if not downright blind.

---

[83] This was to be the basic philosophical conviction that Hilbert considered requisite for mathematics and all scientific thinking, understanding and communication in general. See his "The Foundations of Mathematics", pp. 464-65 and "On the Infinite", *From Frege to Gödel*, van Heijenoort (ed.), pp. 376, 392

8

HUSSERL ON SETS AND THE CAUSES OF THE SET-THEORETICAL PARADOXES[1]

Introduction

The full story of set theory's role in shaping modern logic and in redrawing the boundaries between mathematics and philosophy in both the analytical and the phenomenological traditions is yet to be told and its full implications drawn. In particular, the fact that Edmund Husserl thought and taught about it well before the logic shaped by Bertrand Russell's and Alfred North Whitehead's *Principia Mathematica* came to play a key role in laying the foundations for analytic philosophy has barely been investigated.

Husserl searched for clarity about the meaning of sets all throughout his career. For example, in his late work *Formal and Transcendental Logic*, he described his first book, *Philosophy of Arithmetic*, as an initial attempt on his part "to obtain clarity regarding the original genuine meaning of the fundamental concepts of the theory of sets and cardinal numbers".[2] He was well-versed in the set theories being created by his contemporaries and lucid about their logical, epistemological and ontological implications. As a colleague and good friend of Georg Cantor, the creator of set theory, during the last fourteen years of the nineteenth century, he had a front row seat at the creation of set theory and the discovery of the paradoxes of the transfinite. So he was sort of a victim *avant la lettre* of the crisis in foundations that broke out once Bertrand Russell publicized the famous contradiction about the set of all sets that are not members of themselves that he discovered while studying Cantor's theories. Then, appointed to the University of Göttingen in 1901, Husserl engaged in exchanges with mathematicians who knew the set-theoretical paradoxes before Russell did. In November 1903, David Hilbert wrote to Gottlob Frege that

---

[1] This was originally a paper entitled "Husserlian Sets or Fregean Sets?" presented at the XVI Coloquio Conesul de Filosofia das Ciencias Formais, Teoria dos Conjuntos/Mereologia, held from November 6-10, 2012 in Santa Maria/RS, Brazil.

[2] Edmund Husserl, *Formal and Transcendental Logic*, The Hague: Martinus Nijhoff, 1969 (1929), §27a.

Russell's antinomy was already known in Göttingen, that Ernst Zermelo had found it three or four years earlier after having learned of other, even more convincing, contradictions from Hilbert himself as many as four or five years before.[3] As discussed in Chapter 3, concrete evidence corroborating Zermelo's finding of the paradox is found in a note he sent to Husserl in April 1902.[4]

Guillermo Rosado Haddock drew attention to Husserl's notes on set theory[5] in his 1973 doctoral thesis,[6] but this did not arouse any excitement. Here I seek to provide the conceptual framework for interpreting Husserl's statements in those notes that: 1) the set-theoretical paradoxes show that his contemporaries did not yet have the real and genuine concept of set needed; 2) that if one is clear and distinct with respect to meaning, one readily sees the contradiction involved in the set-theoretical paradoxes; and 3) that the solution to them would lie in demonstrating the shift of meaning that makes it that one is not immediately aware of the contradiction and that once one perceives it one cannot indicate wherein it lies.

To do this I present those of Husserl's ideas that I think are necessary for interpreting those statements. To this I juxtapose issues involved in Frege's use of the extensions that lead to the contradiction about the set of all sets that are not members of themselves within his system and the conclusions that he and Russell came to regarding the causes of that contradiction. Finally, I interpret Husserl's statements in light of what I

---

[3] Gottlob Frege, *Philosophical and Mathematical Correspondence*, Oxford: Blackwell, 1980, p. 51; Volker Peckhaus and Reinhard Kahle, "Hilbert's Paradox", *Report No. 38, 2000/2001*. Institut Mittag-Leffler, The Royal Swedish Academy of Sciences.

[4] Edmund Husserl, "Memorandum of a Verbal Communication from Zermelo to Husserl", in his *Early Writings in the Philosophy of Logic and Mathematics*, Dordrecht: Kluwer, 1994, p. 442; Bernhard Rang and Wolfgang Thomas, "Zermelo's Discovery of Russell's Paradox", *Historia Mathematica* 8, 1981, pp. 16-22.

[5] Edmund Husserl, *Ms A 1 35*, untitled, undated manuscript on set theory available at the Husserl Archives in Cologne, Leuven, and Paris, now partially published in German by Carlos Ierna and Dieter Lohmar as "Husserl's Manuscript A I 35", in Guillermo Rosado Haddock (ed.), *Husserl and Analytic Philosophy*, Berlin: de Gruyter, 2016, pp. 289-319.

[6] Guillermo Rosado Haddock, *Edmund Husserls Philosophie der Logik und Mathematik im Lichte der gegenwärtigen Logik und Grundlagenforschung*, Doctoral Thesis, Rheinischen Friedrich-Wilhelms-Universität zu Bonn, 1973.

have said. My remarks are not about mathematics *per se*, but about set theory and the foundations of analytic philosophy and phenomenology.

Logical laws and laws of meaning

By the time he wrote the *Logical Investigations* in the late 1890s, Husserl considered it very important to distinguish between logical laws and laws of meaning. According to him, logical laws serve to guard against formal or analytical contradiction, what he called *Widersinn*.[7] What violates logical laws, what is contradictory (*widersinnig*), genuinely has a coherent meaning and can be determined to be true or false. However, though meaning is there, no existing object can correspond to the meaning. As examples of contradictions (*Widersinnigkeiten)*, he gave expressions like 'wooden iron', 'round square', 'all squares have five corners' that have meaning, but no object. No thing or fact such as is described by such expressions exists or can exist.[8] In his notes on set theory, Husserl studied the sentences, 'The present emperor of France is blond' and 'The present emperor of France is not blond'. 'The present emperor is blond' implies that France presently has a blond emperor and she has no emperor at all. He contended that the sentence is not valid, because it is objectless, in actual fact or owing to a contradiction.

Along these same lines, he maintained that to the objection that there is no set that contains itself as an element, one need merely respond that that is *widersinnig.*[9]

In contrast to logical laws, laws of meaning serve to distinguish meaningfulness from meaninglessness, sense from nonsense, by providing pure logic with possible coherent, meaningful meaning forms whose formal truth or falsehood and reference to objects logical laws determine. Meanings, Husserl repeated over and over, are governed by *a priori* laws that regulate how they may be combined, fit together and constitute meaningful, coherent meanings instead of chaotic nonsense (*Unsinn*). The impossibility of combining meanings in certain ways is not subjective, but objective, ideal and grounded in the pure essence of meaning.

---

7 See p. 93, n. 16 regarding the hard problems surrounding the translation of the words '*Widersinn*' and '*widersinnig*', '*Widersinnigkeit*' and my choice to use the German words.

8 Edmund Husserl, *Logical Investigations*, London: Routledge and Kegan Paul, 1970 (1900/01), Investigation IV.

9 Husserl, *Ms A 1 35.*

Husserl believed that the primitive, essential distinction between dependent and independent meanings formed the necessary basis for discovering the essential categories of meaning in which were grounded a number of essential laws of meaning. He, like Frege before him and Russell after him, stressed that fundamental differences between dependent meanings and independent meanings lying concealed behind inconspicuous grammatical distinctions are inviolable because they are "founded deep in the nature of things".

Husserl studied how one may be led astray by the fact that meanings of each category may figure in the subject position otherwise reserved for substantival meanings. The words are definitely in the subject position, but their meanings are not the same as they normally are. Not just any meaning can be substituted for *S* or for *p*. Once meaning categories are violated, the coherency of the meaning is lost. The underlining on Husserl's copies of Frege's "Concept and Object" and "Function and Concept" shows Husserl's fundamental agreement with Frege on this matter.[10]

A natural order in formal logic

As discussed at length in Chapter 4, Husserl found a natural order in formal logic and broadened its domain to include two levels above traditional Aristotelian logic, which he saw as being but a small area of pure logic that needed to be distinguished and segregated from the extended sphere of pure logic that includes the mathematical disciplines and is immense in range and wealth of content in comparison. He considered his understanding of the structure of the world of pure logic to be a radical clarification of the relationship between formal logic and formal mathematics and that it led to a definitive clarification of the sense of pure formal mathematics as a pure analytics of non-contradiction.[11]

On the first level of Husserl's hierarchy, the traditional Aristotelian logic of subject and predicate propositions and states of affairs deals with what is stated about objects in general from a possible perspective. In the disciplines of the two higher levels, it is no longer a question of objects as such about which one might predicate something, but of investigating what is valid for higher order objective constructions that are determined

[10] Husserl's copies of these articles are consultable at the Husserl Archives in Leuven, Belgium.

[11] Edmund Husserl, *Introduction to Logic and Theory of Knowledge, Lectures 1906/07*, Dordrecht: Springer, 2008, §§18-19; Husserl, *Formal and Transcendental Logic*, p. 11.

in purely formal terms and deal with objects in indeterminate, general ways.[12]

On the second level, Husserl located the basic concepts of mathematics, the theory of cardinal numbers, the theory of ordinals, set theory, mathematical physics, formal pure logic, pure geometry, geometry as *a priori* theory of space, the axioms of geometry as a theory of the essences of shapes, of spatial objects, but also the pure theory of meaning and being, *a priori* real ontology of any kind, ontology of nature, ontology of minds, natural scientific ontology, the sciences of value, pure ethics, the logic of morality, the ontology of ethical personalities, axiology or the pure logic of values, pure esthetics, ontology of values, the logic of the ideal state or the ideal world government as a system of cooperating ideal nation states, or the science of the ideal state, the ideal of a valuable existence, objective axioms (relating to *a priori* propositions as truth for objects, as something belonging in the objective science of these objects, or of objects in general in formal universality, essence-propositions about objects insofar as they are objective truths and as truths have their place in a truth-system in general.[13]

The third level is that of his theory of manifolds,[14] which we shall not be concerned with here. The key thing to realize at this point is that, according to Husserl's theory, sets and numbers function in an entirely different way on the first level than in set theory and arithmetic, which Husserl found on the second level.

In the case of numbers, in expressions of the first level, for example, '2 men', '3 houses', numbers occur as form, but not as independent objects about which something is predicated. In that case, the sentence "Jupiter has four moons", to use Frege's example in the *Foundations of Arithmetic*,[15] is a statement about Jupiter's moons in which the number characteristic four occurs as form and is thereby dependent. If one says w and x and y and z are φ, Husserl explained, then one has combined the objects $w \ldots z$

---

[12] Husserl, *Introduction to Logic and Theory of Knowledge*, 18c.

[13] Husserl, *Introduction to Logic and Theory of Knowledge*, §§18-19, pp. 434-35; his *Logic and General Theory of Science 1917/18, with supplementary texts from the first version of 1910/11*, Cham, Switzerland: Springer, 2019 (1996), Chapter 11.

[14] Husserl, *Logical Investigations, Prolegomena*, §§69-70; his *Ideas, General Introduction to Pure Phenomenology* (1913), New York: Colliers, 1962; his *Logic and General Theory of Science*, §§71-72; his *Formal and Transcendental Logic*, §33.

[15] Gottlob Frege, *The Foundations of Arithmetic*, Oxford: Blackwell, 2nd rev. ed., 1986 (1884), §57.

by 'and'. The 'and' is form and grounds the coherent form of the plural predication. Corresponding to this is a cardinal number, which is a new thought configuration. It is one thing, he stressed, to make statements about objects in which number properties occur as form, and are thereby dependent, and another thing to make statements about numbers as such in such a way that the numbers are the objects. We can make such forms independent, but then new higher order objects, hypostatizations of forms, emerge that are not objects in their own right. This is why numbers function entirely differently in the propositional logic of the first level than they do in the arithmetic of the second level, where statements about numbers in which numbers are the objects are found, for example:

1. "Any number can be added to any number".
2. "If *a* is a number and *b* a number, then *a* + *b* is as well".
3. "Any number can be decreased or increased by one".
4. "The numbers form a series continuing from 0 *in infinitum*".[16]

Analytics

Instead of pure logic, Husserl taught, one might speak of analytics, or the science of what is analytically knowable in general, the science that establishes and systematically grounds analytic laws.[17] He conceived of the second level of pure logic as an expanded, completely developed analytics in which one proceeds in a purely formal manner since every single concept used is analytic. One calculates, reasons deductively, with concepts and propositions. Signs and rules of calculation suffice because each procedure is purely logical. One manipulates signs that acquire their meaning in the game through the rules of the game. One may proceed mechanically in this way and the result will prove accurate and justified.[18]

In his logic courses, Husserl taught that the mathematical disciplines of the purely logical sphere proceed from given, purely logical concepts and axioms that are grounded in the essence of purely logical categories. It is a matter of a rigorously scientific, a priori theory that builds from

---

16 Husserl, *Introduction to Logic and Theory of Knowledge*, §18c.

17 Edmund Husserl, *Alte und neue Logik, Vorlesung 1908/09*, Dordrecht: Kluwer, 2003, p. 244.

18 Husserl, *Introduction to Logic and Theory of Knowledge*, §§18-19, pp. 434-35; Husserl, *Logic and General Theory of Science*, Chapter 11.

the bottom up and derives the manifold of possible inferences from the axiomatic foundations a priori in a rigorously deductive way.[19]

From the late 1890s on, Husserl held that the "*world of the mathematical and purely logical is a world of ideal objects*, a world of 'concepts'.... *There all truth is nothing other than analysis of essences or concepts*", and pure logical, mathematical laws are laws of essence.[20]

In affirming this, he wanted to make it clear that he was not hypostatizing ideal entities or talking about the unwelcome, obscure "special and irreducible intermediary entities called meanings" that the preeminent analytic philosopher Quine called "illusory".[21]

Husserl said that it was his failure "to obtain clarity regarding the original genuine meaning of the fundamental concepts of the theory of sets and cardinal numbers" in *Philosophy of Arithmetic* that had "compelled" him to recognize the purely logical ideal.[22] It is worthwhile pointing out in this regard that in Russell's article on the philosophical implications of mathematical logic that is translated in Husserl's notes on set theory, Russell affirmed that "all knowledge which is obtained by reasoning, needs logical principles which are *a priori* and universal" and that mathematics and logic force us "to admit a kind of realism in the scholastic sense... to admit that there is a world of universals and of truths which do not bear directly on such and such a particular existence".[23]

Husserl said that his concepts of ideal meanings and contents and the idea of transferring all of the mathematical and a major part of the traditionally logical to the realm of the ideal derived from Hermann Lotze, who had been Frege's teacher. Husserl repeatedly defended the view, which he attributed to Lotze, that pure arithmetic is a branch of logic that had undergone independent development. He taught that the unending profusion of theories that arithmetic develops is already fixed, enfolded in

---

19 Edmund Husserl, *Logik, Vorlesung 1902/03*, Dordrecht: Kluwer, 2001, pp. 32-35, 39; Husserl, *Introduction to Logic and Theory of Knowledge*, §§13c, 19d, 25b.

20 Husserl, *Introduction to Logic and Theory of Knowledge*, §13c.

21 Willard Quine, "On What There Is" (1948), pp. 11-12 and "Two Dogmas of Empiricism" (1953), p. 22 of his *From a Logical Point of View* (2nd rev.), New York: Harper & Row, 1961.

22 Husserl, *Formal and Transcendental Logic*, §27a, §24 and note; his *Introduction to the Logical Investigations, A Draft of a Preface to the Logical Investigations*, The Hague: Martinus Nijhoff, 1975 (1913), pp. 34-35.

23 Bertrand Russell, *Essays in Analysis*, London: Allen & Unwin, 1973, pp. 292-93.

the arithmetical axioms, and deduction effects the unfolding of them following systematic, simple procedures. Each genuine axiom is a proposition that unfolds the idea of cardinal number from some side or unfolds some of the ideas inseparably connected with the idea of cardinal number.[24]

(This is not necessary to my argument here, but because of the literature making Husserl into a sort of Brouwerian intuitionist,[25] it needs to be made clear that Husserl repeatedly, explicitly and emphatically stressed that, because they belong in the world of the purely logical, arithmetic and set theory are not phenomenology. He maintained that as long as we remain in pure theory of meaning and being, we need not concern ourselves at all with cognitive formations, with consciousness. He believed that everything 'purely' logical was an 'in itself,' an 'ideal' that included in its proper essential content (*Wesengehalt*) nothing mental, nothing of acts, subjects, or empirically factual persons of actual reality. He believed that in the case of pure logic, of an 'analytics' in the broadest, radical sense of the word, only certain of the most general cognitive formations enter the picture for purposes of phenomenological elucidation.)[26]

Husserl on sets and the set-theoretical paradoxes

So how do Husserl's ideas about sets and the set-theoretical paradoxes fit into the conceptual framework I have just described?

First, it is imperative to keep in mind that sets have an entirely different meaning in the subject-predicate propositions of the first level of Husserl's hierarchy than they do in the set theory of the second level. In the theory of proposition forms or forms of states of affairs of the first level, individual objects are the terms of the predication. Sets, however, do not occur as objects in the subject-predicate propositions, but function in them as dependent forms.

In contrast, in the set theory of the second level, truth is the analysis of essences or concepts, where "we make judgments universally about sets

[24] Edmund Husserl, *Logik, Vorlesung 1896*, Dordrecht: Kluwer, 2001, pp. 241-42, 271-72; his *Logik, Vorlesung 1902/03*, pp. 19, 32-35, 39; his *Introduction to Logic and Theory of Knowledge*, §15.

[25] For example: Richard Tieszen, *Mathematical Intuition, Phenomenology and Mathematical Knowledge*, Dordrecht: Kluwer, 1989; Mark van Atten, *Brouwer Meets Husserl. On the Phenomenology of Choice Sequences*, Dordrecht: Springer, 2007.

[26] Husserl, *Introduction to the Logical Investigations*, pp. 20, 31.

that in a certain way are higher order objects. We do not make judgments directly about elements, but about whole totalities of elements and arbitrary elements, and the whole totalities, the sets to be precise, are the objects-about-which.

As seen in Chapter 4, he gave these examples of statements about sets on the second level:

1. "2 sets can each be joined into a new set".

2. "2 sets *a b* are each related to one another in such a way that either *a* is part of *b* or *b* is part of *a*, or that they intersect (a set having a part in common), or that it turns out that they are identical, coincide".

3. "The set formed of the elements *A B C* is part of the set formed of the elements *A B C D* containing "more elements".[27]

On the second level, set theory is derived analytically from the concept of set, which if it is to be mathematical must have a "set essence" in view. This set essence is expressed in the relation between a set itself and its elements. An essence relation makes it impossible for the members of the relation to be identical. So it belongs essentially to the concept of set that no set can contain itself as an element without contradiction.

For Husserl, it is part of the idea of set to be a unit, a whole, comprising certain members as parts in such a way that it is something new that is first formed by them. It belongs essentially to the concept of whole that no whole can contain itself as a part. So, as a kind of whole, a set is subject to the formal rules governing wholes and parts that stipulate that a whole cannot, without contradiction, be its own part. So no set can contain itself as a member. Sets are *a priori* different from their members.[28]

Husserl's 1902 exchange with Zermelo turned upon remarks that Husserl had made in 1891, in his review of Ernst Schröder's *Vorlesungen über die Algebra der Logik*,[29] where Schröder had tried to show that bringing all possible objects of thought into a class gives rise to contradictions. In his review, Husserl wrote that in "the sense of the calculus of sets as such, any set ceases to have the status of a set as soon as it is considered as an element of another set; and this latter in turn has the status of a set

27 Husserl, *Introduction to Logic and Theory of Knowledge*, §§18-19.

28 Husserl, *Ms A 1 35*.

29 Edmund Husserl, "Review of Ernst Schröder's *Vorlesungen über die Algebra der Logik*", in his *Early Writings in the Philosophy of Logic and Mathematics*, pp. 52-91.

only in relation to its primary and authentic elements, but not in relation to whatever elements *of* those elements there may be". He warned that if "one does not keep this in mind, then actual errors in inference can arise".[30]

Third, Husserl repeatedly relegated the set theoretical paradoxes to the category of *Widersinnigkeiten*. For him, a set that contains itself as an element was *widersinnig*. By saying that the set of all sets that were not members of themselves is a *Widersinnigkeit*, Husserl was putting it into the same category as the round square, the golden mountain, and the present emperor of France. The formal logical construction "set of all sets which do not contain themselves as parts", he argued, may not be presupposed to be about something that already exists. Just as it is contradictory for a whole to be its own part at the same time, so it is contradictory for a set to be its own member. It proceeds from the paradox that a set that contains itself as an element or a set that does not must be a *Widersinn*. The classification is *widersinnig* as well.

Of what he referred to as "Zermelo's paradox", Husserl wrote that Zermelo argued that a set M that contains each of its partial sets as elements is an inconsistent set. 1) We consider those partial sets that do not contain themselves as elements. 2) In their entirety these form a set M′ that is contained in M. 3) M′ is thus an element of M. 4) M′ is not an element of M′. Proof: were M′ an element of M′, then it would contain a partial set of M (namely M′) that contains itself as element. However, M′ is to contain *ex definitione* partial sets of M that do not contain themselves as elements. 5) Thus M′, since it is not an element of M′, is a partial set of M, which does not contain itself not as element. But all such sets are *ex definitione* contained in the concept of M′, thus in opposition to 4. But M′ is an element of M′. We come to a direct contradiction. If it essentially belongs to the concept of set that (without contradiction) no set can contain itself as an element, then M′ and M are identically the same set, and we show that the whole reasoning was untenable.[31]

[30] Husserl, "Review of Ernst Schröder's *Vorlesungen über die Algebra der Logik*", pp. 84-85 and his "Memorandum of a Verbal Communication from Zermelo to Husserl", p. 442; Rang & Thomas, "Zermelo's Discovery of Russell's Paradox".

[31] Husserl, *Ms A 1 35.*

Frege's recourse to extensions

Husserl, Frege and Russell came to many of the same conclusions about the causes of the set-theoretical paradoxes, so we now need to look at the reasoning that led Frege to introduce sets and at Russell's struggles to avoid the contradiction derivable in Frege's system.

Frege thought that wherever we are concerned about truth, we must attach a reference to proper names and concept-words and that we are making a mistake that can easily vitiate our thinking if we do not do this. So he considered the prime problem of arithmetic to be that of how one apprehends logical objects, in particular numbers.

Operating only on the first level of Husserl's hierarchy, Frege argued that numbers were independent objects that must always be conceived substantivally and not as dependent attributes. He believed that the presence of the definite article 'the' in an expression like 'the number 4' served to class it as an object and that in arithmetic this independence comes out at every turn, as for example in an identity like 4 + 4 = 8. He thought that we should not be "deterred by the fact that, in the language of everyday life, number appears also in attributive constructions" for that "can always be got around". He proposed that:

> "Jupiter has four moons" can be converted into "the number of Jupiter's moons is four"... we can say: "the number of Jupiter's moons is the number four, or 4". Here "is" has the sense of "is identical with" or "is the same as". So that what we have is an identity, stating that the expression "the number of Jupiter's moons" signifies the same object as the word "four".[32]

He added that the independence that he was "claiming for number was not to be taken to mean that a number word signifies something when removed from the context of a proposition, but only to preclude the use of such words as predicates or attributes, which appreciably alters their meaning".

Seeing that many of the inferences that could be made by appealing to his formula for treating what is dependent as independent led to evidently false or nonsensical conclusions, or were sterile and unproductive, Frege settled for the definition: "The Number which belongs to the concept F is the extension of the concept 'concept equal to the concept F'" and for his

[32] Frege, *The Foundations of Arithmetic*, §57.

axiom of extensionality, which he considered to be "an unprovable law" authorizing a transformation to "take place, in which concepts correspond to extensions of concepts…".[33]

Upon learning of the contradiction about the set of all sets that are not members of themselves that Russell derived in the system of *The Basic Laws of Arithmetic*, Frege tested the validity of the chain of inferences leading up to the contradiction and concluded that his law about extensions was false. He confessed that he had been reluctant to use classes, but had found no other answer to the question as to how to apprehend logical objects.[34]

He later described the shift of meaning that had made him not immediately aware of the contradiction. The paradoxes of set theory arise, he said, because a concept is connected with something that is called the set which appears to be determined by the concept and determined as an object. Such a transformation of a concept into an object is inadmissible, because the set formed only seems to be an object, while in truth there is no such object at all. He summed up the "essence of the procedure which leads to the thicket of contradictions":

> The objects that fall under F are regarded as a whole, as an object and designated by the name 'set of *F*s'. This is inadmissible because of the essential difference between concept and object, which is indeed quite covered up in our word languages.… Confusion is bound to arise if a concept word, as a result of its transformation into a proper name comes to be in a place for which it is unsuited.[35]

In *Foundations of Arithmetic*, he had warned that it was a mere illusion to suppose that a concept can be made into an object without altering it.[36]

Russell's attempts to evade the paradoxes

As for Russell, he said that his struggle with the contradiction he derived in Frege's logic had taught him that if a word or a phrase that is

---

[33] Gottlob Frege, *Posthumous Writings*, Oxford: Blackwell, 1979, p. 182.

[34] Gottlob Frege, "Frege on Russell's Paradox" (1903), in *Translations from the Philosophical Writings*, Oxford: Blackwell, 2nd ed., 1960, pp. 234-44.

[35] Frege, *Philosophical and Mathematical Correspondence*, p. 55.

[36] Frege, *The Foundations of Arithmetic*, p. X.

devoid of meaning when separated from its context is wrongly assumed to have an independent meaning, false abstractions, pseudo-objects, and paradoxes and contradictions are apt to result.[37] He had originally believed that:

> When we say that a number of objects all have a certain property, we naturally suppose that the property is a definite object, which can be considered apart from any of all of the objects, which have, or may be supposed to have, the property in question. We also naturally suppose that the objects which have the property form a *class*, and that the class is in some sense a new single entity, distinct, in general, from each member of the class.[38]

However, the contradiction about the classes that are not members of themselves showed him that classes must be something radically different from individuals.[39] He came to believe that if one assumes that the class is an entity, one cannot escape the contradiction.[40] As he explained, "if you think for a moment that classes are things in the same sense in which things are things, you will then have to say that the class consisting of all the things in the world is itself a thing in the world, and that therefore this class is a member of itself".[41]

Russell decided that he needed a way to make classes disappear from the reasoning in which they were present without really completely letting go of them,[42] because he believed that "without a single object to represent an extension Mathematics crumbles".[43]

While wrestling with the problem of fake objects, he saw parallels existing between the problems arising when classes are treated as objects and those arising when descriptions, 'like the present king of France is bald,' are treated as names. So, satisfied that classes and descriptions both fell into the same logical category of non-entities,[44] he reasoned that since:

---

[37] Russell, *Essays in Analysis*, p. 165.

[38] *Ibid.*, pp. 163-64.

[39] Bertrand Russell, *Logic and Knowledge, Essays 1901-1950*, London: Allen & Unwin, 1956, p. 81.

[40] Russell, *Essays in Analysis*, p. 171.

[41] Russell, *Logic and Knowledge*, p. 261.

[42] Russell, *Introduction to Mathematical Philosophy*, p. 184.

[43] Bertrand Russell, *Principles of Mathematics*, London: Norton, 1903, §489.

[44] Claire Ortiz Hill, *Rethinking Identity and Metaphysics, On the Foundations of Analytic Philosophy*, New Haven CT: Yale University Press, 1997.

> we cannot accept "class" as a primitive idea. We must seek a definition on the same lines as the definition of descriptions, i.e. a definition which will assign a meaning to propositions in whose verbal or symbolic expression words or symbols apparently representing classes occur, but which will assign a meaning that altogether eliminates all mention of classes from a right analysis of such propositions. We shall then be able to say that the symbols for classes are mere conveniences, not representing objects called "classes," and that classes are in fact, like descriptions, logical fictions….[45]

Russell believed that his means of drawing objects out of descriptions provided a practical model of how to make non-entities function as entities without incurring contradictory results.

Early in his search for ways to evade (his choice of verb) the problem of the contradiction about the class of all classes that are not members of themselves, Russell thought that "the key to the whole mystery" was to be found by inventing (his choice of verb) a hierarchy of types.[46] It had become clear to him that the contradiction about the classes that are not members of themselves could only be avoided by realizing that no class either is or is not a member of itself, that the entire question as to whether a class is or is not a member of itself is nonsense.[47] So, he invented a hierarchy of classes according to which the first type of classes would be composed of classes made up entirely of particulars, the second type composed of classes whose members are classes of the first type, the third type composed of classes whose members are classes of the second type, and so on. The types obtained would be mutually exclusive, making the notion of a class being a member of itself meaningless".[48] His hierarchy of types was to perform "the single, though essential, service of justifying us in refraining from entering on trains of reasoning which lead to contradictory conclusions. The justification is that what seem to be propositions are really nonsense".[49]

---

45 Bertrand Russell, *Introduction to Mathematical Philosophy*, London: Allen & Unwin, 1919, pp. 181-82.

46 Russell, *Principles of Mathematics*, §104.

47 Russell, *Logic and Knowledge*, pp. 261-62.

48 Russell, *Essays in Analysis*, p. 201; his *Principles of Mathematics*, §§104-105; his *Logic and Knowledge*, p. 264.

49 Bertrand Russell and Alfred North Whitehead, *Principia Mathematica to *56*. Cambridge UK: Cambridge University Press, 2nd ed., 1964 (1927), p. 24.

Russell believed that no solution to the contradictions was technically possible without his theory of types, but he realized that it was not "the key to the whole mystery". After all, it was but an ad hoc effort to restore the hierarchical structure established by the fundamental differences between dependent and independent meanings that ordinarily protects against invalid inference, but was broken by Frege's Axiom of extensionality. He saw that deeper problems caused the old contradiction to break out afresh and he realized that "further subtleties would be needed to solve them".[50]

Interpretation of the statements

In light of what I have said, how do I interpret the statements I said I was going to interpret?

The *first* statement concerned the set-theoretical paradoxes showing that Husserl's contemporaries did not yet have the real and genuine concept of set needed.

Those paradoxes were derived using a concept of set that allows one to form the expression "a set may be a member of itself", which Husserl judged to be *widersinnig*. In contrast, as we have seen, he would derive set theory analytically from the real and genuine a priori concept, or essence, of set, for which no set can be a member of itself and for which reasoning appealing to the notion of sets that do not contain themselves as members is entirely untenable. A set is a kind of whole and is subject to the formal rules governing wholes and parts that stipulate that a whole cannot be its own part.

The *second* statement says that if one is clear and distinct with respect to meaning, one readily sees the contradiction involved in the set-theoretical paradoxes.

It follows from the above that, if we are clear and distinct about the meaning of the real and genuine concepts of "set", "member", and more universally about the meaning of the real and genuine concepts of "wholes" and "parts", we readily see that all talk of sets being members of themselves is *widersinnig*.

As we have seen, for Husserl, being clear and distinct about meaning involved recognizing the primitive, essential, a priori, inviolable differences

---

[50] Russell, *Introduction to Mathematical Philosophy*, p. 135; his *Logic and Knowledge*, p. 333.

between the dependent and independent meanings that form the necessary basis for discovering the essential categories of meaning in which are grounded laws of meaning that provide logic with possible coherent, meaningful meaning forms whose formal truth or falsehood, reference to objects, *Widersinnigkeit* or lack thereof, is determined by logical laws.

For him, being clear and distinct about meaning also involved recognizing that sets have an entirely different meaning in the subject-predicate propositions of the first level of pure logic where they function as dependent forms, than in set theory of the second level where they function as higher order ideal objects and where truth is the analysis of essences or concepts.

In comparison, Frege reasoned on the first level, which obliged him to treat sets and numbers as objects. For example, he mixed the first level subject-predicate proposition "Jupiter has four moons" with what Husserl considered to be the second level arithmetical statement that 2+2=4. He considered numbers to be independent objects that must always be conceived substantivally and not as a dependent attributes.[51] He confused statements about objects in which number properties occur as form, and are thereby dependent, and statements about numbers in which numbers are the objects. This led him to introduce a law which he thought would permit him to treat what he recognized as dependent meanings as independent meanings. By making such forms independent, he generated new higher order objects, hypostatizations of forms that are not objects in their own right.

I interpret the *third* statement about the solution to the set-theoretical paradoxes lying in demonstrating the shift of meaning that makes it that one is not immediately aware of the contradiction and that once one perceives it one cannot indicate wherein it lies as having to do with Husserl's insistence upon the importance of the fundamental distinction between independent and dependent meanings lying concealed behind inconspicuous grammatical distinctions.

Husserl and Frege were in fundamental agreement about what Frege called the "fatal tendency" of our "word languages" to cover up essential differences between concepts and objects and allow a concept word to be transformed into a proper name and so to come to be in a place for which it is unsuited. By unavoidable "awkwardness of language", by "a kind of necessity of language", one mentions an object, when one intends a concept.

---

51 Frege, *The Foundations of Arithmetic*, §106 and note.

Frege had thought that the presence of the definite article 'the' in an expression like 'the number 1' sufficed to class it as an object and that we should not be "deterred by the fact that in the language of everyday life number appears also in attributive constructions" for that "can always be got around". He ultimately concluded that this propensity of language to undermine the reliability of thinking by forming apparent proper names to which no objects correspond had allowed concept-words to be transformed into proper names and come to be in places unsuited to them and so had "dealt the death blow" to his set theory.

On his copy of Frege's "On Concept and Object",[52] Husserl marked the sentence that reads, "Language has means of presenting now one, now another, part of the thought as the subject". And he tellingly underlined the word 'language'. According to his theory about the differences between logical laws and laws of meaning, something that violates logical laws can genuinely have a coherent meaning and can be determined to be true or false, but since it is *widersinnig*, no object can correspond to the existing meaning. So the formal logical construction "set of all sets which do not contain themselves as parts", may not be presupposed to be about something that exists any more that the expression "the present emperor of France" denotes something that exists.

Such shifts of meaning allow the pseudo-objects and type ambiguities to creep into reasoning unnoticed that Russell struggled to eliminate in his attempts to evade the paradoxes. As he once warned, when two words have two different types of meanings, the relations of those words to what they stand for are also of different types and the failure to realize this is "a very potent source of error and confusion in philosophy".[53]

In addition, if, as Frege stressed, concept words and proper names must occupy essentially different places, and it is obvious that a proper name will not fit into the place intended for a concept word,[54] if, as he wrote, there is a radical difference between dependent and independent meanings concepts, which is such that an object can never stand for a concept or concept for an object,[55] then basic rules of inference like the principle of substitutivity of identicals and existential generalization will fail when one is put in the place intended for the other.

---

52 Consultable at the Husserl Archives in Leuven, Belgium.

53 Russell, *Logic and Knowledge*, p. 133.

54 Frege, *Philosophical and Mathematical Correspondence*, pp. 54-55.

55 *Ibid.*, p. 92.

Conclusion

In conclusion, I wish to emphasize that Husserl did not say that set theory itself was false. He considered it to be a legitimate mathematical discipline of the second level of the purely logical sphere. For him, set theory was a matter of a rigorously scientific, a priori theory that proceeds from the purely logical concepts and axioms that are grounded in purely logical categories such as those discovered by the essential distinction between dependent and independent meanings. He concluded that it was faulty reasoning about a faulty concept of set that had led to the set-theoretical paradoxes.

In particular, he found himself at odds with the concept of set underlying popular axioms of extensionality. While Russell's tactic was to invent ways to evade the contradictions,[56] Husserl advocated making a fresh start and deriving set theory from non-contradictory concept of set and element, or more universally of whole and part without resorting to an axiom of extensionality. He was most disparaging when it came to the popular extensional definitions of sets of *Principia Mathematica* and related systems and he was lucid enough to see that Mathematics would not crumble if it did not have "a single object to represent an extension'. All the rigmarole that Russell went through to avoid the contradictions derivable in Frege's system with its axiom of extensionality serves to illustrate what Husserl meant in *Formal and Transcendental Logic* when he said that extensions generate contradictions requiring every kind of artful device to make them safe for use in mathematical reasoning.[57]

In comparison, Husserl's friend and colleague, David Hilbert, determined not to be thrown out of the set-theoretical paradise that Cantor had created,[58] seemed to think that the laws of inference were faulty. As he wrote,

> In their joy over the new and rich results, mathematicians apparently had not examined critically enough whether the modes of inference employed were admissible; for purely through the ways in which notions were

[56] Hill, *Rethinking Identity and Metaphysics.*

[57] Husserl, *Formal and Transcendental Logic*, pp. 74, 76, 83.

[58] David Hilbert, in "On the Infinite", *From Frege to Gödel: A Source Book in Mathematical Logic, 1879-1931*, Jean van Heijenoort (ed.), Cambridge MA: Harvard University Press, 1967 (1925), pp. 376.

> formed and modes of inference used – ways that in time had become customary – contradictions appeared.... In particular a contradiction discovered by Zermelo and Russell had, when it became known, a downright catastrophic effect in the world of mathematics.... The reaction was so violent that the commonest and most fruitful notions and the very simplest and most important modes of inference in mathematics were threatened and their use was to be prohibited.... Just think: in mathematics, this paragon of reliability and truth, the very notions and inferences, as everyone learns, teaches and uses them, lead to absurdities.[59]

In contrast to Hilbert's assessment of the problem, viewed from the angle of Husserl's theories about the inviolability of the laws governing the use dependent and independent meanings, Russell's contradiction is just faithfully telling us that: the set X of x's is not a member of what it is a set of; what is predicated of an object is of a different logical type from the object itself; a concept is not an object; what is dependent is not independent... In short, logic is doing what logic is supposed to do. Blurring distinctions between talk of sets on different levels by allowing the sets as dependent forms of the first level to be transformed into proper names and come to figure on the wrong tier in the hierarchy of meaning breaks the logical structure. Flattening logical structure smooths the way for things to come into places not intended for them. Once logical structure is broken and meaning categories are violated trouble is ahead in the form failures of inference.

Why should *Widersinnigkeiten* producing theories about sets and the foundations of arithmetic have any lasting "downright catastrophic effect in the world of mathematics?" If those theories are producing contradictions, if they lead to the failure of the simplest and most important modes of inference, it is not logical to see that as posing any particular threat to the modes of inferences themselves and does not indicate that their use should be prohibited. It is more reasonable to conclude with Husserl that those logical laws are determining the truth or falsehood of conclusions just as they are supposed to do.

In my opinion, there is nothing particularly paradoxical or mysterious about the contradictions derivable in Frege's logical system. They are just cheap contradictions generated by an unclear theory of meaning. There is no reason at all why the paragon of reliability and truth

[59] *Ibid.*, p. 375.

that is mathematics should "crumble" as a consequence, as Russell once said it might or that basic rules of inference should be abandoned as Hilbert suggested.

9

HUSSERL'S WAY OUT OF FREGE'S JUNGLE[1]

Introduction

Influential twentieth century philosophers and mathematicians turned philosophers leapt upon new theories of representation, judgment, meaning, arithmetic and sets elaborated during the late nineteenth century to remodel, if not all together eliminate, many traditional ideas about what Bertrand Russell once colorfully called the ultimate furniture of the universe. One of the principal strategies adopted by Russell, Rudolf Carnap, Willard Quine and like-minded philosophers was to use logic to throw out the old furniture and replace it with new furniture of their liking.

The full implications of those new theories about the ultimate structure of reality have yet to be drawn because, for many reasons, many avenues of research have yet to be pursued. Here, I wish to add new dimensions to standard discussions by looking at the ontological implications for analytic philosophy of Edmund Husserl's theory that numbers and sets function in an entirely different way in the sphere of propositions and states of affairs than in arithmetic and in set theory.[2] To begin with we need to pay another visit Husserl's world of the purely logical.

Husserl's world of the purely logical

As seen earlier, exploration of what Husserl once called the strange world of the purely logical brought him to detect a natural order in formal logic and to broaden its domain to include two levels above the traditional Aristotelian logic of subject and predicates and states of affairs. He considered this new understanding of the structure of the world of pure logic to be of prime importance for the understanding of logic and philosophy.

---

[1] This was originally a paper entitled "I Loved You for Your Beauty..." presented at the International Conference on Objects and Pseudo-Objects. Ontological Deserts and Jungles from Meinong to Carnap held at the University of Liège, Belgium from May 15-16, 2012. It was dedicated to the memory of Ruth Barcan Marcus and Paul Gochet.

[2] Edmund Husserl, *Introduction to Logic and Theory of Knowledge, Lectures 1906/07*, Dordrecht: Springer, 2008, §18c.

These levels are explored in his *Introduction to Logic and Theory of Knowledge, Lectures 1906/07.*[3] Part I of *Formal and Transcendental Logic* is devoted to describing them. In the introduction, Husserl says that he considered this stratification, which had not yet been fully detected in his *Logical Investigations*, to be of the greatest significance, not only for a real understanding of the genuine sense of logic, but also for all of philosophy. He believed it to be a matter of a radical clarification of the relationship between formal logic and formal mathematics and that with it emerged a definitive clarification of the sense of pure formal mathematics as a pure analytics of non-contradiction.[4]

On the first level of this edifice Husserl placed the traditional Aristotelian apophantic logic of subject and predicate propositions and states of affairs which deals with what is stated about objects in general from a possible perspective. He stressed that, although the concept of predicative judgment stood at the center of formal logic as it developed historically, it was but a small area of pure logic, the extended sphere of pure logic that includes the mathematical disciplines being immense in range and wealth of content in comparison.[5]

According to Husserl's theory of the forms of subject-predicate propositions of this first level, number only occurs as form, but not as an object about which something is predicated. He emphasized that only the forms of the plural numerical predication about objects as such belong in a simple theory of objects in general and the forms of their states of affairs and that in statements, propositions or state of affairs, forms are dependent. We can make such forms independent, he realized, but then new higher order objects, hypostasizations of forms emerge which are not objects in their own right. For Husserl, this means that numbers function entirely differently on this first level than in the arithmetic of the second level.[6]

I shall illustrate Husserl's point about the ontological status of numbers in subject-predicate propositions by borrowing from Frege, for the sake of unity of argumentation, the proposition, "Jupiter has four moons", which the latter used to illustrate his own theory about numbers in *The*

---

3 *Ibid.*, §§18-19.

4 Edmund Husserl, *Formal and Transcendental Logic*, The Hague: Martinus Nijhoff, 1969 (1929), p. 11.

5 Edmund Husserl, *Experience and Judgment*, London: Routledge and Kegan Paul, 1973 (1939), §1; his *Introduction to Logic and Theory of Knowledge*, §18c.

6 Husserl, *Introduction to Logic and Theory of Knowledge*, §18c.

Foundations of Arithmetic (§57).[7] According to Husserl's analysis in *Introduction to Logic and Theory of Knowledge*, this would be a statement about Jupiter's moons in which the number characteristic four occurs as form and is thereby dependent. If one says *w* and *x* and *y* and *z* are *φ*, Husserl reasoned, then one has combined the objects *w*…*z* by 'and'. Here, the 'and' is form and grounds the unitary form of the plural predication. Corresponding to this is a cardinal number. However, Husserl stresses, this is a new thought configuration, for it is one thing to make statements about objects in which number properties occur as form and are thereby dependent and another thing to make statements about numbers as such in such a way that the numbers are the objects. Statements about numbers in which numbers are the objects have their place on the second level of Husserl's hierarchy.[8]

Sets as objects do not occur on Husserl's first level of the logic of subjects and predicates any more than numbers do. He taught that:

> in set theory, we make judgments universally about sets that in a certain way are higher order objects. We do not make judgments directly about elements, but about whole totalities of elements and arbitrary elements, and the whole totalities, the sets to be precise, are the objects-about-which. *Corresponding to every plural is a set, but in the theory of proposition forms, or forms of states of affairs, the set does not occur as object.* In it, the objects-about-which are thoroughly indeterminate *A B*…. Rather, only the plural occurs in it, which constitutes a form of predication about arbitrary objects.[9]

On the two levels rising above the level of subject-predicate propositions, it is no longer a question of objects as such about which one might predicate something, but of investigating what is valid for higher order object formations such as cardinal number and set, which are determined in purely formal terms grounded in the essence of logical forms and deal with objects in indeterminate, general ways.[10] Husserl conceived of the second level as an expanded, completely developed analytics in which one proceeds in a purely formal manner since every single concept used is analytic. One calculates, reasons deductively, with concepts and propositions. Signs and rules of calculation suffice because each procedure is purely

---

[7] Gottlob Frege, *The Foundations of Arithmetic*, Blackwell: Oxford, 2nd ed. rev., 1986, §57.

[8] Husserl, *Introduction to Logic and Theory of Knowledge*, §18c.

[9] *Ibid.*

[10] *Ibid.*, §18d.

logical. One manipulates signs, which acquire their meaning in the game through the rules of the game. One may proceed mechanically in this way and the result will prove accurate and justified.[11]

As already seen, Husserl gave these examples of numbers occurring as objects in arithmetical propositions of the second level:

1. "Any number can be added to any number".
2. "If *a* is a number and *b* a number, then *a* + *b* is as well".
3. "Any number can be decreased or increased by one".
4. "The numbers form a series continuing from 0 *in infinitum*".
5. The different laws of addition, subtraction, multiplication, etc.[12]

Sets also function entirely differently in the set theory of the second level where statements are not made directly about elements, but about whole totalities of arbitrary elements. The set theory of the second level asks what is valid for the higher-order objects called sets. Husserl gave the following examples of the truths about sets as objects-about-which that make up set theory:

1. "2 sets can each be joined into a new set".
2. "2 sets *a b* are each related to one another in such a way that either *a* is part of *b* or *b* is part of *a*, or that they intersect (a set having a part in common), or that it turns out that they are identical, coincide".
3. "The set formed of the elements *A B C* is part of the set formed of the elements *A B C D* containing "more elements".[13]

On the third level of Husserl's hierarchy is his theory of manifolds, discussed amply in earlier chapters, where formal logic deals with whole systems of propositions making up possible deductive theories.

Entering Frege's jungle

Now I want to look at Frege's theory of numbers and sets. Frege considered the prime problem of arithmetic to be that of how one apprehends logical objects, in particular numbers, and he wanted to know what justifies one in recognizing numbers as objects.[14] It is vital to realize

---

[11] Husserl, *Introduction to Logic and Theory of Knowledge*, §§18-19, pp. 434-35; his *Logic and General Theory of Science 1917/18, with supplementary texts from the first version of 1910/11*, Cham, Switzerland: Springer, 2019, §58.

[12] Husserl, *Introduction to Logic and Theory of Knowledge*, §18c.

[13] *Ibid.*

[14] Gottlob Frege, "Frege on Russell's Paradox" (1903), in *Translations from the Philosophical Writings*, Oxford: Blackwell, 2nd ed., 1960 (1952), p. 244.

in addition that the logical objects that Frege believed he needed to apprehend were *independent, self-subsistent* logical objects.

Operating only on the lowest level of Husserl's hierarchy, that of the traditional logic of subjects and predicates, Part IV (§§55-86) of *The Foundations of Arithmetic* is devoted to analyzing the concepts of arithmetic. Frege argued there that to obtain the concept of number, it was a matter of fixing the sense of an identity[15] and that only in the case of objects could there be any question of identity.[16] The first portion (§§55-61) of Part IV is entitled "Every individual number is an independent object" and is devoted to affirming the independency of numbers.

In contrast to Husserl, Frege maintained "that the number studied by arithmetic must be conceived not as a dependent attribute, but substantivally".[17] "Precisely because it forms only an element in what is asserted", he reasoned, "the individual number shows itself for what it is, an independent object". He considered that the presence of the definite article 'the' in expressions like 'the number 1' served "to class it as an object" and that in arithmetic "this independence comes out at every turn, as for example in the identity 1 + 1 = 2".[18] He argued that since it was a matter of arriving at a concept of number usable for scientific purposes, "we should not, therefore, be deterred by the fact that in the language of everyday life number appears also in attributive constructions" for that "can always be got around" and proposed that a subject-predicate statement proposition such as

> "Jupiter has four moons" can be converted into "the number of Jupiter's moons is four"….. we can say: "the number of Jupiter's moons is the number four, or 4". Here "is" has the sense of "is identical with" or "is the same as". So that what we have is an identity, stating that the expression "the number of Jupiter's moons" signifies the same object as the word "four".[19]

Frege concludes his argument with the important proviso that the independence that he is "claiming for number is not to be taken to mean that a number word signifies something when removed from the context

---

[15] Frege, *The Foundations of Arithmetic*, p. x, §§62-70, 106.

[16] Gottlob Frege, *Posthumous Writings*, Oxford: Blackwell, 1979, pp. 182, 120.

[17] Frege, *The Foundations of Arithmetic*, §106 and note.

[18] *Ibid.*, §§57, 106.

[19] Frege, *The Foundations of Arithmetic*, §57.

of a proposition, but only to preclude the use of such words as predicates or attributes, which appreciably alters their meaning".[20]

After devoting several pages to ferreting out some very basic problems that he saw sticking to his theory, and unable to silence questions, doubts and suspicions about the undesirable consequences that he saw proceeding from it, he acknowledged that he could not by those methods obtain any satisfactory concept of number. He said that left unmodified his technique was liable to lead to false or nonsensical conclusions or be sterile and unproductive.

So to forestall the problems that he foresaw would vitiate his theories, against his better judgment, he introduced extensions. He settled for the definition: "The Number which belongs to the concept F is the extension of the concept 'concept equal to the concept F'".[21] He took logical law into his own hands and devised Basic Law V to allow logicians to pass from a concept to its extension. Frege knew well that what he wished to sanction through his law was "forbidden by the basic difference between first and second level relations", but he temporarily convinced himself that, though a proof could "scarcely be furnished" and "an unprovable law" would have to be assumed, a transformation might "take place, in which concepts correspond to extensions of concepts...."[22]

Upon learning of Russell's paradox, Frege tested the validity of the chain of inferences leading up to the contradiction and concluded that his law about extensions was false and his explanations did not suffice to secure a reference for his combinations of signs in all cases. He confessed that he had been reluctant to use classes, but that that was the only answer that he had found to the question as to how to apprehend logical objects.[23] "I do not see how arithmetic can be scientifically established; how numbers can be apprehended as logical objects, and brought under review; unless we are permitted – at least conditionally – to pass from a concept to its extension", he agonized in his study of the contradiction in his 1903 appendix to *Basic Laws II*.[24]

---

20 *Ibid.*, §60.
21 *Ibid.*, §§66-69, 107.
22 Frege, *Posthumous Writings*, p. 182.
23 Gottlob Frege, *Philosophical and Mathematical Correspondence*, Oxford: Blackwell. 1980, pp. 132, 140-41.
24 Frege, *Translations from the Philosophical Writings*, p. 214.

Frege was the first to admit that his logic led into a jungle. When asked late in life about the causes of the paradoxes of set theory, he replied that it was language's propensity to undermine the reliability of thinking by forming apparent proper names to which no objects correspond that had allowed concept-words to be transformed into proper names and so come to be in places unsuited to them that had "dealt the death blow" to his set theory.[25] He warned that the difficulties that this idiosyncrasy of language entangles us in are incalculable and threaten to undermine the reliability of thinking.[26]

He described what he called the "essence of the procedure which leads us into a thicket of contradictions" as consisting in regarding the objects falling under F as a whole, as an object designated by the name 'set of Fs', 'extension of 'F', or 'class of Fs' etc. This is inadmissible, he explained, because of the essential difference between concept and object, which is covered up in our word languages. Such a transformation of a concept into an object is inadmissible, because the set formed only seems to be an object, while in truth there is no such object at all. Experience, he said, had shown him "how easily this can get one into a morass". Confusion, is bound to arise, he warned at the end of his life, if as a result of its transformation into a proper name, a concept word comes to be in a place for which it is unsuited.[27]

Blurring distinctions between dependent and independent meanings by allowing a concept word to be transformed into a proper name and to come to figure on the wrong tier in the hierarchy of meaning broke the logical structure that Frege had professed to be so intent upon preserving and opens the way to confusion. Once logical structure is broken and meaning categories are violated, contradictions, paradoxes, antinomies, fallacies, nonsense, confusion, absurdity, pseudo-objects result. Frege chose a jungle, but he could have had a sterile, unproductive desert. Russell reported that the French mathematician Henri Poincaré had rejoiced over the contradictions, announcing triumphantly, 'mathematical logic is no longer sterile, it begets contradiction'.[28]

---

25 Frege, *Philosophical and Mathematical Correspondence*, p. 55.

26 Frege, *Posthumous Writings*, pp. 269-70; Frege *Philosophical and Mathematical Correspondence*, pp. 54-55.

27 Frege, *Philosophical and Mathematical Correspondence*, pp. 54-55.

28 Bertrand Russell, *My Philosophical Development*, London: Unwin Paperbacks, 1985 (1959), p. 59; his *Principles of Mathematics*, London: Norton, 1903, p. xii.

Russell strives to prune Frege's jungle

Intellectual sorrow descended upon Bertrand Russell in full measure when he came upon the contradiction about classes that are not members of themselves that put an end to an "intellectual honeymoon" unlike any he had ever enjoyed before or would ever again enjoy.[29]

Early in his search for a solution to the problem, Russell believed that "the key to the whole mystery" would be found in the distinguishing of logical types.[30] When two words have two different types of meanings, Russell once warned, the relations of those words to what they stand for are also of different types and the failure to realize this is "a very potent source of error and confusion in philosophy".[31] So he established a hierarchy of classes according to which the first type of classes would be composed of classes made up entirely of particulars, the second type composed of classes whose members are classes of the first type, the third type composed of classes whose members are classes of the second type, and so on. The types obtained would be mutually exclusive, making the notion of a class being a member of itself meaningless.[32]

Russell believed that the theory of types he developed led to the "avoidance" of contradictions and to the detection of the fallacy that produced them.[33] And he believed that no solution to the contradictions was technically possible without it. However, he saw that it was not "the key to the whole mystery".[34] Deeper problems caused them to break out again and "further subtleties" were needed to solve them.

He had originally believed that:

> When we say that a number of objects all have a certain property, we naturally suppose that the property is a definite object, which can be considered apart from any or all of the objects, which have, or may be supposed to have, the property in question. We also naturally suppose that

[29] Russell, *My Philosophical Development*, p. 56.
[30] Russell, *Principles of Mathematics*, §104.
[31] Bertrand Russell, *Logic and Knowledge, Essays 1901-1950*, London: Allen &Unwin, 1956, p. 133.
[32] Bertrand Russell, *Essays in Analysis*, London: Allen & Unwin, 1973, p. 201.
[33] Bertrand Russell and Alfred North Whitehead, *Principia Mathematica to *56*, Cambridge UK: Cambridge University Press, 2nd ed., 1964 (1927), p. 1.
[34] See Bertrand Russell, *Introduction to Mathematical Philosophy*, London: Allen & Unwin, 1919, p. 135; his *Logic and Knowledge*, p. 333.

> the objects which have the property form a *class*, and that the class is in some sense a new single entity, distinct, in general, from each member of the class.[35]

However, the contradiction about the classes that are not members of themselves showed him that classes could not be independent entities. He said that it had taught him that if a word or a phrase that is devoid of meaning when separated from its context is wrongly assumed to have an independent meaning, false abstractions, pseudo-objects, and paradoxes and contradictions are apt to result. He came to believe that if one assumes that the class is an entity, one cannot escape the contradiction about the class of classes that are not members of themselves. As he explained, "if you think for a moment that classes are things in the same sense in which things are things, you will then have to say that the class consisting of all the things in the world is itself a thing in the world, and that therefore this class is a member of itself".[36]

The idea that classes were not entities shed some light on the ontological nature of classes by saying what they were not, but Russell had to do more than that. He had to find a way of making them disappear from the reasoning in which they were present without really completely letting go of them.[37]

As seen in the previous chapter, while struggling to get to the bottom of the problem of fake objects, Russell found parallels existing between the problems that arise when classes are treated as objects and problems that come up when descriptions are treated as names. These analogies plus the success he had with his 1905 theory of definite descriptions gave him an idea as to how classes might be analyzed away much as descriptions had been, and so gave him a concrete idea as to how, as he saw it, he might sweep his problems away.[38]

He saw the theory of definite descriptions as a way of making an object fit to go proxy for what was said about it.[39] This means of drawing objects out of descriptions provided him with a practical model of how to make non-entities function as entities without incurring

---

[35] Russell, *Essays in Analysis*, pp. 163-64.
[36] Russell, *Logic and Knowledge*, pp. 260-65; his *Essays in Analysis*, pp. 163-65, 171.
[37] Russell, *Introduction to Mathematical Philosophy*, p. 184.
[38] Russell, *My Philosophical Development*, p. 49.
[39] Russell & Whitehead, *Principia Mathematica*, p. 187.

contradictory results. But this did not prove to be the key to whole mystery either.

Russell finally felt obliged to introduce the axiom of reducibility to cleanse *Principia Mathematica* of unwanted entities. This specially designed axiom would be "equivalent to the assumption that 'any combination or disjunction of predicates is equivalent to a single predicate'"[40] and would provide a way of dealing with any function of a particular argument by means of some formally equivalent function of a particular type. It would thus yield most of the results which would otherwise require recourse to the problematical notions of all functions or all properties, and so legitimize a great mass of reasoning apparently dependent on such notions.[41] He claimed that it embodied all that was really essential in his theory of classes[42] and he leaned it at every crucial point in his definition of classes in *Principia Mathematica*.[43] He considered that many of the proofs of *Principia* "become fallacious when the axiom of reducibility is not assumed, and in some cases new proofs can only be obtained with considerable labour".[44] He called it "a dubious assumption" and a "defect".[45] "This axiom," he confessed, "has a purely pragmatic justification: it leads to the desired results, and to no others. But clearly it is not the sort of axiom with which we can rest content".[46]

Russell credited Occam's razor with having given him "a more clean-shaven picture of reality". It did not, he said, prove to him the non-reality of entities that it had showed him were unnecessary, but it abolished for him the arguments in favor of their reality. He said he did not think it possible to disprove the reality of integers or points or instants or the Gods of Olympus, but did not believe there was the faintest reason to think they existed.[47]

---

40 Russell, *Essays in Analysis*, p. 250; Russell & Whitehead, *Principia Mathematica*, pp. 58-59.
41 *Ibid.*, p. 56.
42 Russell, *Introduction to Mathematical Philosophy*, p. 191; Russell & Whitehead, *Principia Mathematica*, pp. 58, 166-67; Russell, *Logic and Knowledge*, p. 82.
43 Russell, *Essays in Analysis*, p. 250; Russell & Whitehead, *Principia Mathematica*, pp. 58-59, 75-81.
44 Russell & Whitehead, *Principia Mathematica*, p. xliii.
45 Russell, *Introduction to Mathematical Philosophy*, pp. 192-93.
46 Russell & Whitehead, *Principia Mathematica*, p. xiv.
47 Russell, *My Philosophical Development*, p. 49.

The man who once wrote that "Mathematics, rightly viewed, possesses not only truth, but supreme beauty – a beauty cold and austere… sublimely pure, and capable of a stern perfection[48] concluded that, while the "aesthetic pleasure to be derived from an elegant piece of mathematical reasoning" remained, the "solution of the contradictions... seemed to be only possible by adopting theories which might be true but were not beautiful" and that the "splendid certainty" he had "always hope to find in mathematics had become lost in a bewildering maze".[49] The logic that had appeared so convenient, simple and austerely beautiful had spawned error, contradiction, ugliness and messiness.

Frege's and Russell's problems live on

Bewildering maze or not, analytic philosophers determined not to be driven out of the paradise Frege created for them went on to integrate the logic of *Principia Mathematica* into mainstream philosophy. They called it "classical" logic and trying to solve the jungle of problems it produced became the stuff of logic and much of philosophy in our times.

The emblematic figure in this was Quine, who fought hard to defend what he thought of as the "clear extensional ontology"[50] of his desert paradise safeguarded by strong extensional calculi. He made exposing and bewailing any hint of connivance with unwanted ontological notions one of the main planks of his philosophical program. He recognized that the logic that he loved harbored unsolved difficulties, but he and his followers found it desirable for achieving their ends, elegant, and aesthetically pleasing. He admonished philosophers to remain within the confines of the hard won metaphysically pure territory conquerable by faithful logicians enforcing a policy of extensional cleansing. He warned of the ontological crisis that would erupt were logicians to disobey his strictures and begin a retreat back into what he called "the metaphysical jungle of Aristotelian essentialism". Appealing to philosophers' weaker nature, he actually advised

48 Bertrand Russell, *Mysticism and Logic and Other Essays*, London: George Allen & Unwin Ltd. 1959 (1917), p. 6o.
49 Russell, *My Philosophical Development*, pp. 155-57.
50 Willard Quine, *Ontological Relativity and Other Essays*, New York: Columbia University Press, 1969, p. 152.

philosophers to run away from the problems, to flee creatures of darkness and curiously idealistic ontologies that repudiated material objects.[51]

Fortunately, a handful of philosophers braved the strictures and took a bolder attitude toward limning the true and ultimate structure of reality. They ventured beyond the narrow confines of the sterile environment created by strong extensional calculi and developed intensional languages to analyze the many non-extensional statements which figure significantly in the empirical sciences, law, medicine, ethics, engineering, politics, and much of ordinary philosophy, for example, but which had been deemed unfit for study by the analytic philosophical establishment because they complicate matters by not conforming to the rigid standards for admission into the stark, sterile logical world Quine and so many others have found so beautiful.[52] So, more and more reasons for not shoving reasoning into an extensional mold began gathering right in the "beautiful" desert world they were so intent upon preserving.

The road not taken

As we have seen, Husserl had initially experienced revulsion toward idealistic ontology akin to Quine's and Russell's, but found his early empirico-naturalistic Brentanian approach to arithmetic and sets incapable of providing the continuity and clarity needed in science and knowledge in general.[53] After wrestling with his doubts, he developed a way of finding clarity with respect to the central traits of reality that he believed positioned him "far from any mystico-metaphysical exploitation of 'Ideas', ideal possibilities and such".[54] He had initially interpreted Bolzano's thoughts about ideas, propositions and truths 'in themselves' as metaphysical

---

51 Willard Quine, "The Problem of Interpreting Modal Logic", *Journal of Symbolic Logic* 12, 2, June, 1947, pp. 43, 47; his *Ways of Paradox*, Cambridge MA: Harvard University Press, 1976, pp. 176, 188; his *Word and Object*, Cambridge MA: M.I.T. Press, 1960, pp. 191-232; his "Reference and Modality" (1953), in *From a Logical Point of View* (2nd rev.), New York: Harper & Row, 1961, p. 158; Hill, *Rethinking Identity and Metaphysics, On the Foundations of Analytic Philosophy*, New Haven CT: Yale Uniersity Press, 1997, Chapter 11.

52 Ruth Barcan Marcus, *Modalities*, New York: Oxford University Press, 1993, pp. 5, 8, 76; Hill, *Rethinking Identity and Metaphysics*, p. 124.

53 Husserl, *Logical Investigations*, p. 42

54 Edmund Husserl, "Husserl an Brentano, 27. III. 1905", in his *Briefwechsel, Die Brentanoschule I*, Dordrecht: Kluwer, 1994, p. 39.

abstrusities", as "mythical entities, suspended between being and non-being". Then he realized that the first two volumes of Bolzano's theories about ideas in themselves and propositions in themselves were to be seen as an initial attempt at a unified presentation of the field of pure ideal doctrines, that a complete plan of a "pure" logic was already available there.[55]

The ideal entities so unpleasant for empiricistic logic and so consistently disregarded by it, Husserl began teaching, were not artificially devised either by himself or by Bolzano. They were given beforehand by the meaning of the universal talk of propositions and truths that is indispensable in all the sciences. And that indubitable fact had to be the starting point of all logic, for science was a web of theories, and so of proofs, propositions, inferences, concepts, meanings.[56]

From the mid-1890s on, Husserl defended the view, which he attributed to Frege's teacher Hermann Lotze, that pure arithmetic was basically no more than a branch of logic that had undergone independent development. Lotze, Husserl explained, had correctly recognized cardinal number as a specific differentiation of the concept multiplicity (*Vielheit*) and multiplicity as the most universal logical concept combining objects in general. This most universal concept of multiplicity splits into a series of different special forms and these are the cardinal numbers.[57]

In his logic courses, Husserl taught that all of arithmetic is grounded in the arithmetical axioms. The unending profusion of theories that arithmetic develops is already fixed, enfolded in the axioms, and theoretical-systematic deduction effects the unfolding of them following systematic, simple procedures. The concept of cardinal number is derived from given purely logical concepts and axioms and from perspicuous laws grounded in the essence of these purely logical categories. Each genuine axiom is a

---

55 Edmund Husserl, *Introduction to the Logical Investigations, A Draft of a Preface to the Logical Investigations* (1913), The Hague: Martinus Nijhoff, 1975, p. 37; his "Review of Melchior Palagyi's *Der Streit der Psychologisten und Formalisten in der modernen Logik*" (1903), in his *Early Writings in the Philosophy of Logic and Mathematics*, Dordrecht: Kluwer, 1994, pp. 201-02.

56 Edmund Husserl, *Alte und neue Logik, Vorlesung 1908/09*, Dordrecht: Kluwer, 2003, p. 45; his "Review of Melchior Palagyi's *Der Streit der Psychologisten und Formalisten in der modernen Logik*" (1903), pp. 201-02.

57 Edmund Husserl, *Logik, Vorlesung 1896*, Dordrecht: Kluwer, 2001, pp. 102, 241-42, 271-72; his *Logik, Vorlesung 1902/03*, Dordrecht: Kluwer, 2001, pp. 19, 34; his *Introduction to Logic and Theory of Knowledge*, §15; his *Logic and General Theory of Science*, §36b.

proposition that unfolds the idea of cardinal number from some side or unfolds some of the ideas inseparably connected with the idea of cardinal number. The meaning of cardinal number, he said, was the answer to the question: "How many?" Since each and every thing can be counted as one, he reasoned, to conceive the concept of number, or that of any arbitrarily defined number, we only need the concept of something in general. One is something in general. Anything can be counted as one and out of the units all cardinal numbers are built.[58]

Husserl never tried to transform subject-predicate propositions in which numbers figure as dependent properties into propositions about self-sufficient objects and never invented a law mandating that the way Frege did. For Husserl, concepts like cardinal number and set do not express essential forms of propositions and the laws that pertain to them are not laws for truths grounded in the essence of the proposition in general. They are grounded in the universal idea of objectivity that makes them applicable in every possible field of knowledge. They a priori express possible object prototypes and what is grounded in their formal essence.[59] Reflection upon the naturally broadest universality of the concepts number and set and also upon the concepts unit and element determining them showed him that the theory of sets and that of theory of cardinal numbers relate to any object whatsoever with a formal universality and are derivative formations of the concept of anything-whatsoever. Their fundamental concepts are syntactical formations of the empty something. The theory of cardinal numbers deals with numbers as differentiations of forms of sets and set theory with sets as made of any objects whatsoever that are taken together.[60]

In contrast to Russell's conviction that "without a single object to represent an extension mathematics crumbles",[61] Husserl believed that the essential thing in mathematics was not the objects, but was its method that naturally flows into a purely symbolic technique.[62] He complained that

58 Husserl, *Logik, Vorlesung 1902/03*, pp. 32-35, 39, 49, 231-32, 239-49; his *Introduction to Logic and Theory of Knowledge*, §§13c, 19d, p. 434.

59 Husserl, *Introduction to Logic and Theory of Knowledge*, §18a.

60 Husserl, *Formal and Transcendental Logic*, §§24, 27a.

61 Russell, *Principles of Mathematics*, §489.

62 Husserl, *Introduction to Logic and Theory of Knowledge*, §19a.

extensions generate contradictions requiring every kind of artful device to make them safe for use in mathematical reasoning.[63]

Conclusion

Russell wrote that "The characteristic excellence of mathematics is only to be found where the reasoning is rigidly logical: the rules of logic are to mathematics what those of structure are to architecture. In the most beautiful work, a chain of argument is present in which every link is important on its own account, in which there is an air of ease and lucidity throughout, and the premises achieve more than would be been thought possible, by means which appear natural and inevitable".[64]

Husserl claimed no less and it seems to me that his theory of the purely logical approximates those standards far more surely than the *soi-disant* clean, clear beautiful extensional ontology that analytic philosophy wanted to have and to hold. Never bedazzled by the beauty of what George Boolos called Frege's Eden or David Hilbert called Cantor's paradise,[65] Husserl developed a theory of formal logic that is a blueprint for limning the true and ultimate structure of reality every bit as much as Quine's is.

Husserl's world of the purely logical is not particularly ugly and his theories about numbers, arithmetic and set theory are not particularly bad. They are just untried. Moreover, there is nothing especially beautiful about Russell's bewildering maze, Frege's thicket of contradictions or Quine's fragmented world of rabbit parts, river stages and kinship, where

---

[63] Husserl, *Formal and Transcendental Logic*, §§23b, 26c.

[64] Russell, *Mysticism and Logic*, p. 61.

[65] David Hilbert's memorable words: "From the paradise Cantor created for us must no one be able to drive us." (My translation of "Aus dem Paradies, das Cantor uns geschaffen, soll uns niemand vertreiben können") as recorded in "On the Infinite" in *From Frege to Gödel: A Source Book in Mathematical Logic, 1879-1931*, Jean van Heijenoort (ed.), Cambridge MA: Harvard University Press, 1967, p. 376. Also in Benacerraf, Paul and Hilary Putnam (eds.), *Philosophy of Mathematics, Selected Readings*, Cambridge UK: Cambridge University Press, 1983, 2nd ed. rev. (1964), pp. 183-201. The logical world that Frege created has also been compared to the Garden of Paradise. For example, George Boolos spoke of wanting to "guess at Frege's trains of thought," only to conclude that "we cannot explain how the serpent entered Eden," that Frege had been "hoodwinked." See his, "Whence the Contradiction?" in *Frege: Importance and Legacy*, Matthias Schirn (ed.), Berlin: de Gruyter, pp.1996, pp. 249-50.

the ontologies of physical and mathematical objects are but myths relative to an epistemological view.[66]

The analytic logical establishment said they wanted a beautiful logic, but what they really wanted was a logic that would permit them to undo many of the great issues of traditional ontology, issues which, ironically, the likes of Frege and Cantor did not find distressing. It was indeed a matter of trading ontology for a metaphysics, or really a lack of metaphysics, that they considered aesthetically pleasing. In fact, the logic whose virtues they chose to defend was ultimately neither true nor beautiful.

In conclusion, I see this as yet another indication that, as Frege, Russell and Husserl all concluded, fundamental differences between dependent meanings and independent meanings lying concealed behind inconspicuous grammatical distinctions and ultimately prove inviolable because they are "founded deep in the nature of things"[67] in such a way that contradictions, paradoxes, antinomies, fallacies, nonsense, confusion, absurdity inevitably result when they are not respected and that this is a topic of prime importance for the understanding of major issues in twentieth century western philosophy.[68]

---

[66] Quine, *Word and Object* and his *Ontological Relativity and Other Essays.*

[67] Gottlob Frege, "Function and Concept" (1891), in *Translations from the Philosophical Writings*, p. 41.

[68] Claire Ortiz Hill, "Incomplete Symbols, Dependent Meanings, and Paradox", in *Husserl's Logical Investigations*, Daniel Dahlstrom (ed.), Dordrecht: Kluwer, 2003, pp. 69-93 and my "On Fundamental Differences Between Dependent and Independent Meanings", *Axiomathes, An International Journal in Ontology and Cognitive Systems* 20: 2-3, online since May 29, 2010, pp. 313-32. Both articles are anthologized in Claire Ortiz Hill & Jairo da Silva, *The Road Not Taken, On Husserl's Philosophy of Logic and Mathematics*, London: College Publications, 2013.

APPENDIX

THREE REVIEW ESSAYS

"Circling Gottlob Frege"
Review of *Frege: Importance and Legacy*, Matthias Schirn ed. Berlin: Walter de Gruyter, 1996[1]

Frege: Importance and Legacy is based on papers on logic, philosophy of mathematics, epistemology and philosophy of language presented by some of the foremost American and European Frege scholars at a conference on foundational problems in Frege's works and modern logic held in Munich in July 1991. The stated ambition of its editor, Matthias Schirn, is to display both the breadth and the significance of current Frege research as well as to make good a second claim of the title that Frege left a legacy, a set of questions to be answered (something about which there can, of course, be no doubt).

The discussion of Frege's work over the last fifteen years, Schirn considers, has been motivated by the desire to "locate his work more accurately in the history of logic, mathematics and philosophy", "bring into sharp focus and reassess both his logicism and his arithmetical platonism", "examine more thoroughly particular aspects of his logical theory", "analyze his mathematical work in *Grundgesetze*"; "investigate the various facets of his epistemology", "provide a systematic account of his semantics and to develop further certain central ideas of it" (p . 28). The book itself emphasizes the importance of Frege's philosophy of mathematics, to which 2/3 of the work is devoted; Frege's work on the philosophy of language or epistemology plays a subsidiary role.

---

[1] Originally published in *Diálogos* 73, 1999, pp. 203-13.

Schirn's conviction that "to reveal errors or shortcomings in Frege's work may well go hand in hand with admiration for its major achievements, the power and depth of his argument and the lucidity of both his exposition and his style" (p. 1) sets the tone of the collection and also reveals something of the maturity of the editor's approach. Several of the articles anthologized here raise really pertinent questions of more fundamental significance than one usually finds in the literature on Frege and advance theses that warrant further thorough, competent investigation, thus lending the work a spirit of lively, intelligent inquiry. So the work genuinely represents a step forward in providing a truer likeness of Frege's ideas as based on what he actually wrote and not just on a likable, even fanciful, interpretation of his work which more mirrors what many analytic philosophers have believed or wished he had written.

Looking beyond the titles of the papers, or even the stated intentions of the editor, one finds most of the book directly or indirectly circling in on three important themes: the underlying reason for the inconsistency of the *Grundgesetze* system; Frege's Platonism and the role of logical objects in his thought; and Frege's suggestive, but incomplete, remarks on epistemology.

George Boolos, Michael Dummett and Christian Thiel try to locate the mistake in Frege's reasoning that led to the inconsistency in his system, to what Dummett terms the "colossal blunder" that caused the *Grundgesetze* to go "so disastrously wrong" (p. 253).

Rightly noting that there is as yet no unanimity as to the "real" reasons for the failure, in "On the Structure of Frege's System of Logic", Thiel points the finger at the horizontal which, he argues, invites "inappropriate liberality" in admitting *Wertverläufe* like the class that does not belong to itself, hand in hand with the function names out of which they were formed. He calls these "Trojan expressions" and suggests that excluding them might be a solution to Frege's inconsistency problem (p. 275).

Peter Simons' paper, "The Horizontal", complements Thiel's. Despite the inconsistency, Simons says, Frege's logic "has its own oddities and beauties, and can be studied for its own sake both from an historical and from a logico-aesthetic point of view" for what this reveals about how Frege thought (pp. 281-82). Avoiding doing so in a way in which the inconsistency of the system might impinge on his efforts, Simons pokes into "interstices" of Frege's system which he "had neither the time nor, later, the inclination to investigate" (p. 282). Studying the "massive reinterpretation" that Frege's notation underwent between the *Begriffsschrift* and the *Grundgesetze*, Simons comes to thirteen conclusions regarding Frege's reintroduction and reinterpretation of the horizontal (known by him to be redundant) in the *Grundgesetze*, a change which Simons considers to have had "the greatest interpretative repercussions" and to have brought about a "thorough change of sense" (pp. 285-86).

In "Whence the Contradiction", George Boolos disputes Dummett's claim in *Frege: Philosophy of Mathematics* that "the serpent of inconsistency" entered Frege's paradise via the second-order quantifier, a diagnosis which Boolos calls subtle, powerful and unified, but too recherché. According to Boolos "the culprit is the obvious one, Basic Law V" (pp. 235-36), which he brands as "simply a (higher-order) logical falsehood" (p. 249). It was "not so much Frege's insouciance concerning second-order quantifiers that was responsible for his downfall", Boolos maintains, "as his adoption of a theory about a function from second- to first-order objects that could not possibly be true, facilitated by a lingering attachment to the idea that 'contextual definitions' like Hume's principle and Basic Law V, are, if not logically true, then near enough as could make no difference" (p. 245). What Dummett has taken to be the cause of all the trouble, Boolos thinks, should be considered a 'background condition' (p. 239).

Dummett responds to these criticisms in his usual sweeping, categorical style. Frege, Dummett holds, wanted to know what justifies us in assuming the existence of abstract objects, those of a fundamental mathematical theory, in particular. The basis of his answer was the context principle, by which reference to a range of abstract objects is justified if the senses of sentences involving it can be stipulated without presupposing the existence of those objects. The reference of the terms of the theory had to be stipulated by laying down the values of functions, including concepts, that take their referents as arguments and this procedure was validated by a consistency proof that a unique reference had been stipulated for every well-formed expression. This proof was integral to his entire conception of the manner in which one was to justify introducing a range of abstract objects, but it breaks down in the presence of second-order quantification.

Unfortunately, Dummett, Boolos and Thiel have not inquired very far back in their search for the origins of the inconsistency. They shed light on the workings of the inconsistency as it appeared in the *Grundgesetze*, where its first reared its ugly head. By the time the *Grundgesetze* was published, though, the beast of inconsistency had already been slouching around in Frege's "paradise" for some time. The stage for its disturbing appearance was set in the *Grundlagen* and it was just waiting to be found, the way

Columbus discovered America, once Frege finalized and formalized his theories in a way that one could see upon what the whole construction rested.

Yet, only Boolos peeks back into the *Grundlagen*, offering a two paragraph guess as to how Frege might have been "hoodwinked" into putting forth Basic Law V in connection with 'the Julius Caesar problem' and merely concluding that, though we may guess at Frege's trains of thought, we cannot really explain how the serpent entered Eden (pp. 249-50), a skirting of key issues which would do little to disabuse a cynic of the suspicion that, for fear of unearthing ugly and embarrassing problems deeply embedded in the very foundations of analytic philosophy, those most competent to track down the origins of the inconsistency prefer to wring their hands in consternation rather than to set out in earnest to track down the source of the trouble. Whence Basic Law V? Why did Frege feel forced, as he more than once said, almost against his will, to mandate it in the first place? Instead of circling around the issues why not lasso the critter and find out what tempted Frege to put it in the *Grundgesetze* in the first place?

Asking how a serpent of inconsistency might have entered a logical system implies that some nefarious force has been allowed to worm its way into a logic to commit its villainy there. But logical inconsistency does not mysteriously enter into logical systems from the outside. So the only answer to Dummett's question is that the creator somehow planted it there to begin with. The use of the second-order quantifier or the horizontal could not have unearthed the contradiction until Frege had committed himself to a particular systematization of his ideas that he felt obliged to espouse because he saw no way of avoiding the absurd inferences or sterility of the theory of number he embraced in the *Grundlagen*.

The first purpose of his formal language, Frege said in the *Begriffsschrift* was to provide the most reliable test of the validity of a chain of inferences and to point out every presupposition that tries to sneak in unnoticed so that its origin might be investigated. Now, if that is so, and if one of the great merits of Frege's work is, as so many claim, that he created a system so clear that, to borrow Schirn's phrase, "all expressions wear their logical form on their sleeves" (p. 122), then one should be able to start with Frege at square one and reason with him to find the source of the "colossal blunder".

When Russell pointed out the inconsistency, Frege himself immediately pointed to Basic Law V. Both men wrote quite a bit on the source of the contradiction and came to some very specific, and similar, conclusions. Yet, much of what they wrote on the specific causes of the contradiction has been ignored (or, in Frege's case, lost). For example, the scholar intent upon examining the connections between the theory of classes and the various uses of the definite article which both Frege and Russell ultimately concluded had given rise to the paradoxes still enters practically virgin territory.

As it happens, insight into the origins of the inconsistency is most nearly provided by other papers in this collection. The really probing, thought-provoking remarks that Schirn makes about Frege's philosophy of arithmetic in his introduction and in his "On Frege's Introduction of Cardinal Numbers as Logical Objects" are based on a close, observant and lucid reading of the relevant texts that really comes to grips with the issues involved in Frege's introduction of courses-of-values. So, while intentionally refraining from making direct pronouncements about the inconsistency of Frege's theory, Schirn actually provides much needed insight into what Boolos calls "the genesis of Frege's error in putting forth Basic Law V" (p. 249).

In his paper, Schirn thoroughly characterizes the essential features of Frege's foundational program, conscientiously ferreting out problems inherent in his analysis of numerical statements and the introduction of cardinal numbers as logical objects in the *Grundlagen*. Frege's principal scientific concern, Schirn maintains, was to lay the logical foundations of number theory and analysis. To accomplish this, he reasons, Frege probably believed it mandatory to establish not only the purely logical nature of the natural and real numbers, but also their objectual status.

Schirn concludes the first half of his paper "by claiming that unless someone has succeeded in refuting Paul Benacerraf's ontological argument against number-theoretic Platonism, the conception of numbers as objects remains a dogma bequeathed to us by Frege" (p. 32). In the second half of the paper, Schirn argues that Frege's attempted definitions of number in the *Grundlagen* prove inadequate in "resolving the pervasive indeterminacy of reference affecting the cardinality operator" (p. 32).

Such concern with Frege's Platonism and the role of logical objects in his thought is in fact a major theme of this collection. This is as evident in Bob Hale's and Crispin Wright's critical discussion of Hartry Field's ideas in "Nominalism and the Contingency of Abstract Objects" as it is in Dummett's argument about the crucial role that the contradiction producing second-order quantifiers may have played in fulfilling

Frege's aim of justifying us in assuming the existence of abstract objects. Bob Hale's paper "Singular Terms" is "concerned exclusively with the problem of formulating acceptable criteria for singular termhood, of the general kind required… to subserve the Fregean argument for numbers as objects" (p. 439). In "Frege's Treatment of Indirect Reference", Richard Mendelsohn addresses yet another facet of objecthood as he studies problems of sense and reference in oblique contexts. Even Terence Parson's attempt "to produce theories of truth and meaning, to see what assumptions are needed for what results, and to explore some of the options that are left open" and his conclusion "that theories of truth and meaning turn out to be independent of Frege's doctrine that sense determines reference" (p. 372) can be no, stranger: to such considerations. Platonism of course takes center stage in the book's epistemological discussions of Frege's Third Realm.

In "On Positing Mathematical Objects", Michael Resnik studies the philosophical and methodological issues involved in the theories that Frege, Cantor, Dedekind and Hilbert espoused relative to the introduction (through postulation, creation, definition, discovery) of mathematical objects. Resnik concludes that it is wise to review the lessons we can draw from Frege's realism, Dedekind's structuralism and Hilbert's postulationism. The second half of his paper is devoted to depicting how "we can combine a realist, mathematical structuralism with a postulational epistemology to obtain a coherent philosophical view" (p. 56).

In "Frege versus Cantor: On the Concept of Number", W. W. Tait also situates Frege's achievements in relation to those of Dedekind and Cantor. Frege's discussions of others in his field, Tait maintains, "are often characterized less by clarity than by misinterpretation and lack of charity, and on many matters, both of criticism of other scholars and of substance, his analysis is defective" (p. 72). Tait deems it unfortunate that Frege's evaluation of the efforts of his contemporaries "lives on in much of the philosophical literature, where respected mathematicians... are regarded as utterly muddled about the concept of number and great philosophers, such as Cantor and Dedekind, are treated as philosophical naifs..." (p. 73). "Not only have we inherited from Frege a poor regard for his contemporaries", laments Tait, "but, taking the critical .parts of his *Grundlagen* as a model, we in the Anglo-American tradition of analytic philosophy have inherited a poor vision of what philosophy is (p. 73).

Tait particularly takes aim at Frege's criticisms of Cantor and Dedekind as reflected in Dummett's starry-eyed vision of Frege as "the greatest philosopher of mathematics yet to have written" (pp. 70-71). Focusing on the numerous important and interrelated issues surrounding abstractionism and psychologism, equinumerosity in terms of one-to-one correspondence, extensionality, Tait thoroughly examines the wide-ranging implications of criticisms leveled by Frege and Dummett.

For example, in response to Dummett's contention that Frege undoubtedly gave Hume's principle of equinumerosity "its most exact formulation and its most acute philosophical defense", Tait argues that Frege actually, misunderstood Hume and failed to give Cantor his due (pp. 104-05). In defense of Dedekind and Cantor, Tait writes that in neither case is the abstractionism employed "subject to the criticism that it is psychologistic: For neither of them are numbers psychological objects nor are the laws of number to be understood in any way as subjective." (p. 82). Tait's paper ends with a reminder that Frege's "assumption in the *Grundgesetze* that every concept has an extension was an act of recklessness, forewarned against by Cantor already in 1883 and again ... in 1885" (p. 112).

Frege's pronouncements in the area of epistemology have drawn as much attention on the part of scholars for what he said as for what he did not say. In this collection, Eva Picardi, Gottfried Gabriel and Tyler Burge take up philosophical questions raised by Frege's scant, but tantalizing remarks on the subject.

Picardi opens her discussion of Frege's anti-psychologism by noting that there is hardly a piece of writing by Frege "where he misses the opportunity to stigmatize the evil of psychologism" (p. 307). Judging appeals to Frege's conception of epistemology, whose bare outlines can at best be surmised, to be not only an unpromising but a positively misleading way of approaching Frege's anti-psychologism, she argues that Frege's complaints against psychologism were essentially semantic in nature, that he aimed to defeat psychologism through theory of meaning.

The main fault of psychologism for Frege, she explains, lies in "a mistaken picture of language which turns the objectivity of sense and the communication of thoughts into a mystery" (p. 308). One facet of this is a confusion of logical and psychological laws that results from an extreme form of naturalism whose "chief defect is not just that it disregards the claims of a priori knowledge without offering any alternative account, but that, by embodying a relativistic notion of truth, it issues in a form of extreme subjectivism as regards meaning" (p. 309).

Countering those who would contend that Frege himself fell into a new form of psychologism or Kantian transcendentalism, she maintains that it is precisely Frege's realistic conception of truth, in Dummett's sense (p. 320), which "provides the link between his anti-psychologism in logic and his anti-psychologism in the account of meaning", that for Frege "nothing short of the classical notion of truth can give us a correct account of the meaning we attach to our utterances" (p. 309).

Lastly, to dramatize difficulties that Frege's theory of sense encounters on its own ground, she explores what she calls a feeble suggestion on her part that in his later years Frege may have sought to ward off psychologism by espousing a path for securing objectivity of content which did not go through language, but made a straightforwardly metaphysical appeal to a third non-actual, non-sensible realm of independent entities outside of space and time because he ultimately could not see how else adequately to guarantee the objectivity of sense and thoughts. In an appendix, she hypothesizes that Ernst Mach may have been an unnamed target of attacks in Frege's late writings.

In "Frege's 'Epistemology in Disguise'", Gabriel takes quite the opposite approach. For him, "Frege had an immediate interest in logical and epistemological questions, but only a mediate interest in questions in the philosophy of language". His actual goal, Gabriel considers, was "the construction of a logical language to serve a particular purpose: carrying out the epistemologically motivated logicist program" (p. 332). Frege's main works, Gabriel declares, "can be seen as an attempt to clarify the 'epistemological nature' of arithmetic" and are "dedicated to the epistemological aim of obtaining a new understanding of analytical judgments which differs from Kant's views" (p. 331). Gabriel shows how Frege "provides proof-theoretical criteria for decisions about the epistemic nature of truth and entire sciences", how he uses the gap-free chain of deductions in the hope of finding the exact conditions under which a proposition is true (p. 339). Frege, Gabriel contends, "recognizes non-logical reasons as reasons, and thereby acknowledges epistemology as an argumentative basic discipline which is to be distinguished from the psychology of knowledge" and seems "content with a blurred distinction between logic and epistemology" (p. 345).

Burge too considers Frege's main project to be "to explain the foundations of arithmetic in such a way as to enable us to understand the nature of our knowledge of arithmetic" (p. 347). In "Frege on Knowing the Third Realm", he discusses an "intensification" of the puzzle about the dearth of facts about Frege's theory of knowledge of the foundations in the light of what Burge calls his own short, but incomplete, explanation that Frege believed he had little to add to the traditional rationalist account of knowledge, that he assumed "that we can know arithmetic and its foundations purely through reason, and that individuals are reasonable and justified in believing basic foundational truths" (p. 348).

Burge then discusses Frege's theory that both the thought contents constituting the proof-structure of mathematics and the subject matter of those thought contents (extension, functions) exist in a third realm, different from the realm of physical objects and that of mental entities, to which all logic, and thus all sciences, are committed and are about. In this case, the problem then becomes the very traditional one "of understanding how reason alone could justify one in believing that a thought is true, when the thought has a subject matter that is as independent of anyone's thinking as Frege indicates it is" (p. 349).

All agree that Frege was not effusive on the topic of epistemology *per se*. He was, however, unsparing when it carne to defeating and belittling those holding competing views, mainly psychologizing logicians and formalists, and much of that involved confronting them on epistemological ground. Moreover, as embarrassing as it may be to the heirs of the British empiricist tradition who have embraced Frege, he was perfectly explicit about his hostility toward empiricism which in his mind, as no reader of his could fail to notice, was closely linked with psychologism. This is perfectly clear in his reviews of Cantor and Husserl, but Frege leaves no doubt about this in "On Sense and Meaning" and other important writings. Now this plain expression of animosity towards empiricism on Frege's part could be used to dispel mysteries surrounding his epistemological views, and his rationalism and belief in a third realm in particular. Yet it is totally ignored in the papers anthologized here, which again circle important, and potentially embarrassing, issues.

Such circumspection, however, has been an abiding characteristic of Frege research, which got off to a regrettably late start following the long "don't confuse me with the facts" era during which analytic philosophy thrived in English-speaking countries. This paved the way for the introduction of a fictional Frege who was pleasing to numbers of philosophers and fired their imaginations, leaving behind a goldmine of theses to refute. Ever widening the distance between themselves and the facts, philosophers had lost sight of the origins of analytic philosophy, so that the Frege that so many philosophers finally carne to know and love was rather a free creation of Michael Dummett's mind.

In spite of the undeniable efforts in recent years to locate Frege's work more accurately in the history of logic, mathematics and philosophy, we still do not have an adequate and thorough account of the context in which he thought his thoughts. And many of the thoughts found in this book would grow in sophistication if submitted to a really conscientious examination of his writings (as Schirn or Simons have done) and if thoroughly studied in relation to the intellectual context of the times (as Tait has done). For loath as Frege was to give credit where credit was due, he was not, as he has so often been portrayed, laying the foundations of number theory and analysis in a vacuum. He shared the goals of the most insightful and prophetic of his peers, among them Cantor, Husserl, Dedekind, Weierstrass and Peano.

Frege scholarship is only now coming of age and philosophers really should do some soul searching and ask why it has taken roughly a hundred years for it to reach the level of sophistication reflected in this book. For example, it is perfectly astonishing that, as Thiel notes, Frege's pessimistic conclusion regarding the formulation of an intuitively acceptable notion of set (or class or *Begriffsumfang*) has stimulated so little investigation (p. 268).

This slow maturation of Frege scholarship overall is reflected in the fact that many articles in this collection fill in gaps in the scholarship, or make up for other shortcomings, of other papers anthologized here. For example, much of Boolos' and Dummett's exchange tums on questions involving quantifying over infinitely extensible concepts and would grow in sophistication by examining Frege's and Cantor's exchange of ideas, in the way Tait does in his paper. Likewise, Hale begins his paper on singular terms alluding to the argument "which is at least implicit in *Grundlagen* for the existence of numbers as objects" (p. 438), while, as Schirn's paper makes perfectly clear, the argument for the existence of numbers as objects in the *Grundlagen* is as explicit as could be. And it is impossible to think that, as Boolos and Dummett both maintain, Frege hadn't "the glimmering of a suspicion of the existence of indefinitely extensible concepts" (pp. 234, 235), or that, as Thiel writes, "in Frege's time classes were clearly identified with the extensions of concepts" (p. 269). For in a text, which Tait cites and discusses (p. 109), Cantor, the father of set theory and one of the great specialists on indefinitely extensible sets and inconsistency, warned Frege that it was an error to take the extension of a concept as the foundation of the number concept because only in certain cases is the extension of a concept quantitatively determined.

While it is interesting and informative to find the papers complementing each other in this way, it is nevertheless not completely satisfying to find scholars of this caliber using knowledge which should by now be the common property of all Frege scholars to fill in lapses in the scholarship of their peers. So in mirroring the state of current Frege research this collection also reflects certain shortcomings still present in Frege research itself.

One last remark. In all fairness, it must be noted that Edmund Husserl (whom only Tait mentions briefly) is the invisible presence in practically every paper anthologized here. This is as much the case when Tait disparages Frege's damaging attacks on Husserl's teacher Karl Weierstrass and Husserl's close friend and colleague Georg Cantor, as it is in Tait's and Picardi's discussions of Frege's anti-psychologism. Likewise, the interest Thiel manifests in Boolos' suggestion that Frege's extensions might be replaced by abstract objects with respect to a particular equivalence relation (p. 269) brings to mind Husserl's late nineteenth century campaign to show that the entire formal basis upon which the calculus of classes rests is valid for the relationships between conceptual objects and that one could solve logical problems without making the detour through classes.

In the 1890s, Husserl was already hard at work laying bare the follies of extensional logic, by which he meant a calculus of classes. In the *Philosophy of Arithmetic* he had insightfully criticized Frege's recourse to extensions. He also had much of interest to say about epistemology, Platonism, realism and postulationism in mathematics and about problems encountered when trying rigorously to derive all of mathematics from the concept of cardinal number. He grappled with a good number of the theses advanced in this work, and it is a shame that his philosophy of logic and mathematics has not found a place in it, where it could still shed light on the issues under discussion.

Review of *Frege's Philosophy of Mathematics*, W. Demopoulos (ed.), Harvard University Press, 1995[2]

Frege's Philosophy of Mathematics is a collection of eighteen essays by well-known scholars. It sets out to address three main developments in recent work on Frege's philosophy of mathematics: the emerging interest in the intellectual background of Frege's logicism; the reevaluation of the mathematical content of Frege's *Basic Laws of Arithmetic;* and the rediscovery of what is termed "Frege's theorem" that, within the context of second-order logic, Hume's principle (i.e., the number of Fs = the number of Gs if and only if the Fs and the Gs are in one-to-one correspondence) implies the infinity of the natural numbers. In his introduction, editor Demopoulos calls the "rediscovery of Frege's theorem" a major factor underlying the current, renewed interest in Frege's philosophy of mathematics. It is in fact the central theme of the book.

All but one of the papers anthologized date from the 1980s and 1990s. A major principle governing their selection was evidence of "a sympathetic, if not uncritical, reconstruction, evaluation, or extension of one or another facet of Frege's thought". Worthwhile papers not satisfying that criterion were not included in the collection (p. x). The papers are interrelated and their authors very frequently cite and thank one another in a friendly way.

The idea for the collection originated with Michael Dummett, whom Demopoulos considers to have set an intellectual standard to which most philosophers of his generation aspire. Given this, it is worthwhile to bear in mind that, while calling Frege "the best philosopher of mathematics" in the preface to *Frege: Philosophy of Mathematics*, Dummett opined that the reason why Frege's work in the philosophy of mathematics has been "dismissed as a total failure" is probably that his work "does not prompt any further line of investigation in mathematical logic" and "does not even appear to promise a hopeful basis for a sustainable general philosophy of mathematics". The "evidences of the blindness and lack of generosity which were such marked features of Frege's work after 1891 combine", wrote Dummett, "with his great blunder in falling into the contradiction to suggest that he cannot have much to teach us" (p. xi-xiii).

---

[2] Originally published in *Synthese* 133, 2002, pp. 441-52.

The book is divided into three parts. In their different ways, the articles of Part One aim to situate Frege's efforts within the context of nineteenth century efforts to rigorize analysis and to shield it from the deleterious effects of Kant's ideas about intuitions and the synthetic a priori status of mathematical propositions. First, Alberto Coffa aims to embed logicism in a broader movement whose enemy was Kant, whose goal was the elimination of pure intuition from scientific knowledge and whose strategy was the creation of semantics as an independent discipline. This movement included the rigorization of the calculus, Frege's and Russell's theories of arithmetic, and Poincaré's and Hilbert's geometric conventionalism, which Coffa invites readers to look at as stages in a complex process that began with Bolzano.

Bolzano, writes Coffa, was the first to see that Kant had been wrong to think that all conceptual information available in a judgment was to be used up in the grounding of analytic judgments and that one was to appeal to intuition to ground the rest. Bolzano was thus prepared to "explore the possibility that *all* of our pure a priori knowledge – including synthetic a priori knowledge – could be stated and grounded on concepts alone" (pp. 34-35). He and his followers, maintains Coffa, maneuvered pure intuition out of analysis and into arithmetic where Frege's gigantic fly swatter finally came to squash it out. Poincaré and Hilbert came to take up the cause of geometry. Carnap finally saw what Bolzano and Frege almost saw, namely that logical truth is truth in virtue of logical concepts. The essay closes with the words: "And then came Quine" (p. 40).

The following paper by Paul Benacerraf should be an invitation to analytic philosophers to do some thorough soul searching to determine exactly how and why they ever came to believe the views he contests. In particular, he challenges the thesis that twentieth century logicists were correct to consider Frege's logicism to be a philosophical view closely allied with empiricism. Frege's view, Benacerraf maintains, "was a much more intriguing one and in its spirit directly antithetical to the philosophical motivations of his twentieth-century 'followers'" (p. 48). For Benacerraf, *Foundations* is first and foremost a work of mathematics and not, as he had been taught, a work in the Kantian/empiricist tradition. For him, Frege was no empiricist and establishing the analyticity of arithmetical judgments was not his way of defending empiricism against Kantian attack. If Frege was a logicist, Benacerraf concludes, then he was both the first and last one.

"Frege and the Rigorization of Analysis" by Demopoulos complements Coffa's and Benacerraf's papers. Demopoulos agrees that "when Frege's foundational interests are viewed in their mathematical context, they stand in sharp contrast with the logical empiricist's attempts to show the analyticity of arithmetic and more generally of all a priori knowledge" (p. 69), but then sets out to show that Frege's interest in rigor was closely linked to his rejection of intuition in reasoning and thus had *both* a philosophical and a mathematical dimension. He notes that though that his remarks are "neither novel nor contentious" this aspect of Frege's thought has been unduly neglected.

In "Frege and Arbitrary Functions" John Burgess investigates the question as to whether Frege's notion of function could be said to involve definability or even differentiability restrictions, an issue he considers to have implications for the overall interpretation of Frege's philosophy. Burgess concludes that Frege's notion of function did not involve definability restrictions and that it cannot be decided on the basis of the available texts whether it involved differentiability restrictions. Frege, he argues, cannot be expected to have espoused broader theories about functions that only began to be developed as he abandoned his original work.

Mark Wilson's "The Royal Road of Geometry" teems with facts and reflections about philosophical traditions in nineteenth century geometry that he tries to link to Frege's published views. While it is true that as Wilson contends much "work needs to be done on how the chains of influence might have run in this period" (p. 142 n.), Wilson's principal theses should set alarm bells ringing.

For example, the stated central purpose of the paper is to show that we will better understand the character of Frege's philosophy and the manner in which he conceived his logicism by seeing it as having grown up in the shadow of the methodological concerns arising in geometry (those of complexified projective geometry and of Karl von Staudt's theory of "concept-objects" in particular). Citing *Foundations* and Frege's earlier writings, Wilson argues that, contrary to popular opinion, they "stand at a remarkable distance" from the concerns of those undertaking to rigorize analysis (ex. pp. 148, 159).

Yet surely the principal reason scholars put Frege into the movement to arithmetize (and so to degeometrize) analysis is precisely that he so openly called for a more rigorous treatment of higher analysis. In *Foundations* §§1-4, for example, he specifically called for sharper definitions of the concepts of function, continuity, and limit and of infinity, negative and irrational numbers. There he states his conviction that such a pursuit ultimately leads to analyses of the concept of number and of the simplest propositions holding of positive whole numbers (the leading idea of the *Philosophy of Arithmetic* by Weierstrass' student and assistant Husserl, who starting in the 1890s really did turn to innovations in geometry to find answers to questions about numbers that he could not answer by appealing to Weierstrass' teaching about the derivation of analysis from the concept of positive whole number).

But Wilson bypasses all talk of the *arithmetization* of analysis. And he does not explain away either Frege's declaration in §89 of *Foundations* that in calling the truths of geometry synthetic a priori Kant revealed their true nature, or the claim in §14 that the fact that the kind of innovations in geometry that Wilson discusses are possible shows that, unlike the fundamental propositions of the science of number, the axioms of geometry are independent of the primitive laws of logic and consequently synthetic. In §13 Frege had warned that we "should do well in general not to overestimate the extent to which arithmetic is akin to geometry".

Since both Burgess and Wilson advance arguments to counter what they perceive as being the "anti-Fregean conclusions" of Jaakko Hintikka and Gabriel Sandu in "The skeleton in Frege's cupboard: the standard versus nonstandard distinction" (*The Journal of Philosophy* 89), it is worth noting that those conclusions there are no more hostile to Frege than Dummett's conclusions cited above.

The four articles of Part Two investigate the mathematical content of the *Begriffsschrift* and *Foundations*. Three of them are by George Boolos, who first of all engages an imaginary, but very astute, Kantian interlocutor in a dialogue to show how, and how well, the arguments of the third part of the *Begriffsschrift* might be defended against a certain sort of Kantian attack and to determine the extent to which Frege may have shown that there are many interesting examples of mathematical truths that can be reduced to logic.

Boolos scrutinizes the examples given in part three of the *Begriffsschrift* of judgments that can be proved by purely logical means, but which may at first sight appear to be possible only on the basis of some intuition. Far from dispensing with intuition, the Kantian responds, Frege is "up to his ears" in it. For it is an intuition of precisely the kind he believes that he has shown to be unnecessary that licenses the rule of substitution. Besides, though perhaps formally consistent, the system cannot be interpreted in Frege's way in the absence of some metaphysical doctrine of properties that Frege does not supply. Furthermore, if one reads the second-order quantifier ∃F as "There is a set F...", then the difficulty presented by Russell's paradox immediately arises if the range of "F" is taken to be all sets. In so arguing, the Kantian unearths some of the reasoning behind Frege's later appeal to the extensions that were to guarantee substitutivity in a purely logical way and thus pinpoints weaknesses in Frege's arguments that foreshadow problems that he later faced and that persist to this day.

Boolos replies that "a formalism like that of the *Begriffsschrift* can be used to schematize plural existential generalization, and our understanding of the plural forms involved in this type of inference can be appealed to in support of the claim that Frege's rule [of substitution] is properly regarded as a rule of logic" (p. 174), that "there is a way of interpreting the formulae of the *Begriffsschrift* that is faithful to the usual meanings of the logical operators and on which each comprehension axiom turns out to say something that can also be expressed by a sentence of the form 'if there is something..., then there are some things such that anything... is one of them and any one of them is something...'" (p.177). One does not need to be a Kantian, however, to be skeptical as to how effectively the Kantian's criticisms, which target the very heart of Frege's ill-fated enterprise, have actually been overcome.

Sandwiched in between Boolos' papers is Charles Parsons' 1964 article entitled "Frege's Theory of Number", which is intended to be a contribution towards attaining a clear view of what is true and what is false in Frege's account of arithmetic. Parsons concludes that while the criticisms of the thesis that arithmetic is a part of logic that have been made over the years do suffice to show that it is false, it should not be rejected in the unqualified way it appears to have been by mathematicians like Poincaré, Brouwer and Hilbert. Frege did, Parsons maintains, show that the logical notion of one-to-one correspondence plays a constitutive role in the notion of number.

In "The Consistency of Frege's *Foundations of Arithmetic*", Boolos pursues questions raised by Parsons. There he presents FA, a theory whose underlying logic is standard axiomatic second-order logic written in classical notation and could have been presented as an extension of the system of the *Begriffsschrift*. "Numbers" is postulated as the sole nonlogical supposition of FA. It would express Frege's and Russell's conviction that existence and uniqueness are implicit in the use of the definite article in the form of the principle that for any concept F there is a unique extension of the concept 'equinumerous with F' in support of Hume's principle (the only place, Boolos points out, where Frege appeals to extensions in *Foundations).* Boolos is satisfied that "the principles Frege *employs* in the *Foundations* are consistent. Arithmetic can be developed on their basis in the elegant manner sketched there. And although Frege couldn't and we can't supply a reason for regarding Numbers... as a logical truth, Frege was better off than he has been thought to be" (p. 230).

"The Standard of Equality of Numbers" by Boolos asks whether Hume's Principle could have been used to help Dedekind find a proof from logical truths that there are infinitely many objects. He concludes that Dedekind would not have liked the suggestion and that we cannot accept it either, that there is no reason for regarding Hume's Principle as a truth of logic and it is doubtful that it is a truth at all.

The last and longest part of the book is devoted to the *Basic Laws of Arithmetic* and to salvaging more of Frege's reasoning. Thus Richard Heck begins where Parsons and Boolos have left off by asking whether Frege's formal proofs of the axioms of arithmetic in *Basic Laws* depend only on Hume's principle. The presence of Basic Law V governing value-ranges leading Heck to reply that they do not, he then sets out to demonstrate that except for the ineliminable use of extensions in the proof of Hume's principle itself, all the uses of value-ranges in Frege's proof of the basic laws of arithmetic are easily and uniformly eliminable, that Frege resorted to value-ranges for reasons of convenience, simplicity and elegance.

Building on the conclusions of the preceding essays, in a second paper Heck further argues that the evaluation of Frege's efforts in *Basic Laws* must change. In particular, he undertakes to demonstrate that in *Basic Laws,* in addition to deriving axioms for arithmetic in second-order logic from Hume's principle, Frege gave formal proofs of two celebrated theorems of Dedekind, that the book contains a proof, in Fregean arithmetic that Frege's own axioms for arithmetic determine a class of structures isomorphic to the natural numbers and a proof in pure second-order logic that all structures satisfying these axioms are isomorphic.

Howard Stein's article on the relation of the ancient Greek theory of ratio to Dedekind's work next sets the stage for studies by Peter

Simons, Michael Dummett, Peter Neumann and S. A. Adeleke of the theory of real numbers that Frege was developing when calamity, in the form of Russell's paradox, struck. All of them come to optimistic conclusions about the philosophical insight afforded by Frege's never completed theory. Thus, in reconstructing and venturing to complete Frege's unfinished theory, Simons unearths a number of considerations to show that by affording us a second look at Frege's way of supporting logicism, his aborted theory yields new insight into logicism and raises a number of philosophically interesting questions about it and mathematics in general. Simons also finds aspects of Frege's criticisms of Cantor, Dedekind and Weierstrass perceptive and of relevance now. He does not, though, entertain any illusions that a construction like his could prove any more tenable than the Frege's theory of natural numbers did.

The last three papers tackle questions of consistency. Terence Parsons sets out to show that the first-order portion of Frege's system is consistent and then to explore the significance of the model-construction technique sketched for Frege's claims about the arbitrariness of the identification of truth-values with courses of values. His tactic is to neutralize the effects of the abstraction technique that quickly leads to contradictions in first-order naive set theory. Parsons underscores that to understand his proof one must keep in mind Frege's conviction that truth-values are objects and that terms that denote truth-values can occur syntactically in the same places that other names of objects can. Sentences being truth-values, they then can occur in all the places we would normally expect to find objects, such as flanking the identity sign, and this allowed Frege to use the identity sign for the material conditional. John Bell then undertakes to formulate and prove a stronger version of Parson's result for arbitrary first-order theories. He also shows that a natural attempt to further strengthen his result runs afoul of Tarski's theorem on the undefinability of truth.

In a final paper, entitled "Saving Frege from Contradiction", Boolos pursues his ideas about Hume's principle in an effort to repair damage done by Russell's paradox. Proposing a "New V" in the place of the unsatisfactory V' that Frege proposed in the appendix to *Basic Laws II,* Boolos concludes that the "development of arithmetic outlined in the *Grundlagen* can be carried out in the consistent theory obtained by adding Numbers to the system of the *Begriffsschrift*, as well as in the inconsistent system of the *Grundgesetze*" (p. 452).

As the reader can see this book is, as suits the spirit of the times, largely dedicated to saving or rehabilitating major chunks of Frege's logical project. It might have been entitled *Doctoring Frege's Theories.* Almost all of the saviors have jumped into Frege's reasoning after he had begun fixing his theory with extensions that masked certain shocking consequences of his reasoning up to that point, i.e. once he had used extensions to prove Hume's principle. But, it must be protested, Frege appealed to extensions then precisely because of some very disturbing substitution problems that his theory of identity and arithmetic was already producing, – substitution problems that are the very breeding ground of contradiction and inconsistency. Frege's proof of Hume's principle, as Boolos reminds more than once in "The Standard of Equality of Numbers", is derived from an inconsistent theory of concepts and objects.

This being the case, Richard Heck puts his finger on the book's major weakness (pp. 286-87). It lies in the fact that, as Frege acknowledged in *Foundations* §66-67, left unmodified, the theory of arithmetic he had begun recommending was liable to produce nonsensical conclusions or be sterile and unproductive. In particular, as he wrote, one could never "decide by the means of our definitions whether any concept has the number Julius Caesar belonging to it, or whether that conqueror of Gaul is a number or not" (*Foundations* § 56). Onerous problems of the "Julius Caesar problem" kind induced Frege to introduce the extensions that led to the ill-fated Basic Law V of *Basic Laws*, which he said was the only answer that he had found to the question as to how we apprehend logical objects (quote p. 286).

So Heck is surely right to conclude that the questions really needing answers lie there. "We shall thus not", he writes, "fully understand Frege's philosophy until we understand the enormous significance the question how we apprehend logical objects, and the Caesar problem, had for him…" (p. 287). Demopoulos concurs when he requires that any interpretation of Frege's presentation of the problem in connection with Hume's principle explain how the introduction of extensions overcomes the difficulty that the Julius Caesar problem posed for numbers while not itself succumbing to a similar objection (a major issue in this reviewer's book *Rethinking Identity and Metaphysics*). This problem, Demopoulos maintains, must be addressed in connection with the *Basic Laws,* where extensions are introduced in a way formally analogous to the contextual definition of number. Failure to address it, he warns, "implies not only that Frege's mature theory of number is ungrounded, but that Frege must have known this…" (p. 10). However, although Heck and Demopoulos make this point in the most unequivocal terms, their few pages of comments are, strangely, the only significant mentions of the Julius Caesar problem in the entire book. Conclusion: this excellent book badly needs a Caesarean section.

Lastly, it must be said that the book's general index contains no entries at all for many of the main subjects treated in the book (ex. inconsistency, contradiction, analyticity, rigorization, analysis, synthetic a priori, function) and incomplete listings for topics as basic to the work as Hume's principle, consistency, comprehension, real numbers. Though it lists Kant, it is blind to the many, and more frequent, mentions of the words "Kantianism" and "Kantian", or "anti-Kantian". Meanwhile, minor figures like Otto Hölder seem to enjoy complete listings.

Review of P. W. Humphreys and J. Fetzer (eds.), *The New Theory of Reference: Kripke, Marcus, and its Origins*, Dordrecht: Kluwer, 1998[3]

A session held on December 28, 1994 at the Eastern Division meeting of the American Philosophical Association in Boston had an unwarranted effect, the story of which is chronicled in this book. Quentin Smith of Western Michigan University presented a paper (pp. 3-12) whose stated aim was 'to correct a fundamental and widespread misunderstanding about the origins of the New Theory of Reference' (p. 3). In it, he advanced and defended the thesis that 'the main misunderstanding is that it is widely believed that Kripke originated the main ideas of this theory', whereas 'the key ideas in the New Theory were developed by Ruth Barcan Marcus, in her writings in 1946-1947 ...and especially in her 1961 article on "Modalities and Intensional Languages" ...presented in February 1962 at the Boston Colloquium for the Philosophy of Science' (p. 3), in which Kripke had taken an active part. Smith attributed the misunderstanding to an insufficient familiarity with Marcus's work and to Kripke's failure to acknowledge the influence of her ideas, which he had not initially understood (pp. 9-10).

---

[3] Originally published in *History and Philosophy of Logic* 20, 1999, pp. 125-27.

Taking umbrage, Kripke's colleague at Princeton, Scott Soames next argued (pp. 13-35) that 'what Smith has done is to mistakenly read many of Kripke's arguments and doctrines back into Marcus, and then to insinuate that Kripke is guilty of theft' (pp.14, 29). Soames called Smith's paper shameful, careless and incompetent. Smith, Soames contended, had done Kripke a 'grave injustice', written as if Kripke had 'appropriated the major views expressed in *Naming and Necessity* from Marcus while denying her proper credit, and suggests that it is a scandal that the rest of the profession was thereby duped' (pp. 13, 29). Smith replied (pp. 37-61). Debate and controversy ensued.

In an effort to put the discussion on objective ground, Jaakko Hintikka published the original papers in *Synthese*. Part I of this volume of Synthese Library reproduces them. Part II publishes an additional reply by Soames along with two papers in which another of Kripke's colleagues at Princeton, John Burgess, also attacks Smith. The tone is unnecessarily vituperative. Those papers are followed by a paper by Smith in which he focuses on 'largely unknown contributions' made by Marcus and Peter Geach to the theories of direct, causal or rigid reference found in the New Theory of Reference and argues that that the 'world-definition' of rigid designation associated with Kripke is preferable to the 'direct-reference definition' associated with David Kaplan.

Published in Part III are sections on definite descriptions, modality, identity, referential opacity, substitutivity from the 1961 Harvard dissertation of Dagfinn Føllesdal, another participant in the famous 1962 session. This is followed by an article by Sten Lindström on the model-theoretic semantics for modal logic that Stig Kanger began developing in his 1957 Stockholm dissertation. Comparing Kanger's and Kripke's semantics for modal logic, Lindström finds that Kanger's semantics is adequate for the notion of logical necessity and that Kripke's adequately captures a form of metaphysical necessity, but that neither semantics is capable of adequately handling the notion captured by the other. The task of devising a semantics capable of treating both notions is a still unmet challenge, concludes Lindström (p. 230). In a final essay, Smith continues to try to provide a more accurate and comprehensive account of the 'new' theory in question. His paper includes sections on G. E. Moore's essay on 'The nature of judgment', Føllesdal's doctoral dissertation, Hintikka's early ideas on metaphysical possibility (1957-1963), Cocchiarella and the secondary semantics for logical necessity,

Plantinga's theories, plus more on Geach and, of course, Kripke and Marcus.

The book as a whole presents a wealth of facts and arguments in defence of the various positions taken. There is, however, always something ineluctably elusive about questions of influence and the origins of ideas that is not captured in attention to details. An insightful grasp of the overall picture is required. And this is all the more true when, as is the case here, major issues and important figures are under discussion.

In this case, philosophers really need to acquire a deeper and more sufficient understanding of why and how the 'old' theory of reference took hold. Any proper analysis and appraisal of Marcus's work has to be undertaken in connection with the logical and philosophical exigencies that made that 'old' theory seem to be a clever solution to logical predicaments arising out of the foundations that Frege tried to lay for arithmetic in the first place. Only that will yield the necessary insight into how and why one may or may not conclude that Marcus's earliest ideas mothered and fostered a rival theory eventually able to undermine and overtake the 'old' one. After all, both Frege and Russell ultimately pinpointed issues surrounding descriptions, identity, substitutivity and extensions as being the Achilles heels of logical ideas they both espoused and then abandoned.

It is also important to remember that philosophy has its fashions and its sacred cows. In the late 1940s, Marcus' work on quantified modal logic and the necessity of identity was pioneering and prophetic, but it was hardly fashionable. As is well known, Quine, the fashionable philosopher of the 1950s and 1960s (and a participant in the key 1962 session), made quashing modal and intensional logics one of the principal planks of his philosophical program. One of his targets was Marcus's earliest work. He charged, among other things, that the quantified modal logic of her doctoral thesis had 'queer ontological consequences' and could precipitate an ontological crisis. He warned that her theorem on the necessity of identity was such as to lead us 'back into the metaphysical jungle of Aristotelian essentialism' for which an object must be seen as having some of its traits necessarily and others contingently'. Defying Quine's opprobrium, Marcus fought an uphill battle in defence of the censured theses.

Looking at the evolution of the ideas that went into the making of the 'new' theory within the larger context of the charges that Quine levelled against Marcus helps shed light on the issues raised. And that debate surely prepared the ground for a wider acceptance for ideas that went into the making of a 'new' theory. Although Quine's arguments were mistaken, Soames acknowledges, 'they were enormously influential and they baffled large numbers of the profession for decades' (pp. 14, 16). (Were they duped?). This fact can partially explain how Kripke's views might appear novel, refreshing, astonishing, yet were ready to take hold.

A study of the Marcus-Quine exchange also makes it seem improbable that, as Soames categorically states, there 'is no way that the formal system of Marcus's early papers could have significant consequences about ordinary names and descriptions in natural language' (p. 11); or that, as Burgess maintains, Marcus's earliest work 'is only indirectly relevant to present study' (p. 89). The very nature of Quine's very public and influential complaints, ill-founded or not, established its relevance. Why else might Quine have repeatedly challenged the 'champion' of quantified modal logic to explain away his puzzlement about the logical behaviour of statements like '9 = the number of the planets' in modal contexts?

Another important part of the overall picture is, of course, the development of possible worlds logic, which in the hands of Hintikka, Kripke and others eventually proved to be a particularly effective device for exposing logical form and viewing the inner workings of analytic philosophy's brave new logic. Explorers of possible worlds were to make discoveries that helped to confirm the results of Marcus's earlier ventures into the world of modality and intensionality. For one thing, possible worlds logic put a spotlight on problems associated with extensionality, identity, failures of substitutivity and existential generalisation. It thus had a hand in undermining Quine's hegemony and in vindicating Marcus of many of his charges. This too created a more hospitable environment for the further development of ideas along the lines of those she had defended since Kripke was knee high to a grasshopper. In addition, the disarming, folksy style of Kripke's *Naming and Necessity* could warm an audience to his ideas in a way that Marcus's earliest formal work could not have effected.

In spite of the acrimonious tone introduced by Soames and sustained by him and Burgess, the book as a whole presents a wealth of philosophical arguments that reach deep into the heart of the philosophical enterprise as many have understood it in this century, thus providing much thought provoking material.

One final remark. In the introduction the editor's note that 'a few listeners walked out in apparent protest' (p. vii). There are numerous reasons why a person might leave a three hour session. This reviewer attended the session and, sickened by something eaten the evening before, was obliged to leave the room on at least two occasions, something difficult to do discreetly because the only door was located at the front of the room.

BIBLIOGRAPHY

Becker, Oskar, "The Philosophy of Edmund Husserl" (1930), *The Phenomenology of Husserl, Selected Critical Readings*, R. O. Elveton (ed.), Chicago: Quadrangle Books, 1970, pp. 40-72.

Benacerraf, Paul and Hilary Putnam (eds.), *Philosophy of Mathematics, Selected Readings*, Cambridge UK: Cambridge University Press, 1983, 2nd ed. rev. (1964).

Bolzano, Bernard, *Paradoxes of the Infinite*, London: Routledge, 1950 (1831).

Bolzano, Bernard, *Theory of Science (Wissenschaftslehre)*, Dordrecht: Reidel, 1973 (1837).

Brentano, Franz, *Psychology from an Empirical Standpoint*, London: Routledge and Kegan Paul, 1973 (1874).

Brück, Maria, *Über das Verhältnis Edmund Husserls zu Franz Brentano, Vornehmlich mit Rücksicht auf Brentanos Psychologie*, Würzburg: K. Tritsch, 1933.

Cantor, Georg. *Briefbücher I (1884-1888), II (1890-1895). III (1895-1896)* (Cod. Ms. 18), consultable at the Niedersächsische Staats- und Universitätsbibliothek Göttingen, Abteilung Handschriften und Seltene Drucke.

Cantor, Georg, *Georg Cantor Briefe*, Herbert Meschkowski and Winfried Nilson (eds.), Berlin: Springer, 1991.

Cantor, Georg, *Gesammelte Abhandlungen*, Ernst Zermelo (ed.), Berlin: Springer, 1932.

Cantor, Georg, "*Grundlagen einer allgemeinen Mannigfaltigkeitslehre, Ein mathematisch-philosophischer Versuch in der Lehre des Unendlichen*" (1883), in his *Gesammelte Abhandlungen*, pp. 165-246.

Cantor, Georg, "Mitteilungen zur Lehre vom Transfiniten", *Zeitschrift für Philosophie und philosophische Kritik*, 91 (1887), pp. 81-125; 92 (1888), pp. 240-65, in his *Gesammelte Abhandlungen*, pp. 378-439.

Cantor, Georg, "Rezension von Freges *Grundlagen der Arithmetik*", *Deutsche Literaturzeitung* VI (20), 1885, pp. 728-29.

Centrone, Stefania, *Logic and Philosophy of Mathematics in the Early Husserl*, Dordrecht: Springer, 2010.

Centrone, Stefania (ed.), *Essays on Husserl's Logic and Philosophy of Mathematics*, Dordrecht: Springer, 2017.

Coniglione F., Roberto Poli & Robin Rollinger (eds.), *Abstraction and Idealization. Historical and Systematic Studies, Poznan studies in the philosophy of the sciences and the humanities* 82, Amsterdam: Rodopi, 1999.

Couturat, Louis, *De l'infini mathématique*, Blanchard, Paris, 1986 (1873).

Dahlstrom, Daniel (ed.), *Husserl's Logical Investigations*, Dordrecht: Kluwer, 2003.

Dauben, Joseph, *Georg Cantor, His Mathematics and Philosophy of the Infinite*, Princeton: Princeton University Press, 1979.

Dummett, Michael, *Frege, Philosophy of Mathematics*, Cambridge MA: Harvard University Press, 1991.

Dummett, Michael, *The Interpretation of Frege's Philosophy*, Cambridge MA: Harvard University Press, 1981.

Dummett, Michael, *Origins of Analytic Philosophy*, Cambridge, MA: Harvard University Press, 1994.

Føllesdal, Dagfinn, "Gödel and Husserl", in *From Dedekind to Gödel*, Jaakko Hintikka (ed.), Dordrecht: Kluwer, 1995, pp. 427-46.

Føllesdal, Dagfinn, "Introductory note" to Kurt Gödel's "The Modern Development of the Foundations of Mathematics in the Light of Philosophy", in Gödel's *Collected Works* III, New York: Oxford University Press, 1995, pp. 364–73.

Frege, Gottlob, *The Basic Laws of Arithmetic I*, Berkeley CA: University of California Press, 1963 (1893).

Frege, Gottlob, *Collected Papers on Mathematics, Logic und Philosophy*, Oxford: Blackwell, 1984.

Frege, Gottlob, "A Critical Elucidation of Some Points in E. Schröder's *Vorlesungen über die Algebra der Logik*" (1895), in *Translations from the Philosophical Writings of Gottlob Frege*, 2nd ed., pp. 86-106.

Frege, Gottlob, *The Foundations of Arithmetic*, Oxford: Blackwell, 1980 (1884).

Frege, Gottlob, *The Foundations of Arithmetic*, Oxford: Blackwell, 2nd rev. ed., 1986 (1884).

Frege, Gottlob, "Frege on Russell's Paradox" (1903), in *Translations from the Philosophical Writings of Gottlob Frege*, 2nd ed., pp. 234-44.

Frege, Gottlob, "Function and Concept" (1891), in *Translations from the Philosophical Writings of Gottlob Frege*, Geach & Black (eds.), 3rd ed., pp. 21-41.

Frege, Gottlob, *Gottlob Freges Briefwechsel mit D. Hilbert, E. Husserl, B. Russell, sowie ausgewählte Einzelbriefe Freges*, Gottfried Gabriel et al. (eds), Hamburg: Meiner, 1980.

Frege, Gottlob, *Nachgelassene Schriften*, Hamburg: Meiner, 1969.

Frege, Gottlob, "On Concept and Object" (1892), in *Translations from the Philosophical Writings of Gottlob Frege*, 3rd ed., 1980, pp. 42-55.

Frege, Gottlob, *Philosophical and Mathematical Correspondence*, Gottfried Gabriel et al. (eds.), abridged by Brian McGuinness, Oxford: Blackwell, 1980.

Frege, Gottlob, *Posthumous Writings*, Hans Hermes et al. (eds.), Oxford: Blackwell, 1979.

Frege, Gottlob, "Review of Dr. E. Husserl's *Philosophy of Arithmetic*" (1894), in his *Collected Papers*, pp. 195-20.

Frege, Gottlob, "Review of Georg Cantor, *Zur Lehre vom Transfiniten: Gesammelte Abhandlungen aus de Zeitschrift für Philosophie und philosophische Kritik* [Contributions to the Theory of the Transfinite: Collected Articles from ZPhphK] (1892)", in his *Collected Papers*, pp. 178-81.

Frege, Gottlob, *Schriften zur Logik und Sprachphilosophie aus dem Nachlass*, 2nd ed. rev., Hamburg: Meiner, 1978.

Frege, Gottlob, *Translations from the Philosophical Writings of Gottlob Frege*, Peter Geach and Max Black (eds.), 2nd ed., 1960 (1952).

Frege, Gottlob, *Translations from the Philosophical Writings of Gottlob Frege*, Peter Geach and Max Black (eds.), Oxford: Blackwell, 3rd ed., 1980 (1952).

Frege, Gottlob, *Wissenschaftlicher Briefwechsel.* Hans Hermes et al. (eds.) Hamburg: Meiner, 1976.

Gerlach, Hans Martin and Hans Rainer Sepp (eds.), *Husserl in Halle,* Bern: Peter Lang, 1994.

Gilson, Lucie, *Méthode et Métaphysique selon Franz Brentano*, Paris: Vrin, 1955.

Gilson, Lucie, *La Psychologie descriptive selon Franz Brentano,* Paris: Vrin, 1955.

Gödel, Kurt, "The Modern Development of the Foundations of Mathematics in the Light of Philosophy", in his *Collected Works* III, New York: Oxford University Press, 1995, pp. 374-87.

Gödel, Kurt, "What is Cantor's continuum problem?", in his *Collected Works* II, New York: Oxford University Press, 1990 (1964), pp. 254-70.

Goodrick-Clarke, Nicholas, *The Occult Roots of Nazism, Secret Aryan Cults and their Influence on Nazi Ideology,* New York: I. B. Tauris, 1985.

Grattan-Guinness, Ivor, "Georg Cantor's Influence on Bertrand Russell", *History and Philosophy of Logic* 1, 1980, pp. 61-93.

Grattan-Guinness, Ivor, "How Russell Discovered His Paradox", *Historia Mathematica* 5, 1978, pp. 127-37.

Grattan-Guinness, Ivor, "Psychology in the foundations of logic and mathematics: the cases of Boole, Cantor and Brouwer", *History and Philosophy of Logic* 3, 1982, pp. 33-53.

Grattan-Guinness, Ivor, *The Search for Mathematical Roots, Logics, Set Theories and the Foundations of Mathematics from Cantor through Gödel*, Princeton NJ: Princeton University Press, 2000.

Grattan-Guinness, Ivor, "Towards a Biography of Georg Cantor", *Annals of Science* 27 (4), 1971, pp. 345-91.

Haack, Susan, *Philosophy of Logics*, Cambridge UK: Cambridge University Press, 1978.

Haaparanta, Leila (ed.), *Mind, Meaning and Mathematics, Essays on the Philosophical Views of Husserl and Frege*, Dordrecht: Kluwer, 1994.

Haaparanta, Leila and Heikki Koskinen (eds.), *Categories of Being, Essays on Metaphysics and Logic*, Oxford: Oxford University Press, 2012.

Hackett, Paul (ed.), *Mereologies, Ontologies, and Facets: The Categorical Structure of Reality*, Lanham MD: Lexington Books, 2018.

Hallett, Michael, *Cantorian Set Theory and Limitation of Size*, Oxford: Clarendon, 1984.

Hartimo, Mirja (ed.), *Phenomenology and Mathematics*, Dordrecht: Springer, 2010.

Hilbert, David, Extracts from Hilbert's *Denkschrift* for Leonard Nelson, undated, consultable at in the Niedersächsische Staats-und Universitäts-bibliothek Göttingen, Abteilung Handschriften und Seltene Drücke, translated into English in Hill & da Silva 2013, pp. 386-87.

Hilbert, David, "The Foundations of Mathematics" (1927), in van Heijenoort (ed.), pp. 464-79,

Hilbert, David, "Neubegründung der Mathematik, Erste Mittheilung", *Abhandlungen aus dem mathematischen Seminar der Hamburgischen Universität* 1, 1922, pp. 157–77.

Hilbert, David, "On the Foundations of Logic and Arithmetic" (1904), in van Heijenoort (ed.), pp. 129-38.

Hilbert, David, "On the Infinite" (1925), in van Heijenoort (ed.), pp. 369-92, also in Benacerraf & Putnam (eds.), pp. 183-201.

Hill, Claire Ortiz, "Abstraction and Idealization in Georg Cantor and Edmund Husserl", in F. Coniglione, Roberto Poli, Robin Rollinger (eds.), and in Hill & Rosado Haddock.

Hill, Claire Ortiz, "Cantor's Paradise, Metaphysics and Husserlian Logic", in Haaparanta & Koskinen (eds.), pp. 217-40, and in Hill & da Silva.

Hill, Claire Ortiz, "Did Georg Cantor Influence Edmund Husserl?" *Synthese* 113, October 1997, pp. 145-70, and in Hill & Rosado Haddock.

Hill, Claire Ortiz, "Frege Attacks Husserl and Cantor", *The Monist* 77(3): 1994, pp. 347-57, and in Hill & Rosado Haddock.

Hill, Claire Ortiz, "Frege's Letters", in Hintikka (ed.), pp. 97-118, and in Hill & da Silva.

Hill, Claire Ortiz, "Husserl and Frege on Substitutivity", in Haaparanta (ed.), pp. 113–40, and in Hill & Rosado Haddock.

Hill, Claire Ortiz, "Husserl and Hilbert on Completeness", in Jaakko Hintikka (ed.), pp. 143-63, and in Hill & Rosado Haddock.

Hill, Claire Ortiz, "Husserl on Axiomatization and Arithmetic", in Hartimo (ed.), pp. 47-71, and in Hill & da Silva.

Hill, Claire Ortiz, "Husserlian Sets or Fregean Sets?" *Notae Philosophicae Scientiae Formalis*, volume 2, no. 1, May 2013, pp. 22-32, http://gcfcf.com.br/pt/files/2013/07/Hill-Claire-Ortiz-NPSF-vol.2-n.1.pdf

Hill, Claire Ortiz, "Husserl's *Mannigfaltigkeitslehre*", in Hill & Rosado Haddock, pp. 161-77.

Hill, Claire Ortiz, "Incomplete Symbols, Dependent Meanings, and Paradox", in Dahlstrom (ed.), pp. 69-93, and in Hill & da Silva.

Hill, Claire Ortiz, *La logique des expressions intentionnelles,* Mémoire de Maitrise, Université de Paris-Sorbonne, April 1, 1979, published online on Academia.edu and ResearchGate.com.

Hill, Claire Ortiz, "On Fundamental Differences between Dependent and Independent Meanings", *Axiomathes, An International Journal in Ontology and Cognitive Systems* 20: 2-3, online since May 29, 2010, 313-32 (DOI 10.1007/s10516-010-9104-1), and in Hill & da Silva

Hill, Claire Ortiz, "On Husserl's Mathematical Apprenticeship and Philosophy of Mathematics", in Tymieniecka (ed.), *Phenomenology World Wide*, pp. 76-92, and in Hill & da Silva.

Hill, Claire Ortiz, "One Dogma of Empiricism", in Reicher and Marek (eds.), pp. 30-38, and in Hill & da Silva.

Hill, Claire Ortiz, "Phenomenology from the Metaphysical Standpoint", *Diálogos*, XLIII, 91, January 2008, pp. 19-35.

Hill, Claire Ortiz, "Reference and Paradox", *Synthese*, 138, 2, January 2004, pp. 207-32, and in Hill & da Silva.

Hill, Claire Ortiz, *Rethinking Identity and Metaphysics, On the Foundations of Analytic Philosophy*, New Haven CT: Yale University Press, 1997.

Hill, Claire Ortiz, "Review of E. Husserl's *Allgemeine Erkenntnistheorie (1902/03), Vorlesung*", *History and Philosophy of Logic*, 24 (2003), pp. 76-78.

Hill, Claire Ortiz, "Review of E. Husserl's *Alte und Neue Logik 1908/09*", *History and Philosophy of Logic*, 26 (2005), pp. 159-62.

Hill, Claire Ortiz, "Review of Edmund Husserl's *Logik und allgemeine Wissenschaftslehre* (Husserliana vol. XXX)", *History and Philosophy of Logic* 19, 1998, pp. 115-17.

Hill, Claire Ortiz, "Review of E. Husserl's *Logik, Vorlesung* (1896) and *Logik, Vorlesung* (1902/03)", *The Review of Modern Logic*, Vol. 10, nos. 1 & 2 (September 2004-February 2005) Issue 31, pp. 145-54.

Hill, Claire Ortiz, "Tackling Three of Frege's Problems: Edmund Husserl on Sets and Manifolds", *Axiomathes* 13, 2002, pp. 79-104, and in Hill & da Silva.

Hill, Claire Ortiz, "The Varied Sorrows of Logical Abstraction", *Axiomathes* 1-3, 1997, pp. 53-82, and in Hill & Rosado Haddock.

Hill, Claire Ortiz, *Word and Object in Husserl, Frege and Russell, the Roots of Twentieth Century Philosophy*, Athens OH: Ohio University Press, 1991, 2001.

Hill, Claire Ortiz and Guillermo Rosado Haddock, *Husserl or Frege? Meaning, Objectivity, and Mathematics*, La Salle IL: Open Court, 2000.

Hill, Claire Ortiz and Jairo José da Silva, *The Road Not Taken, On Husserl's Philosophy of Logic and Mathematics*, London: College Publications, 2013.

Hintikka, Jaakko (ed.), *From Dedekind to Gödel, Essays on the Development of the Foundations of Mathematics*, Dordrecht: Kluwer, 1995.

Husserl, Edmund, "A. Voigt's 'Elemental Logic,' in Relation to my Statements on the Logic of the Logical Calculus" (1893), in his *Early Writings in the Philosophy of Logic and Mathematics*, pp. 121-30.

Husserl, Edmund, *Allgemeine Erkenntnistheorie, Vorlesung 1902/03*, Elisabeth Schuhmann (ed.), Dordrecht: Kluwer, 2001.

Husserl, Edmund, *Alte und neue Logik, Vorlesung 1908/09*, Elisabeth Schuhmann (ed.), Dordrecht: Kluwer, 2003.

Husserl, Edmund, *Aufzätze und Rezensionen* (1890–1910), Bernhard Rang (ed.), Dordrecht: Kluwer, 1979, for the most part translated in his *Early Writings in the Philosophy of Logic and Mathematics.*

Husserl, Edmund, "Aus der Einleitung der Vorlesung Erkenntnistheorie und Hauptpunkte der Metaphysik 1898/99", in his *Allgemeine Erkenntnistheorie*, pp. 225-55.

Husserl, Edmund, *Briefwechsel, Die Brentanoschule I*, Dordrecht: Kluwer, 1994.

Husserl, Edmund, "The Concept of General Arithmetic" (1890), in his *Early Writings in the Philosophy of Logic and Mathematics*, pp. 1-6.

Husserl, Edmund, *The Crisis of European Sciences and Transcendental Phenomenology*, Evanston IL: Northwestern University, 1970 (1954), translation of his *Die Krisis der europaïschen Wissenschaften und die tranzendentale Phänomenologie, eine Einleitung in die phänomenologische Philosophie* (1936).

Husserl, Edmund, *Early Writings in the Philosophy of Logic and Mathematics*, Dordrecht: Kluwer, 1994, primarily a translation by Dallas Willard of writings published in Husserl's *Aufzätze und Rezensionen* (1890–1910).

Husserl, Edmund, "Essay III, Double Lecture: On the Transition through the Impossible ('Imaginary') and the Completeness of an Axiom System", in his *Philosophy of Arithmetic, Psychological and Logical Investigations with Supplementary Texts from 1887-1901*, pp. 409-73, translation of his "Das Imaginäre in der Mathematik", published in his *Philosophie der Arithmetik, mit ergänzenden Texten (1890-1901)*, pp. 430-51.

Husserl, Edmund, *Experience and Judgment*, London, Routledge and Kegan Paul, 1973, translation by James S. Churchill of his *Erfahrung und Urteil: Untersuchungen zur Genealogie der Logik* (1939).

Husserl, Edmund, *Formal and Transcendental Logic*, The Hague: Martinus Nijhoff, 1969, translation by Dorion Cairns of his *Formale and transzendentale Logik, Versuch einer Kritik der logischen Vernunft* (1929).

Husserl, Edmund, "From Husserl's Sketches for his Review of Schröder", in his *Early Writings in the Philosophy of Logic and Mathematics*, pp. 421-41.

Husserl, Edmund, "Husserl an Brentano, 27. III. 1905", in his *Briefwechsel, Die Brentanoschule I*, pp. 37-39.

Husserl, Edmund, *Husserl: Shorter Works*, P. Mc Cormick & F. Elliston (eds.), Notre Dame IN: University of Notre Dame Press, 1981.

Husserl, Edmund, *Ideas, General Introduction to Pure Phenomenology*, New York: Collier Books, 1962, translation by W. R. Boyce Gibson of his *Ideen zu einer reinen Phänomenologie und phänomenologischen Philosophie, Erstes Buch: Allgemeine Einführung in die reine Phänomenologie* (1913).

Husserl, Edmund, *Ideas Pertaining to a Pure Phenomenology and to a Phenomenological Philosophy, Second Book, Studies in the Phenomenology of Constitution*, Dordrecht: Kluwer, 1989.

Husserl, Edmund, *Introduction to Logic and Theory of Knowledge, Lectures 1906/07*, Dordrecht: Springer, 2008, translation by Claire Ortiz Hill of his

Einleitung in die Logik und Erkenntnistheorie, Vorlesungen (1906–07), Ullrich Melle (ed.), Dordrecht: Kluwer, 1984.

Husserl, Edmund, *Introduction to the Logical Investigations, A Draft of a Preface to the Logical Investigations*, E. Fink (ed.), The Hague: Martinus Nijhoff, 1975 (1913), translation of his "Entwurf einer 'Vorrede' zu den Logischen Untersuchungen" (1939).

Husserl, Edmund, "Letter from Edmund Husserl to Carl Stumpf" (1890/91), in his *Early Writings in the Philosophy of Logic and Mathematics*, pp. 12-19.

Husserl, Edmund, *Logic and General Theory of Science 1917/18, with supplementary texts from the first version of 1910/11*, Cham, Switzerland: Springer, 2019, translation by Claire Ortiz Hill of his *Logik und allgemeine Wissenschafts-theorie, Vorlesungen 1917/18, mit ergänzenden Texten aus der ersten Fassung 1910/11*, Ursula Panzer (ed.), Dordrecht: Kluwer (1996).

Husserl, Edmund, *Logical Investigations*, London: Routledge and Kegan Paul, 1970, translation by J. N. Findlay of his *Logische Untersuchungen* (1900-01).

Husserl, Edmund, *Logik, Vorlesung 1896*, Elisabeth Schuhmann (ed.), Dordrecht: Kluwer, 2001.

Husserl, Edmund, *Logik, Vorlesung 1902/03*, Elisabeth Schuhmann (ed.), Dordrecht: Kluwer, 2001.

Husserl, Edmund, "Memorandum of a Verbal Communication from Zermelo to Husserl", in his *Early Writings in the Philosophy of Logic and Mathematics*, p. 442.

Husserl, Edmund, *Ms A I 35* Untitled, undated manuscript on set theory consultable at the Husserl Archives in Cologne, Leuven and Paris, now partially published in German by Carlos Ierna and Dieter Lohmar as "Husserl's Manuscript A I 35", in Rosado Haddock (ed.), pp. 289-319.

Husserl, Edmund, "On the Concept of Number, Psychological Analyses" (1887), in his *Philosophy of Arithmetic, Psychological and Logical Investigations with Supplementary Texts from 1887-1901*, pp. 305-57 and in *Husserl: Shorter Works*, P. Mc Cormick & F. Elliston (eds.), pp. 92-120, translations of his "Ueber den Begriff der Zahl" published in his *Philosophie der Arithmetik, mit ergänzenden Texten (1890-1901)*, pp. 289-339.

Husserl, Edmund, "On the Logic of Signs (Semiotic)" (1890), in his *Early Writings in the Philosophy of Logic and Mathematics*, pp. 20-51.

Husserl, Edmund, "Personal Notes" (1906-1908), in his *Early Writings in the Philosophy of Logic and Mathematics*, pp. 490-500.

Husserl, Edmund, *Philosophy of Arithmetic, Psychological and Logical Investigations with Supplementary Texts from 1887-1901*, Dordrecht: Kluwer, 2003 (1891), translation by Dallas Willard of his *Philosophie der Arithmetik, mit ergänzenden Texten (1890-1901)*, Lothar Eley (ed.), The Hague: Martinus Nijhoff, 1970.

Husserl, Edmund, "Psychological Studies in the Elements of Logic", (1894), in his *Early Writings in the Philosophy of Logic and Mathematics*, pp. 139-70.

Husserl, Edmund, "Recollections of Franz Brentano" (1919), in *Husserl: Shorter Works*, P. McCormick & F. Elliston (eds.), pp. 342-49 and in McAllister, pp. 47-55.

Husserl, Edmund, "Report on German Writings in Logic from the Years 1895-1899, First Article", in his *Early Writings in the Philosophy of Logic and Mathematics,* pp. 207-24.

Husserl, Edmund, "Report on German Writings in Logic from the Years 1895-1899, Third Article", in his *Early Writings in the Philosophy of Logic and Mathematics,* pp. 246-59.

Husserl, Edmund, "Report on German Writings in Logic from the Years 1895-1899, Fifth Article", in his *Early Writings in the Philosophy of Logic and Mathematics*, pp. 280-302.

Husserl, Edmund, "Review of Ernst Schröder's *Vorlesungen über die Algebra der Logik*" (1891), in his *Early Writings in the Philosophy of Logic and Mathematics*, pp. 52-91.

Husserl, Edmund, "Review of Palagyi's Der Streit der Psychologisten und Formalisten in der modernen Logik" (1903), in his *Early Writings in the Philosophy of Logic and Mathematics*, pp. 197-206.

Husserl, Edmund, *Studien zur Arithmetik und Geometrie*, Ingeborg Strohmeyer (ed.), The Hague, Martinus Nijhoff, 1983.

Husserl, Edmund, *Vorlesungen über Bedeutungslehre Sommersemester 1908*, Ursula Panzer (ed.), Dordrecht: Kluwer, 1987.

Husserl, Malvine, "Skizze eines Lebensbildes von E. Husserl", *Husserl Studies* 5, 1988, pp. 105-25.

Jones, Henry, *A Critical Account of the Philosophy of Lotze, the Doctrine of Thought*, Glasgow: James Maclehouse and Sons, 1895.

Jung, Carl, *Jung on Evil*, Murray Stein (ed.), London: Routledge, 1995.

Jourdain, Philip E .B., "Gottlob Frege" (1912), in Frege's *Philosophical and Mathematical Correspondence*, pp. 179-206.

Leclercq, Bruno Sébastien Richard and Denis Seron (eds.), *Objects and Pseudo-Objects Ontological Deserts and Jungles from Brentano to Carnap*, Berlin: de Gruyter, 2015.

Linke, Paul, "Gottlob Frege as Philosopher" (1946), in Poli (ed.), pp. 49-72, translation by Claire Ortiz Hill of "Gottlob Frege als Philosoph", *Zeitschrift für philosophische Forschung*, 1, Heft 1, 1946-1947, pp. 75-99.

Livadas, Stathis, *Contemporary Problems of Epistemology in the Light of Phenomenology, Temporal Consciousness and the Limits of Formal Theories*, London: College Publications, 2012.

Lotze, Hermann, *Logic*, New York: Garland, 1980 (1888).

Marcus, Ruth Barcan 1993, *Modalities*, New York: Oxford University Press.

Marty, Anton, "Über subjektlose Sätze und das Verhältnis der Grammatik zur Logik und Psychologie", *Vierteljahrsschrift für wissenschaftliche Philosophie* 19, 1895, pp. 19-87, pp. 263-334.

McAllister, Linda, *The Philosophy of Brentano*, London: Duckworth, 1976.

Nelson, Leonard, Extracts from Leonard Nelson's Letter of December 29, 1916 to David Hilbert consultable at the Niedersächsische Staats- und Universitätsbibliothek Göttingen, Abteilung Handschriften und Seltene Drücke, translated in Hill & da Silva 2013, pp. 388-91.

Osborn, Andrew, *The Philosophy of E. Husserl in its Development to his First Conception of Phenomenology in the Logical Investigations*, New York: International Press, 1934.

Peckhaus, Volker, *Hilbertprogramm und Kritische Philosophie, Das Göttinger Modell interdisziplinärer Zusammenarbeit zwischen Mathematik und Philosophie*, Göttingen: Vandenhoeck & Ruprecht, 1990.

Peckhaus, Volker and Reinhard Kahle, "Hilbert's Paradox", *Report No. 38, 2000/2001*, Institut Mittag-Leffler, The Royal Swedish Academy of Sciences.

Picker, Bernold, "Die Bedeutung de Mathematik für die Philosophie Edmund Husserls", *Philosophia Naturalis* 7, 1962, pp. 266–355.

Poli, Roberto (ed.), *The Brentano Puzzle*, Aldershot: Ashgate, 1998.

Quine, Willlard, *From a Logical Point of View* (2nd rev.), New York: Harper & Row, 1961.

Quine, Willard, "Identity, Ostension, and Hypothesis" (1950), in his *From a Logical Point of View*, pp. 65-77.

Quine, Willard, "On What There Is" (1948), in his *From a Logical Point of View*, pp. 1-19.

Quine, Willard, "Ontological Relativity", in his *Ontological Relativity and Other Essays*, pp. 26-68.

Quine, Willard, *Ontological Relativity and Other Essays*, New York: Columbia University Press, 1969.

Quine, Willard, "The Problem of Interpreting Modal Logic", *Journal of Symbolic Logic*, 12, 2, June 1947, pp. 43-48.

Quine, Willard, "Quantifiers and Propositional Attitudes", *Journal of Philosophy*, 53 (1956), pp. 177-87.

Quine, Willard, "Reference and Modality" (1953), in his *From a Logical Point of View*, pp. 139-59.

Quine, Willard, "Two Dogmas of Empiricism" (1953), in his *From a Logical Point of View*, pp. 20-46.

Quine, Willard, *Ways of Paradox*, Cambridge MA: Harvard University Press, 1976.

Quine, Willard, *Word and Object*, Cambridge MA, M.I.T. Press, 1960.

Rang, Bernhard and Wolfgang Thomas, "Zermelo's Discovery of Russell's Paradox", *Historia Mathematica* 8, 1981, pp. 16-22.

Raynova, Yvanka B., "Jean-Paul Sartre, A Profound Revision of Husserlian Phenomenology", in Tymieniecka (ed.), *Phenomenology World Wide*.

Reicher, M. E. and J. C. Marek (eds.), *Experience and Analysis, Erfahrung und Analyse* (Proceedings of the International Wittgenstein Conference on held in Kirchberg am Wechsel, August 2004).

Rosado Haddock, Guillermo, *Edmund Husserls Philosophie der Logik und Mathematik im Lichte der gegenwärtigen Logik und Grundlagenforschung*. Doctoral Thesis, Rheinischen Friedrich-Wilhelms-Universität zu Bonn, 1973.

Rosado Haddock, Guillermo, "Interderivability of Seemingly Unrelated Mathematical Statements", *Diálogos* 59 (1992), pp. 121-34 and in Hill & Rosado Haddock.

Rosado Haddock, Guillermo, "On Antiplatonism and its Dogmas," *Diálogos* 67 (1996), pp. 7-38, and in Hill & Rosado Haddock.

Rosado Haddock, Guillermo, "On Husserl's Distinction between States of Affairs (*Sacherverhalt*) and Situation of Affairs (*Sachlage*)", *Phenomenology and the Formal Sciences,* T. Seebohm et al. eds., Dordrecht: Kluwer, 1991, pp. 35-48, and in Hill & Rosado Haddock.

Rosado Haddock, Guillermo, "On Husserl's Two Notions of Sense", *History and Philosophy of Logic* 7, 1, 1986, pp. 31-41, and in Hill & Rosado Haddock.

Rosado Haddock, Guillermo, "On the Semantics of Mathematical Statements", *Manuscrito* 19, no. 1, 1996, pp. 149-75.

Rosado Haddock, Guillermo, "Remarks on Sense and Reference in Frege and Husserl", *Kant-Studien* 73, Heft 4 December, 1982, pp. 425-39.

Rosado Haddock, Guillermo, "To be a Fregean or to be a Husserlian: That is the Question for Platonists", *Advances in Contemporary Logic and Computer Science*, W. Carnielli and I. D'Ottaviano (eds.), American Mathematical Society, 1999, and in Hill & Rosado Haddock.

Rosado-Haddock, Guillermo (ed.), *Husserl and Analytic Philosophy,* Berlin: de Gruyter, 2016.

Roy, J.-M., Jean Petitot, Francisco Varela and Bernard Pachoud (eds.), *Naturalizing Phenomenology, Issues in Contemporary Phenomenology and Cognitive Science*, Stanford CA: Stanford University Press, 1999.

Russell, Bertrand, *Essays in Analysis*, London: Allen & Unwin, 1973.

Russell, Bertrand, *Introduction to Mathematical Philosophy*, London: Allen & Unwin, 1919.

Russell, Bertrand, *Logic and Knowledge, Essays 1901-1950*, R. C. Marsh (ed.), London: Allen & Unwin, 1956.

Russell, Bertrand, *My Philosophical Development*, London: Allen and Unwin, 1975, 1985 (1959).

Russell, Bertrand, *Mysticism and Logic and Other Essays*, London: Allen & Unwin Ltd., 1959 (1917).

Russell, Bertrand, "The Philosophical Implications of Mathematical Logic", *The Monist* 22 (Oct. 1913), pp. 481-93 and in his *Essays in Analysis*, pp. 284-94, partially translated in Husserl Ms A I 35.

Russell, Bertrand, *Principles of Mathematic,* London: Norton, 1903.

Russell, Bertrand and Whitehead Alfred North, *Principia Mathematica to *56*, Cambridge UK, Cambridge University Press, 2nd ed., 1964 (1927).

Sartre, Jean-Paul, "Intentionality: A Fundamental Idea of Husserl's Phenomenology", *Journal of the British Society of Phenomenology* 1, 2, May 1970, pp. 4-5.

Schirn, Matthias (ed.), *Studies on Frege* vol. 1, Stuttgart: Bad Cannstatt: Frommann-Holzboog Verlag, 1976.

Schmit, Roger, *Husserls Philosophie der Mathematik: platonische und konstructivische Moment in Husserls Mathematik Begriff*, Bonn: Bouvier Verlag, 1981.

Schoen, Henri, *La Métaphysique de Hermann Lotze, ou la philosophie des actions et des réactions réciproques*, Paris: Librairie Fischbacher, 1902.

Scholz, Heinrich, "Briefe an Husserl 8. III 1936", in E. Husserl's *Briefwechsel vol. VI, Philosophenbriefe,* Dordrecht: Kluwer, 1994 (1936), pp. 379-80.

Scholz, Heinrich and Friedrich Bachmann, "Der wissenschaftliche Nachlass von Frege", in *Actes du congrès international de philosophie scientifique,* vol. VIII: *Histoire de la logique et de la philosophie scientifique,* pp. 24-30, Paris: Hermann, 1936.

Schuhmann, Karl, *Husserl-Chronik*, The Hague: Martinus Nijhoff, 1977.

Schuhmann, Karl, "Husserls doppelter Vorstellugsbegriff: die Texte von 1893", *Brentano Studien*, 3, 1990-91, pp. 119-36.

Seebohm, Thomas, Dagfinn Føllesdal and J. N. Mohanty (eds.), *Phenomenology and the Formal Sciences*, Dordrecht: Kluwer, 1991.

Sepp, Hans Rainer (ed.), *Edmund Husserl und die phänomenologische Bewegung*, Freiburg: Alber, 1988.

Simons, Peter, *Philosophy and Logic in Central Europe from Bolzano to Tarski*, Dordrecht: Kluwer, 1992

Sluga, Hans, *Gottlob Frege*, London: Routledge & Kegan Paul, 1980.

Smith, Barry, *Austrian Philosophy, the Legacy of Franz Brentano*, La Salle IL: Open Court, 1994.

Smith, Barry, "On the Origins of Analytic Philosophy", *Grazer philosophische Studien*, 35, 1989, pp. 153-73.

Stumpf, Carl, *Erkenntnislehre*, Leipzig: Barth, 1939.

Sugarman, Richard, "Emmanuel Levinas: the Ethics of 'Face to Face'/the Religious Turn", in Tymieniecka (ed.), *Phenomenology World Wide.*

Tieszen, Richard, "Kurt Gödel and Phenomenology", *Philosophy of Science* 59, no. 2, 1992, pp. 176-94.

Tieszen, Richard, *Mathematical Intuition, Phenomenology and Mathematical Knowledge*, Dordrecht: Kluwer, 1989.

Tymieniecka, Anna-Teresa (ed.), *Phenomenology and Existentialism in the Twentieth Century*, Book I, *New Waves of Philosophical Inspirations*, Dordrecht: Springer, 2009.

Tymieniecka, Anna-Teresa (ed.), *Phenomenology World Wide*, Dordrecht: Kluwer, 2002.

van Atten, Mark, *Brouwer Meets Husserl, On the Phenomenology of Choice Sequences*, Dordrecht: Springer, 2007.

van Atten, Mark, "Construction and Constitution in Mathematics", *The New Yearbook for Phenomenology and Phenomenological Philosophy* 10, 2010, pp. 43-90.

van Heijenoort, Jean (ed.), *From Frege to Gödel: A Source Book in Mathematical Logic, 1879-1931*,Cambridge MA: Harvard University Press, 1967.

Veraart, Albert, "Geschichte des wissenschaftlichen Nachlasses Gottlob Freges und seiner Edition. Mit einen Katalog des ursprünglichen Bestands der nachgelassenen Schriften Freges", in Schirn (ed.), pp. 49-106.

Wang, Hao, *Beyond Analytic Philosophy*, Cambridge MA: M.I.T, Press, 1986.

Wang, Hao, *A Logical Journey, From Gödel to Philosophy*, Cambridge MA: M.I.T. Press, 1996.

Wang, Hao, *Reflections on Kurt Gödel*, Cambridge MA: MIT Press, 1987.

Willard, Dallas, "Husserl's Critique of Extensionalist Logic: 'A Logic that Does Not Understand Itself'", *Idealistic Studies* IX, no. 2 (May), pp. 142-64, 1979.

Willard, Dallas, "Husserl on a Logic That Failed", *The Philosophical Review*, LXXXIX, no. 1, January 1980, pp. 46-64.

Willard, Dallas, *Logic and the Objectivity of Knowledge*, Athens OH: Ohio University Press, 1984.

Index

www.ingramcontent.com/pod-product-compliance
Lightning Source LLC
LaVergne TN
LVHW050510100826
845148LV00002B/292

* 9 7 8 1 8 4 8 9 0 4 5 1 4 *